Where to go next? Which crag will be my next challenge? How to get there? These are the first questions which come to my mind when I'm looking for a new rock climbing destination. Since there are so many good crags in Europe I find it hard to make up my mind. Luckily, with

the Rock Climbing Atlas guidebooks this has become so much easier. As before, this new guide gives a clear view of all the best crags around, even those secret spots you could never find. The guide helps with accommodation around the crag and the best and cheapest ways to get there and move around. This is very convenient and helps me to make the trips as good as they can get.

Enjoy reading the 3rd guide in this series a
South Western Europe and Morocco have to

GN00501653

We are living in an ever more virtual world. With a simple click of the mouse we can fly with Google Earth over the most remote corners of the world, and reduce our planet to a mere image on the screen of a mobile phone.

Even so, it's still stories and personal accounts, and, above all, photos that inspire dreams in me, from which concrete plans and goals develop. Personally, this Rock Climbing Atlas is therefore much more than just a climbing guide: it's a temptress, and a wonderful inspiration to keep discovering new and exciting areas!

Rock Climbing Atlases provide valuable information about both well known climbing areas and, more importantly, those many lesser known areas that are really worth discovering. They are GPS devices for our passion and the endless climbing possibilities that exist.

Stay on the edge.

Stefan Glowacz

Published by: Rocks Unlimited Publications
Printed by: Roto Smeets GrafiServices, Utrecht

Graphical design: Irene Pieper from NIHIL Climbing
Authors: Wynand Groenewegen & Marloes van den Berg
Editor: Daniel Jaeggi

This Rock Climbing Atlas does not contain any topos or detailed route information because we would like to encourage our readers to purchase local climbing guidebooks. The proceeds of guidebook sales tend to support local climbers and underpins route development, and we hope that our actions, and those of our readers, may contribute to the preservation and enhancement of the climbing areas we describe.

Although we have put every effort and taken reasonable care in preparing this guide, we cannot guarantee and we do not accept any liability for the accuracy or completeness of the content. Prices can go up, campsites shut down, climbing areas close, new routes appear, airline schedules change, etc. Please visit our website www.rockclimbingatlas.com for updates and please let us know if you find anything to be inaccurate or missing. Our email address is info@rockclimbingatlas.com. Feedback, comments, and suggestions are highly appreciated.

The publisher, authors and the editor accept no responsibility for any consequences arising from the use of this guide, and do not accept any liability for any damages or injuries incurred. The Rock Climbing Atlas is not a climbing safety book and has no instructions or directions with regards to any aspect of climbing safety. You are strongly advised to seek professional instruction before participating in any climbing related activity. Climbing is an activity with a danger of personal injury or death. Participants should be aware of and accept these risks and be responsible for their own involvement.

The inclusion of a crag in this guide confers neither the right of access to the crag or the surrounding land, nor the right to climb on the crag.

First edition January 2008

ISBN-13: 978-90-78587-03-3

Copyright © Rocks Unlimited Publications

© All rights reserved. No part of this publication may be reproduced, copied, put on the internet, stored in a retrieval system, or transmitted in any form by any means, electronic, mechanical, recording, photocopying, or otherwise, without prior written permission of the publisher.

South Western Europe & Morocco

Rock Climbing Atlas

Sardinia, Italy

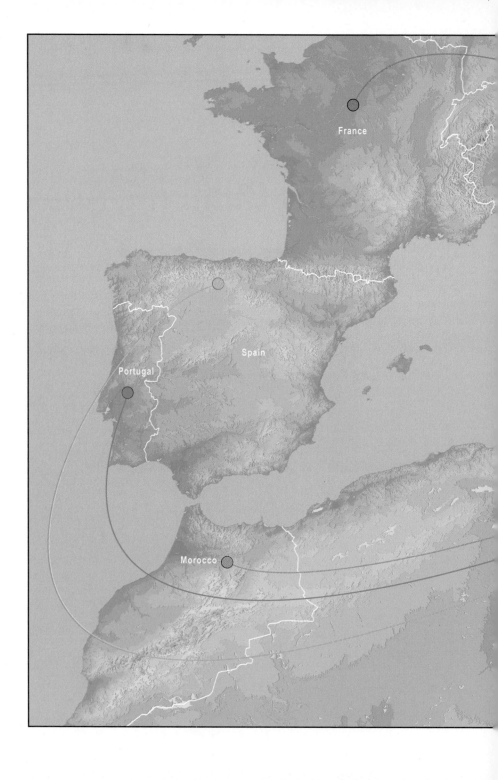

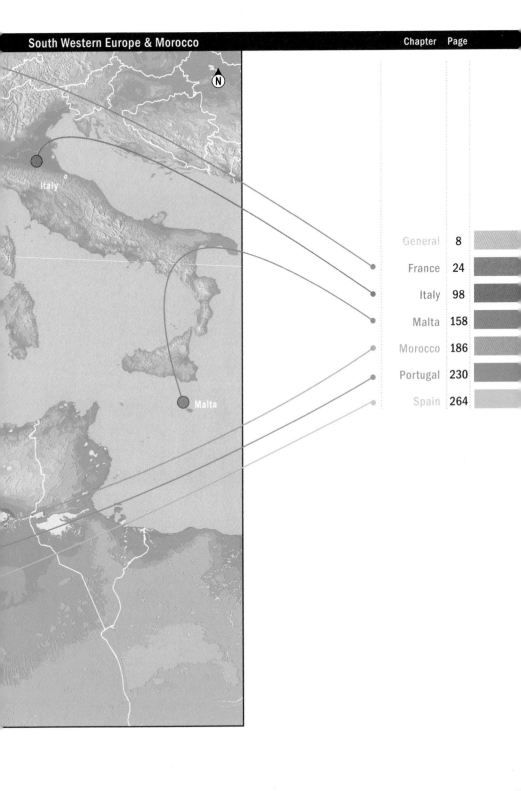

Alexander Huber
Berghaus, sponsored athlete

Leo Houlding

Anniken Binz

Rob Jarman

www.berghaus.com

BERGHAUS and ⬚ are registered trade marks of Berghaus Limited. © Berghaus Limited 2007.

Contents

Planning your next climbing trip and you don't know where to go? Looking for a reason to escape the bad winter weather? Why spend a whole winter climbing indoors anyway if all you're doing is waiting for the sun to start shining again? Maybe you didn't know that there are so many low-cost airlines crossing Europe year round that it is not only easy to travel abroad for a week but fairly cheap too. Some of Europe's most sun-drenched climbing areas are conveniently located close to major package holiday destinations that are completely abandoned outside the summer season - cheap and sunny, what more could you want!

Whatever type of climbing holiday you are looking for, whether you are an experienced climber or a complete beginner, whether you need to please your partner and the family too or whether it is only adventure you are looking for, South Western Europe & Morocco has something to suit every taste. So get your gear together and get out there!

This guide provides you with all the essential facts about climbing in South Western Europe & Morocco. We have included the most interesting climbing areas in France, Italy, Malta, Morocco, Portugal, and Spain - these will surely give you enough to go on for years and years! Everything you need to start planning your trip is included - how to get to each area, what season is best, what the climbing is like, where to sleep (including the most appealing and cheapest options), what to do on rest days, and

which crags are family friendly. We don't provide you with topos or detailed route descriptions - we strongly believe in sustainable tourism and encourage you to buy the local topo, supporting the local climbers and economy - but we give you more than enough to choose your next destination, and to get you to the crags ready to go.

We cover a wide range of areas in this Rock Climbing Atlas but there are clearly dozens more top venues in South Western Europe that we couldn't include for space reasons. Among these, probably Ceüse and Buoux stand out as obvious omissions - they are both well known world-class venues and should be on the hit-list of any hard climber. However, we felt we were able to strike a better balance by including instead some other really worthwhile areas that aren't perhaps as popular. So we have made a selection based on the beauty of the area, the number and quality of the routes (the area should be big and challenging enough to keep you busy for around a week), the quality of the climbing (in terms of protection, route enjoyment, and rock quality), and accessibility, including ease of accommodation. In compiling the guide, we not only relied on information and opinions from local climbers, but we also visited all the areas ourselves. We aim to tell it like it is and don't hesitate from mentioning both the good and the bad!

Enjoy reading and we hope your next climbing holiday is a great one!

The layout of The Rock Climbing Atlas has been designed to be extremely easy to use. Each country has its own extensive introduction after which the climbing areas are described in more detail. The crags within each climbing area are then described. We use only symbols where necessary and the written descriptions are supplemented by many photos. In this way, we hope to give you the best, and most accurate, description of the climbing possibilities.

Country introduction

We will always start with some general comments about each country, to give you a feel for the place and to present some general information. This is followed up by some more specific **Climbing information**. We also give a brief overview of the major **Climbing areas** in the country by showing these on the country map. Herewith we quote the number of routes in that area, which often is an accumulation of different crags, and whether it is a sport, trad, DWS or bouldering area.

Climbing area not included in this Rock Climbing Atlas

Climbing area included in this Rock Climbing Atlas

Sport climbing

Traditional climbing

Bouldering

Deep Water Soloing

Total number of routes

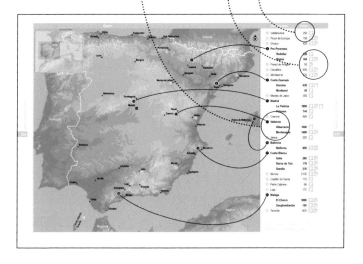

We then present a lot of practical information. In the **Climate** section there is information about the average climate in the country, including average temperature and rainfall figures. We pick the figures to be most representative of the conditions in the climbing areas in the country, but be aware that these are averages and that variations can be extreme! Later, in the individual 'Climbing area / When to go' sections the specific weather conditions for the climbing area are given plus a recommendation for **When to go**.

Getting there gives you the most important information about the best and cheapest travel options to get to the country from abroad. Where applicable, we give you options for travel by plane, train, bus, car and boat. In many cases we give you details of websites containing up to date travel and ticket information.

Moving around provides you with similar information for travel within the country. We try to provide you with travel information for both public transport and car, except when it's impossible to get to the climbing areas by public transport. Car rental can be very useful if flying into a country and we give details of the best places to hire a car. We also provide information about how to get from the airport to the centre of town, and the bus and train stations.

Next we describe the **Accommodation** options with average prices, including campsites, guest-houses and hotels. The local **Food & Drinks** is also described and here we give average costs for eating out in restaurants, having a cappuccino or a beer in a bar and the costs of supermarket food. Moving onto climbing related things, we tell you where you can pick up **Local climbing guidebooks** and topos/route information for the climbing areas we describe. The information provided here is general and will tend to include locations of climbing shops in large towns and cities - local outlets are described in the climbing area sections. Finally we give **Facts about the country**, including important information such as visa requirements, emergency numbers, currency and exchange rates, safety, language, mobile phone usage, internet access and if the water from the tap is safe to drink.

Month	Average temperature (°C)	Average rainfall (mm)
Jan	6	35
Feb	7	37
March	10	39
April	12	44
May	15	43
June	21	31
July	24	11
Aug	25	11
Sept	21	34
Oct	14	47
Nov	9	52
Dec	6	44

Climate table Madrid

Climbing area information

Here you'll find a general description of the climbing area along with information about the best time of year to go. A map shows the whole area with the various crags and, along with further sketches and GPS waypoints, should be enough to allow you to get to each crag painlessly. However, it goes without saying that a general map of the area or the country is always useful!

► Recommendable

Spring

Spring   Summer   Autumn   Winter

► Not recommendable

Winter

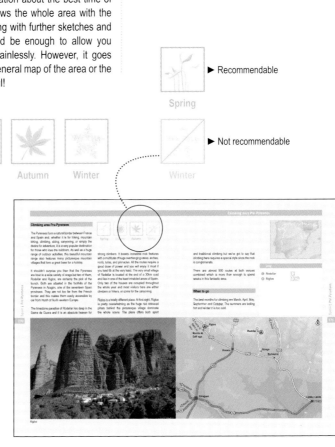

The next section tells you **How to get to the area** and **how to move around** and provides precise details of how to reach the climbing area. We will always tell you if the crags are accessible with public transport or if you'll need your own car. If public transport is an option, we'll give you as much information as possible but we don't publish exact timetables, since this information is very liable to change. Still, we'll give you frequencies and journey times, which should allow you to make good plans. We try to give you fare information where possible and we always quote prices for 2nd class travel. Of course, we also give links to websites with local travel information.

Where to stay tells you about the local accommodation. Where camping is an option, we'll always include campsites as well as possible other types of (cheap) accommodation.

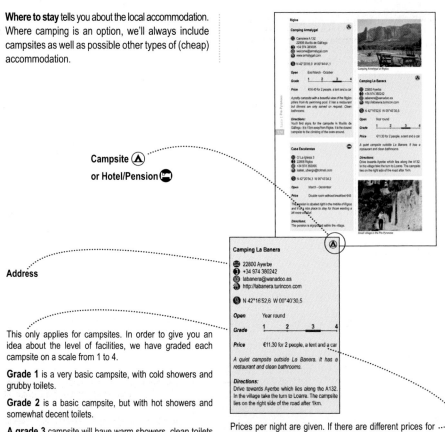

Campsite (A)

or Hotel/Pension

Address

This only applies for campsites. In order to give you an idea about the level of facilities, we have graded each campsite on a scale from 1 to 4.

Grade 1 is a very basic campsite, with cold showers and grubby toilets.

Grade 2 is a basic campsite, but with hot showers and somewhat decent toilets.

A grade 3 campsite will have warm showers, clean toilets and a few other facilities such as a bar and a playground for children.

A grade 4 campsite is luxurious with all kind of facilities.

Prices per night are given. If there are different prices for the low and the high season this is stated as well. High season normally is July and August. Prices for hotels are for a double room with an en-suite bathroom, unless otherwise stated.

Where to buy groceries tells you about the local shops and the best and cheapest places to buy supplies.

In the Country Introduction section there is information given about the relevant climbing guidebooks. In the **Where to find the local climbing guidebook** section, detailed information about the local guidebooks is given, as well as addresses of the shops where you can buy them. If there is no local guidebook, we tell you where you can find information and/or topos on the internet. Of course,

websites come and go so check *www.rockclimbing atlas.com* for the latest information.

Finally, we tell you **What else is there to see & do** in the area besides climbing. We wrote this section particularly for those on longer trips or those climbing as part of a general (family) holiday, but everyone appreciates good rest days too! We don't intend to give a complete overview of all possible activities but we highlight those we think are the most interesting.

Crag details

In this section we present the most important information about the crags. Besides some general comments about the crag and the climbing, there is a comprehensive **Crag details** page where all the required information can be found at a glance.

One star means the climbing is fantastic in terms of quality of the routes and the setting.
Two stars means a visit is absolutely mandatory.

The **GPS waypoints** of the parking and/or the exact location of the crag are provided. We use the grid latitude / longitude hddd°mm'ss.s.

This gives the **time** required to get to the crag **on foot** from either the campsite Ⓐ or car-park 🅿 .

Sport climbing
Traditional climbing
Bouldering
DWS Deep water soloing

Route length, minimum and maximum. Maximum length is given for the longest multi pitch or trad routes where applicable.

We give a grade for the **quality of protection**. This always only applies to the sport routes at each crag and not to trad routes.

Grade 1: shouldn't try this one unless you prefer to go solo....

Grade 2: distances between bolts exceed 4 metres. You have to have good nerves or shouldn't climb above your level.

Grade 3: approximately every 3 metres a bolt

Grade 4: approximately every 2 metres a bolt

Family friendly means there is sufficient flat ground at the crag to take little children along and the approach from the parking or campsite is not too taxing. If applicable we give this information per sector.

The number in the middle of the pie chart indicates the **total number of routes**. This applies to the sport routes and multi pitch routes count as one route, unless otherwise stated. With regard to the **grade range** the most difficult pitch in a multi pitch route is included. We used the French sport grade system.

Sport route: a route that is protected with drilled bolts.
Multi pitch routes: sport routes of at least two rope lengths.
Trad routes: routes on which the leader has to place all protection. On these routes you will always need to take friends, nuts and slings although there might be some fixed protection.

Symbols

Roads

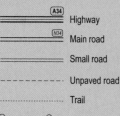

═══════ (A34)	Highway
═══════ (N34)	Main road
═══════	Small road
- - - - - - -	Unpaved road
··················	Trail
⚲——1 km——⚲	Distance
▪▬▪▬▪▬▪▬▪	Rail road

Landscape marks

River	River
Stream	Stream
City or Village	City or Village
Sea or Lake	Sea or Lake
Forest	Forest
Crag	Crag
Boulders	Boulders

Symbols

P	Car-park	✈	Airport
🏷	Signpost	🚌	Bus station / Stop
Bridge	Bridge	🚆	Train station
Ⓝ	North	🏠	House
🛒	Supermarket	⛪	Church
🍴	Restaurant	⛰	Mountain hut
🏨	Hotel / Pension	◼	Monastery
Ⓐ	Campsite	💧	Water source

The next page shows a **Detailed drawing** with the exact location of the crag, unless it is very obvious where it is. We must note that the map scale used is only approximate and features should not be interpreted literally. Where useful, we also include some point to point distances.

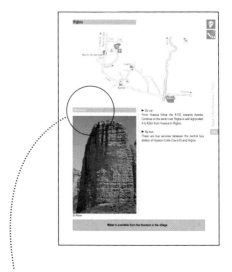

Finally, **Directions** the crags by car and/or by public transport is given.

Steve Mclure finds a rare rest on Tortuga Island (7c+), Sierre de Toix, Costa Blanca, Spain

Destinations for families with children

A family climbing holiday clearly requires an area with enough additional activities. Ideally it should also be possible to take the whole family to the crags so they can get some easy climbing done too. On this basis, the most family friendly destinations covered in this Rock Climbing Atlas are undeniably Sardinia and Arco in Italy, Orpierre and Corsica in France, Mallorca in Spain, and the Algarve in Portugal.

Cala Gonone on Sardinia is an excellent family destination and it probably is the most visited crag and for good reason. There is a wide range of climbing styles and difficulties and it has some sectors lying right on the beach. Lots of nearby accommodation, a great atmosphere, and many other activity options top this package.

Arco is the best-known climbing destination in Italy but the area is not just a magnet for climbers alone - Arco is an outdoor paradise in general! There are many family-oriented campsites near Arco that offer everything children need, including swimming pools and activity programs. The area encompasses a staggering 80 sectors with more than 2000 routes and many crags are suitable for taking young children to.

Orpierre in France has good family campsites too and, combined with the large number of easier routes, it already attracts a lot of families. Children can enjoy themselves at the swimming pool at the campsite while the adults climb some routes

nearby - it is only 10 minutes on foot from the village to the crags - or they can climb some easier routes too.

Corsica, another wonderfully island in the Mediterranean, is a great location for a rock climbing trip. The climbing is well developed with many different areas and most of the crags are situated inland. Middle-grade climbers have a lot to choose from, in particular. The 'Vallée de la Restonica' is one of Corsica's most important crags. This stunning mountain setting lies south west of Corte and is a highlight for many - hikers as well as climbers. The majority of the routes are 5th and 6th grade and it is an ideal place to take children too. The valley itself, as well nearby Corte, has several campsites.

Mallorca is one of those perfect sun-drenched islands with an abundance of limestone that also serves as a major package holiday destination. The sport climbing venues on the island are quite evenly spread. There are a number of crags on the coast but the majority are inland. Deep water soloing is becoming more and more popular in Mallorca too. Despite the island's reputation as a tourist hot spot you can be there in high season without being bothered by the crowds; the island is of a reasonable size and the nightmare package holiday resorts are quite concentrated. The best option if you are with a family is to rent a villa located somewhere in the centre of the island. These are very pleasant places and often come with a private swimming pool providing for lots of fun for the children. Some of the crags, like the beach venue Cala Magraner, are perfect spots for taking the family along (although in mid summer it will be too hot).

The Algarve in Portugal can be ranked as a family destination since there are loads of holiday resorts that are not too far from the climbing spots. Especially if one half of the family enjoys the beach and the sea more than rocks, it can make an ideal destination. In the far south of the Algarve you'll find Rocha da Pena, a very worthwhile crag inland from Faro. Further west there are the sea cliffs

> the rucksack <
faszination & perfektion bis ins detail

www.rock-snake.com

ROCK SNAKE
mountain gear

near Sagres with a combination of DWS, sport, and trad climbing.

Finally it is worth mentioning that two of Europe's best bouldering spots, Fontainebleau in France and Albarracin in Spain, are great family destinations too.

Cheap climbing destinations

With so many cheap flights crossing Europe traveling a bit to get some fantastic climbing done is a completely feasible option. However, budget still must be respected! Here we give some suggestions for climbing areas that don't require having a car to get to the crags and where accommodation is cheap.

El Chorro in Spain really is a superb low-cost destination. The outstanding limestone, the quality of the routes, and the exceptional setting are the reasons for its world-class status. The nearby airport of Malaga is served by many low cost airlines and there's a climber-run campsite close to the climbing. This pretty much seals the deal! There are direct trains from the airport to the main train station, Málaga Renfe. From here there is one daily direct train to El Chorro. At the Camping Finca la Campana it is possible to camp (€6 p.p.p.n), sleep in a bunk room (€11 p.p.p.n) or rent a bungalow from €38 for 2 people to €88 for a group of 8 per night. Campers can make use of the kitchen.

Montanejos, 90km from València, is a real climbers' paradise. The setting is simply beautiful and lush, centred on a big lake called Embalse de Arenoso. The climbing here is mainly on pocketed limestone and there is a combination of bolted and traditional routes. There is a choice of more than 1400 routes spread out over 80 sectors. There are several low-cost airlines flying between València and other European cities. Buses run between València and Montanejos making it easy to reach. In Montanejos the best and cheapest option is to stay at the friendly Albergue El Refugio just outside the village and near the climbing sectors. The price is €15 p.p.p.n. in the bunk room including breakfast and dinner.

Alan Sarhan enjoying the difficult routes at The Gorges du Tarn, photo by Eoin Lawless

South west of Barcelona, near the city of Reus, lies one of the top crags in Spain, Siurana. This is a place to push your limits - it is not really for beginners! It's also worth mentioning that Siurana is one of those places where you can come alone; the welcoming campsite there is a great place to meet other climbers. You can camp here (€10 for 2 persons) or rent a bungalow (€35 to €60 per day for a bungalow up to 4 people). From the campsite you can walk to the sectors. The usual low cost airlines fly to Barcelona but also check out the option of flying to Reus - Ryanair operates direct flights from the UK, as do various charter airlines. From Barcelona there are trains to Reus and from here you continue by bus to Cornudella de Montsant. From here you need to hitchhike the last 7.7km to Siurana.

The Gorges du Tarn in France is a beautiful gorge situated in the south of France, north west of Montpellier. It offers over 400 routes and it surely is on par with Buoux and Ceüse, and highly

The stunning Sector Los Miradores, Estrecho del Mijares of Montanejos

recommended for those who climb 7a and above. The nearest airport is Montpellier but it will be cheaper to fly either to Nîmes or Marseille. Budget airlines operate flights to the latter two cities, Marseille being served most frequently. From Marseille it is possible to travel by train to Montpellier and from here to Millau by bus. From Millau you need to take a taxi to Les Vignes or to ask someone to take you along. Once in Les Vignes you'll find a wide choice of accommodation and the cheapest option is to camp at one of the campsites for less than €10 per day for 2 people. The campsites are 2.2km to 4.5km away from the crags.

Desert tour in Morocco

Orpierre in France is known as a very good destination for beginners and intermediate climbers. It is possible to get there by public transport although the last part requires hitchhiking. Book a budget flight to Grenoble, Marseille, or Nice. Of these Marseille and Nice are major destinations and you can often find very good deals as the competition between the low cost airlines is intense. To get to Orpierre you first need to go to Laragne-Montéglin. As Laragne-Montéglin is connected by train to Marseille Saint-Charles Rail Station it is best to fly to Marseille. The journey takes 3 hours. From Nice it takes 5½ hours. From Laragne-Montéglin you will need to hitchhike first to Eyguians and the last 6km onwards to Orpierre. There is only one campsite in Orpierre itself (€16 for 2 persons) and there are several options to rent a gîte. These self catering apartments or cottages are dotted around in quiet spots throughout the village. Expect to pay between €200 and €800 for 2 to 6 persons per week. From the village it only is a 10 minute walk to the crags.

Val di Mello in Italy, sometimes referred to as Europe's Yosemite, has a very special atmosphere and stunning scenery, and the climbing is just great. The small mountain village of San Martino lies at the start of the Val di Mello. It's a very pretty and a convenient place to stay as it offers a good choice of accommodation all within walking distance of the climbing. Camping costs €16 for 2 people. The best airport is Milan Bergamo - it is not far away from the Val di Mello and is served by several budget airlines. Getting to the Val di Mello from Bergamo airport by public transport involves a combination of buses and trains.

Finally, everyone knows about Fontainebleau! Not only is the climbing magical, but it's easy to get to from just about everywhere (by train, plane or - if you're feeling enterprising - hitching a lift!), there's a huge range of climbing within walking distance of one of the campsites, and it's very feasible to rock-up on your own and get loads of climbing done. Various budget airlines serve Paris and it's also a major railway hub. Once in the centre, catch a train to Fontainebleau itself and hitch a lift to the La Musardière campsite. Camping for 2 people costs €15 and the Trois Pignons area is on your doorstep!

Climbing and sightseeing in Morocco

For many climbers, Morocco is not a destination that readily pops up on the radar. Yet, besides being an exceptionally interesting country to discover, Morocco also boasts some exceptional climbing that is completely unlike anything else you'll find in Europe. There are three main climbing areas in Morocco; the areas are completely different from each other so where you should go really depends on your preferred climbing style. For bolt clipping it is best to head for the Todra Gorge. High limestone cliffs change colour in a magical effect as the day unfolds; weirdly shaped rock formations and tall green palm trees form the setting of Morocco's most popular climbing venue. There are over 400 single and multi pitch routes spread over different sectors that are all easy to reach. The quality and variety for such a small area is

Nympha Stassen in control on Renato butta la pasta (6b+), Sector Belvedere, Arco, Italy, photo by Paul Lahaye

immense and the potential for further development is mind-boggling. Many regular tourists visit the Todra Gorge too so it is rather easy to get there from Marrakesh, and the choice of accommodation is excellent.

If you fancy more adventure and love multi pitching then head to the beautiful Taghia Gorge. Deep canyons, overhanging red walls, peaks reaching 3000 metres, and verdant valleys create the breathtaking scenery of the gorge. Right in the middle lies the remote village of Taghia at 1900 metres. It is a bit of a mission to get there but once in the friendly Berber village you'll find yourself in a completely different world where you'll loose all sense of time. You will stay in a basic gîte run by a Berber family and enjoy your meals with them. There are 115 equipped routes - up to 800 metres long - on perfect limestone although it must immediately be said that the entry requirement is a steady 6b. A great way to combine climbing in the Taghia and Todra gorges is to walk between them! This trek is highly recommended and you'll experience some of the best scenery in the High Atlas.

The third area, Tafraoute, is also relatively unknown among climbers, though normal tourists - attracted by the beautiful surroundings - are slowly finding their way here. This is the place to come for bouldering or pure trad climbing. There are literally thousands of granite boulders to explore (with a lot of potential for new problems) and there are great trad routes on solid quartzite. Either way climbing here will be an adventure!

Wherever you choose to go in Morocco make sure to soak up the culture too. Take a tour in the Sahara or go trekking in the mountains and you will have an unforgettable holiday!

Combine climbing with other activities

If climbing is not the only thing you're interested in then there are many places where you can mix in other activities. Portugal, for example, is the place on the Atlantic for surfers of all kinds, whether regular surfing, wind, or kite. It has a huge range

Go both sailing and climbing in Corsica

of waves and swells, and is a popular destination with surfers of all abilities. It is also a good place to learn to surf - there are lots of places offering surf lessons and packages. Near Lisbon, the crags and the best surfing beach are close to each other. The Algarve has similarly favourable combinations. In other words, Portugal is a magic destination for a combined surf-climb trip!

The clear waters of the Maltese archipelago are also a real treat for beach bums, scuba divers, and wind surfers. Here climbing can be perfectly combined with any water-activity. Plus, Malta has 7,000 years of history and is literally saturated with cultural gems that really can't be missed. There are wonderful excavated temples from the Neolithic period, well preserved Baroque palaces, Renaissance cathedrals, ancient forts, and many museums. Malta truly is a diverse, and romantic, destination.

The most adventurous destination in this Rock Climbing Atlas is undeniably Morocco. Climbing at one of the three areas is easily combined with hiking in the mountains, a trip to the desert or sightseeing in one of its famous cities such as Marrakesh. Make sure to see as much of Morocco as possible, you won't regret it!

Jack Geldard on the eighth pitch (7a+) of Les Rivieres Pourpres, Tagia Gorge, Morocco, photo by David Pickford

Quick scan

Climbing area	Crag	Spring	Summer	Autumn	Winter	Easy routes	Moderate routes	Difficult routes
France								
Fontainebleau	Fontainebleau	●	●	●	●	●	●	●
Orpierre	Orpierre	●	●	●			●	●
Gorges du Tarn	Gorges du Tarn	●	●				●	●
Verdon	Gorges du Verdon	●	●	●			●	●
Les Calanques	Les Calanques	●		●	●	●	●	●
Corsica	Rocher des Gozzi	●		●			●	●
	Col de Bavella	●		●			●	●
	Restonica	●		●			●	●
Italy								
Finale	Finale Ligure	●		●			●	●
Val di Mello	Val di Mello	●	●	●			●	●
Arco	Arco	●	●	●	●	●	●	●
Sardinia	Domusnovas	●	●	●	●	●	●	●
	Isili	●	●	●	●	●	●	
	Jerzu	●	●	●	●	●		●
	Baunèi	●	●	●	●	●	●	●
	Gala Gonone	●	●	●	●	●	●	●
Malta								
Malta	Wied Babu	●		●	●	●	●	
	Blue Grotto	●	●	●	●	●	●	
Gozo	Mġarr ix-Xini	●		●	●	●		●
	Dwejra	●	●	●	●	●	●	●

Making the most of the short winter days in the Calanques, photo by Thomas Rijniers

Climbing area	Crag		🗡	☀	🍃	❄	Easy routes	Moderate routes	Difficult routes
Morocco									
Todra Gorge	Todra Gorge		●		●	●	●	●	●
Taghia Gorge	Taghia Gorge		●		●	●		●	●
Tafraoute	Jebel el Kest		●		●	●	●	●	
	Tafraoute boulders		●		●	●		●	●
Portugal									
Lisbon	Sintra		●	●	●	●		●	
	Farol da Guia		●	●	●	●	●	●	
	Baía Do Mexilhoeiro		●	●	●	●	●	●	●
Algarve	Rocha Da Pena		●	●	●	●	●	●	●
	Sagres		●	●	●	●		●	●
Spain									
Pre-Pyrenees	Rodellar		●		●			●	●
	Riglos		●		●		●	●	●
Madrid	La Pedriza		●		●		●	●	
	Patones		●		●			●	●
Malaga	El Chorro		●		●	●		●	●
	Desplomilandia		●		●	●		●	●
Costa Blanca	Sella		●		●	●		●	●
	Gandia		●		●	●	●	●	●
	Sierra de Toix		●		●	●	●	●	
València	Albarracín		●		●			●	●
	Montanejos		●		●			●	●
Costa Daurada	Siurana		●		●	●		●	●
	Montsant		●		●	●		●	●
Mallorca	Mallorca		●	●	●	●	●	●	●

...the heart of
European climbing...

France

Eric Chaxel on Katia strophe (7b), Gorges du Tarn,
photo by Paul Lahaye

No other nation embraces sport climbing as fully as the French. Not surprising, since they have lots of it! The further south you go in France, the more bolted crags you encounter and there really is something for everyone's taste, at any time of the year.

France still sits right at the top of the European heap and not only for its status in the climbing world. Whether it's the food and wine, the landscape, the culture, or a Mediterranean feel you're looking for, it's very likely that you'll find it in Europe's second largest country. Its landscape varies from flat empty plains to high mountains with a wealth of lush green forests and sparkling rivers. The Mediterranean coast includes the popular tourist area, the French Riviera – its hot, dry summers and mild winters make it a popular beach area. Geographically, mountains and hills cover two thirds of the country. The highest point is the famous Mont Blanc (4808m), on the border of France and Italy, and it is the highest mountain in Western Europe. Still, France's most famous landmark is undeniably its Eiffel Tower in Paris.

In addition to the old standbys walking, cycling, and skiing - and the traditional French jeu de boules! - France has an extremely wide range of outdoor activities. Rafting and canoeing are very popular, and practically every stretch of river, particularly in the gorges and ravines of the Pyrenees, the Alps, and the Massif Central, has places renting boats or organizing excursions. These same mountainous areas are also prime rock climbing territory. The French are very keen on bolted routes, which invite even the more cautious climbers to lead. Generally you just have to look for the name of the route at the base of the crag (it will be painted), you climb it using only a set of quickdraws following the bolt line, and when you get to the top, you will find a perfect belay anchor, usually two bolts and a chain, from which you will be lowered down by your partner. Can it be more relaxed than this?!

Climbing information

Almost every climber is familiar with names like Buoux or Ceüse from photos of these sport's hot shots in the climbing magazines. These are undeniably great areas and sport climbers operating at the higher levels will no doubt wish to visit them. In this chapter, however, we sample some other destinations in France, lesser known maybe but still popular, that offer a wide range of climbing. Some of these are perfect for beginners whereas others are more suitable for advanced climbers. We also give you a selection of places that are good to visit both in summer and winter.

Sunset in the Calanques

Climbing area Fontainebleau

Welcome to the Europe's boulderers' heaven! The countless problems are spread out in the forest of Fontainebleau. The area is well documented and the boulders are clearly marked which makes it a superb destination for beginners and advanced, for young and old!

Climbing area Orpierre

Orpierre is known as one of the best low and middle grade crags in France. The compact limestone has loads of 4th, 5th and 6th grade routes that are well-bolted. The area is named after the rustic village at the base of the climbing.

Climbing area Gorges du Tarn

The breathtaking Gorges du Tarn is an excellent destination for those who climb 7a and above. The gorge lacks good easier routes. The fantastic scenery attracts thousands of tourists each year, who come to enjoy the environment and canoe on the Tarn river.

Climbing area Gorges du Verdon

The Verdon is for many the most famous climbing destination in France. The dramatic scenery, beautiful nearby lakes, and inspiring climbing draws many people here. It's a great place and climbing here is a unique experience - getting to the start of the routes involves airy abseils from the rim of the gorge!

Climbing area Les Calanques

The Calanques is one of the largest rock climbing areas in France. The variety of climbing is huge and the location right on the Mediterranean Sea will blow your mind.

Climbing area Corsica

The island where Napoleon Bonaparte was born hosts some splendid granite crags. Corsica itself is a relaxed but very popular island and gets real busy in summer. The island lacks good routes above 7b but is a good destination for 5th and 6th grade climbers.

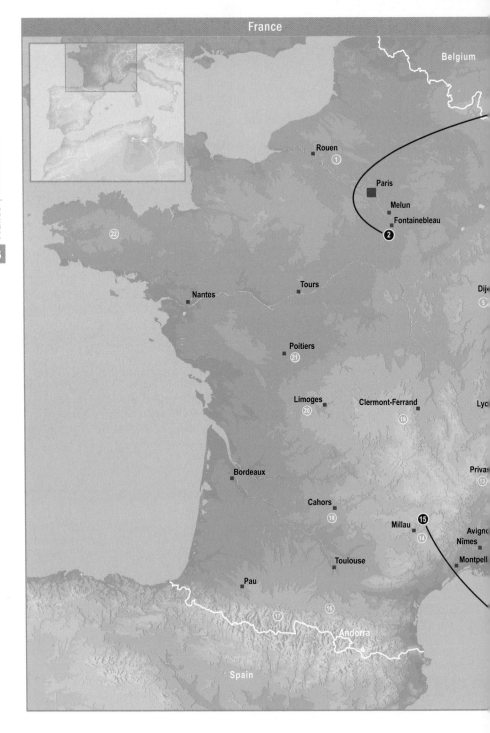

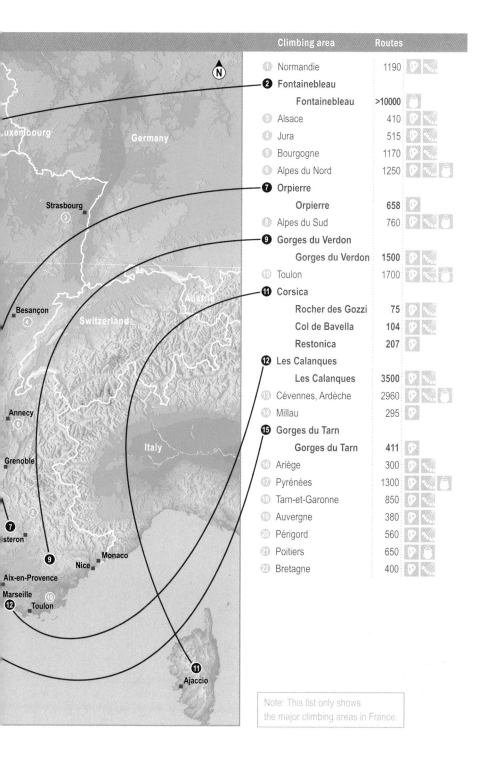

Climbing area	Routes	
① Normandie	1190	
② Fontainebleau		
Fontainebleau	>10000	
③ Alsace	410	
④ Jura	515	
⑤ Bourgogne	1170	
⑥ Alpes du Nord	1250	
⑦ Orpierre		
Orpierre	658	
⑧ Alpes du Sud	760	
⑨ Gorges du Verdon		
Gorges du Verdon	1500	
⑩ Toulon	1700	
⑪ Corsica		
Rocher des Gozzi	75	
Col de Bavella	104	
Restonica	207	
⑫ Les Calanques		
Les Calanques	3500	
⑬ Cévennes, Ardèche	2960	
⑭ Millau	295	
⑮ Gorges du Tarn		
Gorges du Tarn	411	
⑯ Ariège	300	
⑰ Pyrénées	1300	
⑱ Tarn-et-Garonne	850	
⑲ Auvergne	380	
⑳ Périgord	560	
㉑ Poitiers	650	
㉒ Bretagne	400	

Note: This list only shows the major climbing areas in France.

Climate

There are four climatic regions in France that are all affected by the sea in some way. In the west, a true moderate sea climate can de found, driven by the Atlantic. France's interior sees a more continental climate that includes hotter summers and full winters with low-ish rainfall - for example, Paris sees an average July temperature of 18 degrees Celcius and January temperatures of 2 degrees Celcius. The mountains, of course, have their own climate where winters are bitterly cold and prolonged. Naturally, they also see more precipitation, and in winter lots of snow. Most of the villages in the high valleys receive more than 50 days of snow each year. The south, up to 60 km from the Mediterranean coast, experiences a true Mediterranean climate with hot and dry summers and mild winters.

Month	Average temperature (°C)	Average rainfall (mm)
Jan	2	50
Feb	3	45
March	8	53
April	11	55
May	14	70
June	19	85
July	21	54
Aug	20	90
Sept	17	91
Oct	12	76
Nov	7	80
Dec	3	57

Climate table Lyon

Summertime in France

A painter in Orpierre

Getting there

By plane

Air France and, scores of other airlines, link Paris with every part of the world. Some other French cities with international air links (mainly to places within Europe) include Bordeaux, Lyon, Nice, Marseille, Strasbourg and Toulouse. These cities are often served by European low cost airlines.

By train

Rail services connect France with the rest of Europe. You can book tickets and get information from Rail Europe (*www.raileurope.com*). The Channel Tunnel (*www.eurotunnel.com*) has a high-speed rail link to England.

By bus

Paris has bus services to and from every part of Europe. Buses are slower and less comfortable than trains, but they are cheaper. Check *www.eurolines.com*.

By ferry

The quickest passenger ferries and hovercrafts to England run between Calais and Dover, and Boulogne and Folkestone. But there are numerous other routes linking Brittany and Normandy with

England as well. Start your search at *www.ferry-to-france.co.uk*, *www.aferry.to* or *www.directferries.co.uk*.

 By car

France is easily reached from any other European country by car. From the UK a car can be taken on the train or on the ferry. Border crossings are no issue.

Moving around

Generally it's best to have your own car in France. Areas where you don't necessarily need one are Fontainebleau, Gorges du Tarn, and Orpierre. Car rental is possible at all airports in France. As always, it is best to book a rental car in advance via the internet. France's airports have efficient bus transfers to the city centers from where you can get connecting trains or buses.

 By public transport

France has an excellent rail network, operated by the state-owned SNCF (*www.sncf.com*), which reaches almost every part of the country. Thanks to the high-speed TGV trains (*www.tgv.com*) the journey time between major cities has become shorter and internal travel is normally easier by rail than by air. Check out their websites for travel information. Many towns and villages that are not on the train network are linked by intra-département bus lines making it fairly easy to get nearly everywhere on public transport.

Traditional hamlet in the lush Gorges du Tarn, photo by Paul Lahaye

Lunch is very important in France

 By car

Many of France's main motorways are subject to tolls based on the distance traveled. Don't forget to factor in these costs. For example, Lille - Paris - Lyon - Nice costs nearly €80 one way for a normal car.

 By ferry

It is possible to get to Corsica by ferry on which you can take your own car. See the Corsica section for more information.

Accommodation

All kind of accommodation is available in France - idyllic small campsites, charming bed & breakfasts, simple gîtes, self-catered apartments, five-star fully-fledged family campsites, and comfortable hotels. As a climber you are most likely to end up camping and, luckily, every little corner in France has a campsite. Camping and the outdoor life is a little national habit! Prices range from €10 to €26 for two people, a car and a tent but most campsites are only open from around Easter to the end of October. Most areas, fortunately, offer other type of accommodation in winter. Apartment prices range between €200 and €800 for 4-persons per week. A bed in a gîte would normally cost about €15 to €20 per person per night including breakfast and possibly dinner. A double room in a budget hotel starts at €25 per night.

Food & drinks

The French consider cooking an art and its cuisine is extremely diverse. France's geographic and climatic diversity provides the locals with all types of ingredients and this, together with France's long and varied history, defines its food. Actually it is often said that an understanding of French food culture will lead to an understanding of France itself.

Meals range from the very basic, such as the traditional baguette with cheese and an inexpensive red wine, to very complicated dinners than involve many different courses and different wines taken over several hours. It is common in many parts in France to take a two hour break for lunch. Aside from bread and water, wine and cheese are always part of every French meal. In France wine is considered a standard part of everyday meals and is neither expensive nor reserved for special occasions. In addition to its use in cooking, cheese is very often served on a platter as its own course after the main meal but before dessert.

Costs for eating out are low compared to Northern Europe, but you should still expect to pay €25 for a complete dinner, including wine, in a mid-range restaurant. Having a coffee or a small beer in a typical French bar would cost around €1.50. In touristy areas this price can easily triple.

Corte, Corsica

Climbing guidebook

The climbing areas covered in this chapter are all well documented in a range of guidebooks. These are on sale at book shops, tobacco shops, or campsites located at the climbing areas. A good outdoor gear shop in France that has a number of branches is Au Vieux Campeur. They are based in several big cities such as Paris, Lyon, and Toulouse. See their website for opening hours and addresses: *www.au-vieux-campeur.fr.*

France's landscape is never dull

Au Graton Farci

Bon appétit.

PETZL

Corsica has fantastic scenic climbing, photo by Bertrand Maurin

Facts & figures

Population:	58 million
Religion:	Roman Catholic (±80%)
Capital:	Paris
Time zone:	GMT+1
Telephone code:	+33

Money

Currency:	Euro (€)
ATM machines:	widespread

Language

The official language of France is French.

Goodmorning	
	Bonjour
Thank you	
	Merci
Goodbye	
	Au revoir
Yes / No	
	Oui / Non
Right / Left / Straight	
	à droite / à gauche / tout droit
Rock climbing	
	Escalade

Visas & formalities

EU	Other European nationalities	USA / Canada	All other nationalities
No visa required for a period of up to 90 days.			Most other nationalities do not require a visa for a period of up to 90 days. Check *www.diplomatie.gouv.fr* for more information.

Safety

France is a safe place to travel around. However, pretty crime and car theft are extremely common, especially in the south of France and particularly in Marseille. Do not leave anything whatsoever in your car. If you don't trust the situation, leave the windows slightly open to avoid them from being broken into.

Use of mobile phone

There is wide GSM coverage.

Internet access

Internet cafés are found in most towns and cost around €4 to €5 per hour.

Emergency numbers

General:	112
Police:	112
Fire brigade:	112
Ambulance:	112

Water

Tap water is usually safe to drink. However a lot of French buy bottled water as the water from the tap can taste terrible.

Climbing area Fontainebleau

Fontainebleau is without doubt the world's number one bouldering destination. Fontainebleau (often just called "Bleau", or "Font" in Britain) is both the name of a large forest and a small town with a Renaissance palace, just 60km south of Paris. This beautiful area is literally covered with thousands of fantastic sandstone boulders and it also is a favourite weekend getaway for Parisians. The forest is a national park covering 20,000ha and it has highly interesting flora and fauna. The soil in the forest is very sandy - caused by the erosion of the sandstone! - and this helps to make most of the landings very favourable and it adds to the fantastic setting of the boulders. It really feels like a perfect climbers' playground!

The sandstone boulders are spread throughout the forest; in total there are over 130 different areas to choose from. You would need a lifetime to climb them all. All kinds of problems can be found - from

| Spring | Summer | Autumn | Winter |

smooth slabs to steeply overhanging rock using anything from tiny crimps to full sized pockets and, of course, the infamous "Bleau Sloper". The height can vary a lot too - anything from 2m and 6m – and there are a few micro-routes posing as problems knocking around! No matter where you choose to go to you'll always find something to suit your taste since Fontainebleau is a perfect place both for beginners and for the very strong, and everyone in between. You'll even find children's circuits making it an ideal destination for families too.

Cul du Chien, Les Trois Pignons

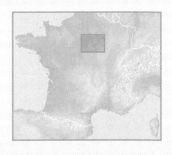

When to go

Fontainebleau is a true year-round bouldering destination. Even though winter months can be wet it is the best season to climb since the rock has much more friction when cool and dry. If you're ticking hard problems, this is the time to come. Naturally spring and autumn are much more comfortable. Summer is fine too since many boulders lie in the shade in the forest - however warm rock and wet hands mean you'll have to drop your grade a bit. It is a great summer destination for a family holiday.

Crag

Ⓐ Fontainebleau

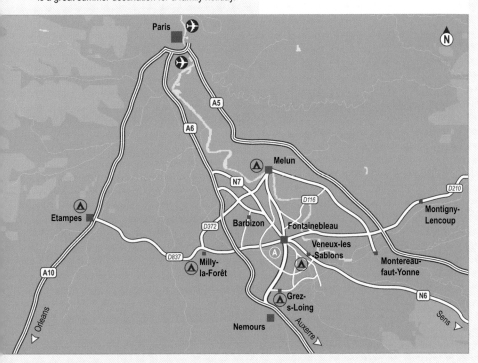

How to get to the area & how to move around

Having a car is a distinct advantage as it allows you to really explore the different areas. However, if you're content to limit yourself to the Trois Pignons region (not such a limitation actually, there's tons of great climbing here!), then hitching to the La Musardière campsite and walking to the boulders is very feasible. Since navigation in the huge forest is quite difficult and most areas are disseminated among the sandy valleys and plains it is advisable to buy the IGN blue map TOP25 number 2417-OT. With this map you cannot get lost!

 By public transport

It is possible to get by train to Fontainebleau and then take your bicycle or hitch. There is an hourly train departing from the train and subway station of Paris 'Gare de Lyon' to 'Bois-le-Roi' (just north of Fontainebleau) and 'Fontainebleau - Avon'. If you're hitching to get to La Musardière, get off the train at the latter and catch a lift west along the D409 to Milly-la-Fôret.

 By car

Both the A5 and A6 motorways skirt the forest. The best approach is on the A6 that crosses the forest on its western part - pick your exact exit depending on your end destination. If coming from the north, leave the A5 at Mélun and head into the forest on either the N6 or D64, again depending on your final destination.

The Royal Château of Fontainebleau

Where to stay

There are quite a number of campsites in the area but most of them only open between March/April and October/November. Outside this period the best option is to rent a gîte which is especially good value if you are in a group. Try: *www.gites-de-france.com*. Prices start at €250 per week for a 4 person gîte in low season and about €350 per week in high season.

One of the cheaper hotels based in Fontainebleau is the Ibis. It has zero character but a double room without breakfast in the centre of Fontainebleau costs €75.

Camping Les Pres

✉ 1, Chemin des prés
77880 Grez-sur-Loing
☎ +33 01 64457275
@ camping-grez@wanadoo.fr
🌐 www.camping-grez-fontainebleau.info

📍 N 48°19'04,7 E 02°41'56,7

Open	March 15 - November 11

Grade | 1   2   **3**   4

Price | €9.40 for 2 people, a tent and a car

Camping Les Pres is a preferred cheap place to stay by many boulderers. It is conveniently situated south of the forest. In the morning it is only a five minute walk to the bakery in Grez sur Loing for fresh croissants. The campsite has a separate bivouac field where open fires are allowed.

Directions:
From Fontainebleau take the N7 to Bourron-Marlotte and Grez-sur-Loing. The turn for the campsite is very easy to miss and comes just after the bridge on the right.

Camping Les Courtilles du Lido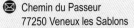

✉ Chemin du Passeur
  77250 Veneux les Sablons
☎ +33 01 60704505
@ lescourtilles-dulido@wanadoo.fr
🖥 www.les-courtilles-du-lido.fr

📱 N 48°23'00,1 E 02°48'06,4

Open   April 15 - September 20

Grade   1 —— 2 —— **3** ——— 4

Price   €14 for 2 people, a tent and a car;
            mobile homes are €221 to
            €700 per week for 4 to 7 people

The campsite lies east of the forest. There is a tennis court, swimming pool, bar and pizzeria. The owners also rent out mobile homes.

Directions:
From Fontainebleau follow the N6 to Veneux les Sablons. The campsite is well signposted.

Philipp Schmidt-Wellenburg on one of many typical slabby problems of Bleau, photo by Eoin Lawless

Fontainebleau centre

Camping La Musardière

✉ Route de grandes vallées
  91490 Milly la Forêt
☎ +33 01 64989191
@ lamusardiere@infonie.fr

📱 N 48°23'40,7 E 02°30'22,8

Open   February 16 - December 1

Grade   1 —— 2 —— **3** ——— 4

Price   €18.60 for 2 people, a tent and a car;
            mobile homes are €25 to €47
            per night for 2 to 6 people

Good clean campsite with swimming pools, very nicely situated in the forest. The campsite is a perfect base to explore the very popular region of 'Les Trois Pignons' and is very close to lots of climbing. Mobile homes are also for rent.

Directions:
On the A6 take exit 13 for Milly-la-Forêt. The campsite is signposted. Coming from Fontainebleau, take the D409 to Milly-la-Forêt. After passing Arbonne, the road crosses the A6 motorway (look out for this if you're hitching!) - the turn-off for the campsite is a little further on the left and is signposted.

Barry O'Dwyer on a hard 7a at Franchard Cuisinere in March,
photo by Eoin Lawless

Haras de la Fontaine Gîtes

✉ 3, rue de la Fontaine
  77167 Poligny
☎ +33 01 64780117
@ amiel@harasdelafontaine.com
🏠 www.france-gite-fontainebleau.fr

Price   €324 - €498, depending on
            the month for a 8 person gîte

*This place rents several nice gîtes of varying
sizes. See their website for detailed information
and prices.*

*Irene Pieper pushing it on Zen (7a),
photo by Jo Montchaussé*

Where to buy groceries?

There is a huge shopping centre at Villier-en-Bière
which is located on the N7 about 10km from Bas
Cuvier. There is a big Carrefour, a Decathlon that
sells climbing gear and lots of other shops. It is
not open on Sundays. Milly-la-Forêt has a good
range of local shops, or there's a moderately sized
Intermarché a little further north, for which you'll
see signs.

Where to find the local climbing guidebook

There are many available guides and the best one
will depend on the grade you climb. We recommend
you buy maps and guides before arriving, as they
can be tricky to find. Try *www.cordee.uk.co* or *www.
bleau.info*.

It you don't happen to have bought it beforehand,
go to the Tourist Office in Fontainebleau (4, Rue
Royale), which is near the palace. The Decathlon
at Villier-en-Bière sells some topos too. You can
also try your luck at the southern car park for Les
Trois Pignons - the SOeScalade van rocks up at
the weekend and main holiday periods during the
warmer months, and sells inexpensive climbing
gear and topos, and does cheap resoles.

*Kevin Moroney on Carnage (7b+), Bas Cuvier,
Fontainebleau, photo by Eoin Lawless*

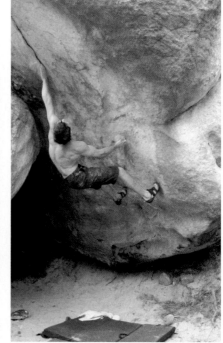

Boulder impressions, photos by Daniel Jaeggi

Bleau De Grès 6 describes many 5th and 6th grade problems.

Fontainebleau Magique is the Jingo Wobbly guide to mainly orange and blue circuits (3a-5b).

Au Grès des Trois Pignons is a topo covering the entire Les Trois Pignons area.

Fontainebleau Off Piste lists the harder problems in the main areas, grade 6 and above, and also some lesser-known problems off the beaten track.

Fontainebleau Climbs lists many areas and describes circuits of all difficulties.

Fontainebleau 7+8 lists all problems grade 7 and higher.

What else is there to see & do

Fontainebleau
Fontainebleau is a pleasant town that has a cinema and loads of restaurants and cafes where you can hide from the rain or just relax. The Royal Château of Fontainebleau is also well worth a visit. The château dates back to the sixteenth century and shows marks of each monarch and emperor who lived there, amongst them Napoleon. It's right in the centre of the town and its gardens are free to the public. It's a nice alternative to seeing Versailles.

Biking and hiking
The forest of Fontainebleau is full of walking and cycling trails, also marked on the IGN blue map TOP25 number 2417-OT.

Bouldering!
If the weather closes in on you and threatens to make you weak through inactivity, there is a bouldering wall in Arbonne to keep you fit!

Young Rick Lahaye enjoying the white circuit at Franchard Cuisiniere, photo by Mike Lahaye

Fontainebleau

There are over 130 different areas hidden in the forest, with thousands of boulders. Where you should go really depends on the grades you're looking to climb. We give a few suggestions below but for a complete overview of all areas have a look at *www.bleau.info*.

Most problems are grouped together in colour-coded circuits which can be easily followed around. Each problem is marked with a number in coloured paint - by following the numbers you will get to do a broad range of problems of similar difficulty. There are even special circuits for children.

One important thing to take into account, especially if you're not too familiar with bouldering, is that the Fontainebleau grading system is different to the sport climbing grading. As a rule of thumb (at least in the middle grades), drop a digit from your sport climbing grade to get an idea of the kind of problems you could be attempting; if you can climb a 7a sport route on sight, a 6a problem should be doable on sight.

Circuit colour coding:
White: very easy and low boulders especially
            for children.
Yellow: 2a - 3b
Orange: 3a - 4b
Blue: 4a - 5b
Red: 5a - 6b
Black (and sometimes White): 6a – 8b

Suggested areas for beginners:
● Canche aux Merciers
● Rocher des Potêts
● Diplodocus
● Le Rocher de la Reine
● L'éléphant

Suggested areas for intermediate boulderers:
● Bas Cuvier
● Cul du Chien
● Bois Rond
● 95.2
● La Roche aux Sabots

Suggested areas for strong boulderers:
● Bas Cuvier
● Cuvier Rempart
● Apremont
● Franchard Cuisinière
● Franchard Isatis
● Drei Zinnen

Suggested areas that have white circuits for families with young children:
● Beauvais
● Franchard Ermitage
● Roche aux Sabots
● Gorges d'Apremont
● Canche aux Merciers
● J.A. Martin
● Rocher Canon
● Rocher Saint-Germain
● Mont Aigu
● Maisse le Patouillat
● Buthiers
● Etréchy
● Mondeville
● La Padôle
● L'éléphant

Time for a beer in Fontainebleau

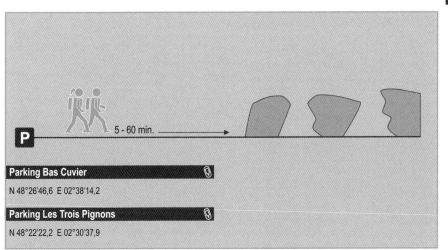

5 - 60 min.

Parking Bas Cuvier

N 48°26'46,6 E 02°38'14,2

Parking Les Trois Pignons

N 48°22'22,2 E 02°30'37,9

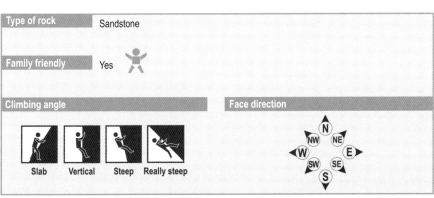

Type of rock	Sandstone
Family friendly	Yes

Climbing angle

Slab   Vertical   Steep   Really steep

Face direction

N NW NE W E SW SE S

Number of routes & Grade range

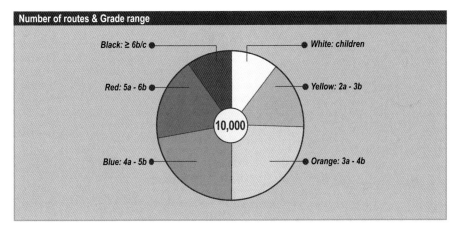

Black: ≥ 6b/c

Red: 5a - 6b

Blue: 4a - 5b

White: children

Yellow: 2a - 3b

Orange: 3a - 4b

10,000

Climbing area Orpierre

Spring   Summer   Autumn   Winter

Orpierre is named after the very small and pretty medieval village at the base of the climbing. Situated in the Buëch valley in the beautiful Alpes-de-Haute-Provence département, Orpierre is known as a very good destination for beginners and intermediate climbers - the majority of the routes are 5th and 6th grade. There is also plenty to do for those that climb harder but these routes are of lower quality, to be honest.

It's not just the crags and the concentration of easy routes that attract the climbers - the setting is very special and the area is well worth a visit just to experience it. This part of the Haute-Provence has many small, pretty villages and fantastic flora and fauna. But there are also larger towns nearby, like Sisteron, which are good for nights out or sightseeing.

Another big advantage is that it only is a 10 minute walk from the village to the crags. Since Orpierre offers good accommodation and even has one campsite in the village, it is a favorite with families: kids can enjoy themselves in the swimming pool at the campsite while parents climb nearby. Or, as a place to make "first steps", it's unbeatable. So, if all of this appeals to you, head for the Haute-Provence!

Sector Le Puy lies just above the pretty village of Orpierre

When to go

Even though there are always climbers around from March to November it is best to stay away in summer (due to the heat) and just come during spring and autumn. Still, climbing in summer remains possible. Orpierre has a very dry climate: it only rains (or snows!) 25% of the time each year. Bring warm clothes for the evenings as the village is at an altitude of 700m.

Crag

Ⓐ Orpierre 🅿

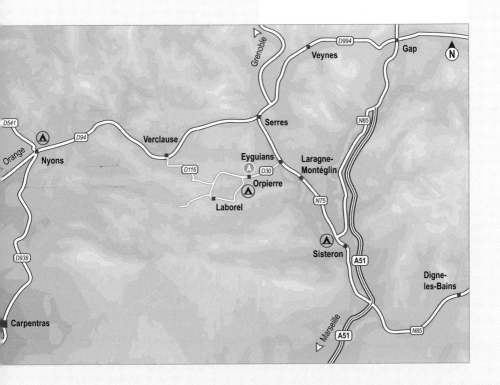

How to get to the area & how to move around

You can get to the area by public transport but the last part requires hitching a lift. Therefore it is more convenient to rent a car but, once in Orpierre, you don't need one to get to the climbing.

 By public transport

Book a budget flight to Grenoble, Marseille, or Nice. Of these Marseille and Nice are major destinations and you can often find very good deals as the competition between the low cost airlines is intensive.

The get to Orpierre you first need to get to Laragne-Montéglin. As Laragne-Montéglin is connected by a direct line to Marseille Saint-Charles Rail Station [3h12, €23], Marseille is your best-bet airport. See 'By public transport' at the 'Climbing area Gorges du Tarn' section for information on transport between the airport and the railway station. From Nice it takes 5½ hours by train [€50.70]. From Laragne-Montéglin you will need to hitchhike, first to Eyguians and the last 6km onwards to Orpierre.

 By car

Orpierre is situated north west of Sisteron. From Paris take the motorway to Lyon, Grenoble, Gap and finally Sisteron. It is 720km from Paris.

Sector 4h and Adrech

Vincent Massuger on Elle a tout d'une grande (6a+), Sector Adrech

Where to stay

There is only one campsite in Orpierre itself but it only opens during the tourist season. Luckily there are also several possibilities to rent a gîte in Orpierre. These self-catering apartments or cottages are situated in peaceful locations throughout the village, often on roads where cars are not allowed. They also can be rented on a half-pension basis.

One of the better-known gîtes, Les Drailles, is run by Pierre-Yves Bochaton, one of the local activists and bolter. Call 0033 04 92663120 or go to *www. orpierre.info* for more information.

It totally depends on the number of people, the period of the year, the type of gîte, and the level of service but expect to pay between €200 and €800 for 2 to 6 people per week. The following gîte owners are based in or around Orpierre:
- *www.gites-lemoulin.com*
- *www.mirjam.web.com*
- *www.lapastarelle.com*

The GR946 goes right through Orpierre

Camping des Princes d'Orange

✉ 05700 Orpierre
☎ +33 04 92662253
@ campingorpierre@wanadoo.fr
🏠 www.camping-orpierre.com

📱 N 44°18'40,4 W 05°41'48,1

Open   April 1 - October 28

Grade
1 ——— 2 ——— 3 ——— 4

Price   €20 for two people, a car and a tent;
€255 to €550 for a 4 to 6 person
mobile home or chalet per week

Nicely located campsite only a few minutes on foot from the village and the climbing. It has a pool, a simple restaurant, and they rent mobile homes and chalets as well.

Directions:
The campsite is clearly signposted in the village.

Camping des Princes d'Orange in Orange is only a few minutes walk from the climbing scene

Hôtel Le Céans

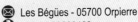

✉ Les Bégües - 05700 Orpierre
☎ +33 04 92662422
@ le.ceans@infonie.fr
🏠 www.le-ceans.fr

Open   March 15 - November 1

Price   a double room without breakfast
€47 to €61

The hotel has 24 rooms and comes with a tennis court and a swimming pool.

Directions:
Coming from Eyguians on the D30 go right through Orpierre. The hotel is 5km further down the road.

The tiny streets in Orpierre

Also available

Rock Climbing Atlas - South Eastern Europe

This edition covers the best climbing areas in:
Bulgaria, Croatia, Hungary, Macedonia, Romania and Slovenia

Sector Château

Leading difficult routes is no problem for Rick Lahaye, La Oullya Une (7a+)

Where to buy groceries?

There is only one small shop (epicerie) in Orpierre. There is a large Intermarché supermarket along the N75.

Where to find the local climbing guidebook

The Orpierre topo is for sale at the epicerie, the campsite in Orpierre, and at Vertigo Sport for €20 (the climbing shop on the main square). The topo covers the sectors surrounding the village and also some crags in nearby towns. It is a well-designed book but, unfortunately, it uses drawings instead of photos. This makes it tricky every now and then to find the right route.

What else is there to see & do

Sisteron
Only 20 minutes drive southeast of Orpierre, Sisteron is very well worth a day trip. The town is rich with monuments and old buildings, and is built on a remarkable rock-structure. The rocks look like razor blades and even have routes on them. It is actually a fun destination to go climbing for a few hours if you happen to be in town.

Outdoor activities
The climbing shop in Orpierre can organise various outdoor activities, including guided canyoning.

Walking & Biking
The beautiful and peaceful area surrounding Orpierre is great to explore on foot or by bike. If you require any information on hiking or biking tours, contact the Tourist Office.

Tourist Office Orpierre
- ✉ Le Village – 05700 Orpierre
- ☎ +33 04 92663045
- @ ot.orpierre@wanadoo.fr
- 🌐 www.orpierre.fr

Stephanie Bardeli concentrating on N comme cornichon (7a+), Sector Château

When driving into the village the first rock formation you will see is Sector Quiquillon. This imposing rock dominates the scene and will whet your appetite for the multi pitch routes on it. Sector Quiquillon is one of 9 sectors that together make Orpierre one of France's finest easy-grade climbing destinations.

The climbing area is well developed – the paths are clearly marked and most routes are completely bolted. A lot of your climbing effort will involve crimp routes on mainly vertical rock but there are also plenty of pocketed challenges. Those after 5th and 6th grade routes should head to the nearby sectors north of the village, Sectors Cascade or Belleric, not far away from Parking 1. Those climbers looking for mainly 7th grade routes the overhanging Sector Château is the place to be! The sectors closer to the village are visited most often as the approach to those from P2 is longer. It depends a bit on the sector but a helmet is no unnecessary luxury due to some loose rock, particularly at Sector Adrech.

The climbing shop in the village can provide any information you should require. They also offer canyoning and Via Ferrata trips. There is a toilet and water is available at the Parking du Belleric just behind the big car park in the village.

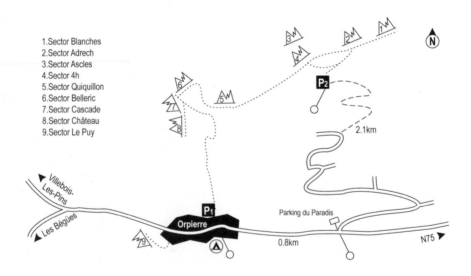

1.Sector Blanches
2.Sector Adrech
3.Sector Ascles
4.Sector 4h
5.Sector Quiquillon
6.Sector Belleric
7.Sector Cascade
8.Sector Château
9.Sector Le Puy

Directions

▶ By Car
Coming from Sisteron take the N75 / E712 to Serres. Orpierre is signposted on this road. It is 8km on the D30 from Eyguians to Orpierre.

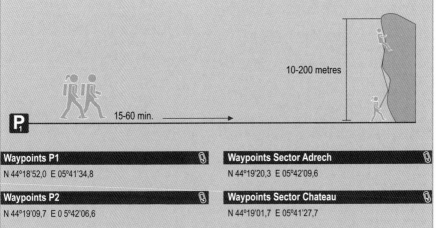

10-200 metres

15-60 min.

Waypoints P1
N 44°18'52,0 E 05°41'34,8

Waypoints P2
N 44°19'09,7 E 0 5°42'06,6

Waypoints Sector Adrech
N 44°19'20,3 E 05°42'09,6

Waypoints Sector Chateau
N 44°19'01,7 E 05°41'27,7

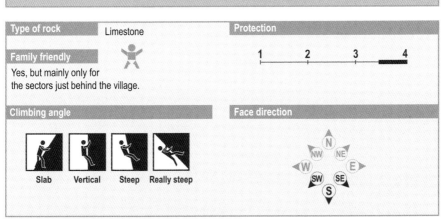

Type of rock
Limestone

Family friendly
Yes, but mainly only for
the sectors just behind the village.

Protection
1   2   3   4

Climbing angle
Slab   Vertical   Steep   Really steep

Face direction
N NW NE W E SW SE S

Number of routes & Grade range

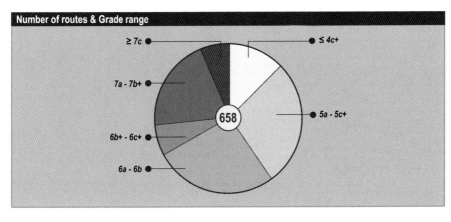

≥ 7c
≤ 4c+
7a - 7b+
5a - 5c+
6b+ - 6c+
6a - 6b

658

Climbing area Gorges du Tarn

The Gorges du Tarn is a beautiful gorge situated in the south of France, north west of Montpellier. The dramatic rock-faces on both sides of the gorge are carved out by the river Tarn, which finds its source on Mont Lozère in the Cévennes Mountains and flows through several French départements. This very impressive part of France attracts a large number of tourists each year. Especially in the months of July and August the gorge is crowded with people enjoying nature and the many other possible activities. The area is great for hiking and caving although most tourists come to enjoy kayaking or canoeing on the river itself.

The Gorges du Tarn is also an important climbing area in France with over 400 routes and is surely on par with Buoux and Ceüse for quality. However, there are not many easy routes in the Tarn so be warned - this is really a place for those climbing

Spring   Summer   Autumn   Winter

7a and above. The limestone is heavily featured, often overhanging and covered with pockets. Often stamina rather than power is required to complete the routes successfully.

As the gorge is a popular tourist destination you'll have no problems finding somewhere suitable to stay.

One of many picturesque villages in Gorges du Tarn

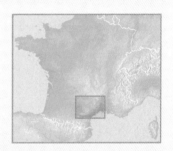

When to go

It is best to visit the Gorges du Tarn during spring and autumn. Summers are normally too hot and the place gets very crowded with tourists anyway. You also have to contend with high accommodation prices during these months. Still, there are enough shady sectors to make climbing feasible in summer.

Crag

Ⓐ Gorges du Tarn

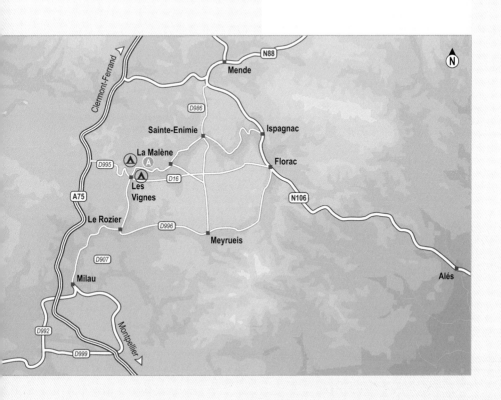

How to get to the area & how to move around

A car is pretty handy but not really necessary. There are plenty of drivers willing to give lifts, otherwise it is no more than 5km from any of the campsites to any of the sectors.

 By public transport

The nearest airport is in Montpellier but it will be cheaper to fly to either Nîmes or Marseille. Budget airlines operate flights on these two, Marseille being served most frequently.

To get to the gorge you first need to get to Millau, via Montpellier. There are trains between Marseille and Montpellier. Take one of the shuttle buses from Marseille Airport to Marseille Saint-Charles Rail Station [€8.50, 25 min]. These leave every 20 minutes. From here take the train to Montpellier via Nîmes [€28, 2½ h]. From Montpellier continue to Millau by bus [4h to 5h30, €32]. See *www.voyages-sncf.com* for train schedules and prices. From Millau take a taxi to Les Vignes or wherever else you are staying.

 By car

The Gorges du Tarn is situated east of the A75/E11 between exits 39 to 45. This is the motorway between Clermont-Ferrand and Montpellier. Exit 45 takes you to Millau.

Where to stay

The Gorges du Tarn has a wide range of accommodation. There are a number of hotels and numerous campsites, however these usually only open between April 1st and October 15th. It's most convenient to stay in or around Les Vignes, close to the climbing. If you're on foot, it is a bit of a hike (2.2km to 4.5km) to get to the climbing from Les Vignes or any of the other campsites but completely doable.

Camping Le Beldoire

✉ 48210 Les Vignes
📞 +33 04 66488279
🏠 www.camping-beldoire.com

📍 N 44°17'13,3 E 03°14'03,0

Open	May 1 - Sep 15
Grade	1 2 3 4
Price	€10.30 to €16.30 for 2 people, a car and a tent

This three star campsite is conveniently located between Les Vignes and the climbing sectors. You can pitch your tent right next to the water. It has a swimming pool, a snack bar, and a small shop that sells fresh bread in the morning.

Directions:
The campsite lies just outside Les Vignes along the D907, in the direction of St Enimie.

Magali Gauthier on Que la fete commence (7b), Sector Le Grand Toit, photo by Paul Lahaye

Riverside camping

*Mathieu Bergot on Ten years after (7b), Sector Le Navire,
photo by Paul Lahaye*

Camping La Blaquiere

✉ 48210 Les Vignes
☏ +33 04 66485493

▣ N 44°18'13,7 E 03°16'06,7

Open   May 1 - September 10

Grade   1 ———— 2 ———— **3** ———— 4

Price   €11.80 to €15.50 for 2 people, a car
             and a tent; bungalows or mobile
             homes from €210 to €500 per week
             depending on the season

*The campsite has nice shady pitches next to the
Tarn. They rent bungalows and mobile homes.
Pizzas and snacks are served in the restaurant.
From the campsite it's an easy walk to sector Les
Baumes Hautes.*

Directions:
The campsite is some 5km from Les Vignes, in the
direction of St Enimie.the D907, in the direction of
St Enimie.

Camping Terrados

✉ 48210 Les Vignes
☏ +33 04 66488337

▣ N 44°16'41,8 E 03°13'47,6

Open   April 1 - October 15

Grade   1 ———— **2** ———— 3 ———— 4

Price   €11.20 for 2 people, a car and a tent

*Basic two star campsite next to the Tarn river.
There are a lot of spots in the shade - the only
downside is the river rapid right next to the
campsite. This might keep you from sleeping…*

Directions:
The campsite is located in Les Vignes.

*Sebastian Schwertner on Prise de carre (7b),
Sector Calmez-vous, photo by Paul Lahaye*

Hôtel du Gévaudon

48210 Les Vignes
+33 04 66488155
hrgevaumaj@wanadoo.fr

N 44°16'39,8 E 03°13'39,1

Open   March 1 - November 15

Price   €38.50 for a double room without breakfast

Basic hotel with a bit run-down rooms.

Directions:
The hotel is located right in the centre of Les Vignes.

Hôtel Le Parisien

48210 Les Vignes
+33 04 66488151

N 44°16'32,1 E 03°13'34,4

Open   April 1 - September 20

Price   €39 for a double room without breakfast

Small but elegant hotel that overlooks the Tarn.

Directions:
The hotel is on the edge of the village along the road towards Le Rozier.

Les Vignes

Laura Steinbusch on 6eme Sens (6b), Sector Shadocks, photo Paul Lahaye

There are plenty of places to rent a kayak

Where to buy groceries?

The villages along the Tarn only have small shops. Your wallet will thank you if you do your shopping in Millau or Mende.

Where to find the local climbing guidebook

The topo called "Le Tarn" is for sale for €23 at the Tabac shop in Les Vignes, in Le Rozier, and at most campsites (including Le Beldoire just outside Les Vignes). It uses photos of the rocks and has pretty clear drawings. The only drawback is that the topo is a little outdated - since the publication date many new sectors and routes have been opened up.

Those looking for short approaches should go to the Tarn!

What else is there to see & do

Kayaking & canoeing
Kayaking and canoeing on the Tarn is very popular. Expect to pay between €20 and €30 per person for 20km to 25km.

Biking
The gorge is a beautiful place to go biking - both on and off road. Most campsites rent bikes but bringing your own is clearly the better option, especially if you value using good kit.

Sainte-Enimie
This medieval village lies in the heart of the gorge. It is said to be one of the most beautiful villages in France and is a highly popular tourist attraction. This is no wonder as the picturesque houses in the truly stunning setting are highly photogenic.

Rest day heaven!

Gorges du Tarn

The bulk of the climbing in the Gorges du Tarn takes place just north east of Les Vignes. The sectors are all situated very close to each other next to the D907 road that winds through the beautiful gorge. This is for sure a good destination for those who appreciate short walk-ins!

Many strong climbers head for The Tarn as the majority of the routes are in the 7th grade and can be considered real 3 star gems! The vertical and overhanging faces are peppered with pockets;

stamina is an absolute essential in order to top-out. Most routes are at least 15 metres high and there are also a number of pitches that are between 50 and 70 metres long. As this is a purebred sport climbing destination the routes are very well bolted.

To date, only a very small part of the gorge has been developed and there should be plenty more to come. Make sure you check out the impressive Sector Le Grand Toit with the big roof.

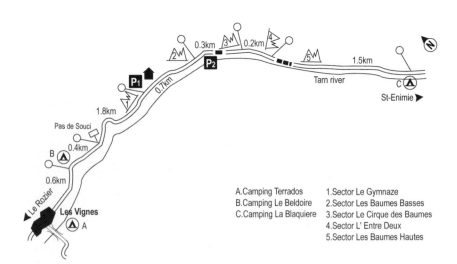

A.Camping Terrados
B.Camping Le Beldoire
C.Camping La Blaquiere

1.Sector Le Gymnaze
2.Sector Les Baumes Basses
3.Sector Le Cirque des Baumes
4.Sector L' Entre Deux
5.Sector Les Baumes Hautes

Directions

► By Car
From Millau follow the signs to Le Rozier and Les Vignes and the gorge is very well marked.

France | Gorges du Tarn | Gorges du Tarn

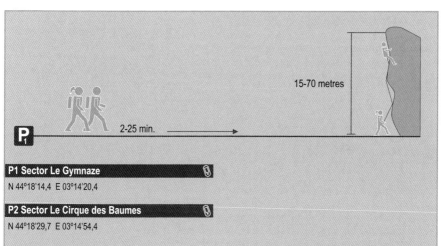

15-70 metres

2-25 min.

P1 Sector Le Gymnaze

N 44°18'14,4 E 03°14'20,4

P2 Sector Le Cirque des Baumes

N 44°18'29,7 E 03°14'54,4

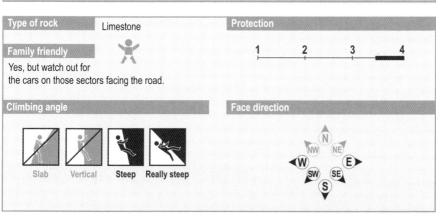

Type of rock

Limestone

Family friendly

Yes, but watch out for
the cars on those sectors facing the road.

Protection

1   2   3   4

Climbing angle

Slab   Vertical   Steep   Really steep

Face direction

N
NW   NE
W   E
SW   SE
S

Number of routes & Grade range

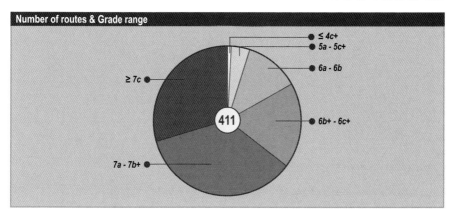

≤ 4c+
5a - 5c+
6a - 6b
≥ 7c
411
6b+ - 6c+
7a - 7b+

Climbing area Verdon

Spring   Summer   Autumn   Winter

The Gorges du Verdon is a truly unique place in Europe and one of the greatest tourist attractions of France. This spectacular canyon straddles the departements of Var and the Alpes de Hautes Provence. The gigantic cliffs, up to 700m high, of calcareous rock are the result of the erosion of the Verdon river. The 21km long canyon varies in width between 6m and 100m at the bottom and 200m to 1500m at its rim. In the midst of a nature reserve rich in flora and fauna, there is no doubt that this is one special place!

The Gorges du Verdon is also considered by many world-class climbers to be the ultimate multi pitch sport climbing destination. There are over 1500 routes on perfect limestone and the deep cliffs provide all kinds of different climbing styles with soaring cracks, towering pillars, and apparently endless vertical walls with occasional challenging overhangs to surmount. The fun starts on the way

in, abseil descents being the only way to the start of the routes! As soon as you drop down into the void, there is no other way out than climbing the 20-400 meters back to where you started.

Besides the truly fantastic and unique climbing, the Verdon is also a great place for canyoning, rafting, biking, and hiking. The lake Le Lac Ste Croix is also nearby so you can combine climbing with some days on the water learning to sail or windsurf. In short, it is a great place for the adventurous multi-pitch sport climber but it's also a great multi-activity destination for everyone.

Sunset at the Gorges du Verdon

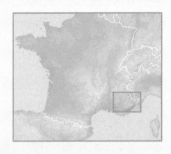

When to go

The best months for climbing are April, May, June, September, and October. July and August are too hot - most sectors face south. Still, climbing is possible in summer if you start a bit later in the day as the sun at many sectors disappears around 3pm.

Crag

 Gorges du Verdon

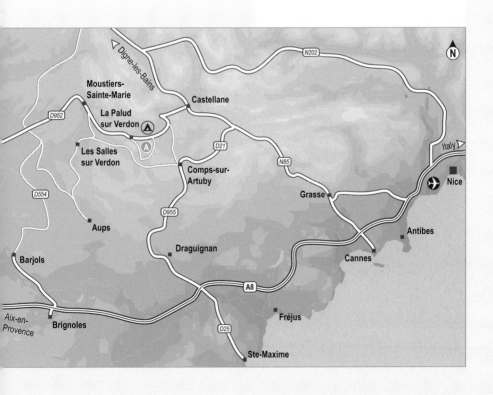

How to get to the area & how to move around

You need to have your own wheels to get to the different sectors. Unfortunately, at the time of research there were no places offering bike rental.

 By public transport

You could get to La Palud sur Verdon by bus but, as we said, once there you still need a car to get to the different sectors. There are daily direct buses from Nice and Marseille.

 By car

La Palud sur Verdon lies between Le Lac Ste Croix and Castellane and it is the central point from which to branch out into the gorge. The road is very twisty and it can take up to one hour to cover the 20km from Le Lac Ste Croix, especially in high season.

Les Gorges du Verdon

Where to stay

Your choice of accommodation in the Verdon is simply huge - from simple campsites to refugees, and apartments to luxury hotels. The best place to stay is in La Palud sur Verdon as this is closest to the climbing.

Having fun at La Lac de Ste-Croix

Camping Municipal Le Grand Canyon

✉ Route de Castellane
04120 La Palud sur Verdon
☎ +33 492773813
🖥 campinglapalud@wanadoo.fr

📍 N 43°46'49,2 E 06°20'55,4

Open	April 13 - September 20

Grade 1 —— **2** —— 3 —— 4

Price   €10 for 2 people, a car and a tent

This is a basic but neat and quiet campsite just outside La Palud sur Verdon. It has spacious pitches with a few trees.

Directions:
It is the first campsite on the road from La Palud sur Verdon to Castellane.

There are numerous hiking trails in the Verdon!

Camping de Bourbon

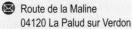

✉ 04120 La Palud sur Verdon
☎ +33 492773817

🔵 N 43°46'41,8 E 06°20'18,3

Open   April - September

Grade   1   2   3   4

Price   €10.20 for 2 people, a car and a tent

Probably the campsite most favored by climbers. It is nothing more than a grass field with some trees, it has clean toilets, and you can make use of the kitchen.

Directions:
It is just before the centre of La Palud sur Verdon on the right hand side coming from Moustiers.

Auberge de Jeunesse

✉ Route de la Maline
    04120 La Palud sur Verdon
☎ +33 492773872
@ lapalud@fuaj.org
🏠 www.hihostels.com

🔵 N 43°46'31,2 E 06°20'31,0

Open   April 15 - October 1

Grade   1   2   3   4

Price
For members of Hostelling International the price is €14.90 per person per night including breakfast and clean sheets. Non-members pay €2.90 extra per night, for which they get a stamp. After six stamps they obtain a members' card that is valid for one year. Camping is €5.90 per person per night.

This is a newly opened youth hostel in a quiet spot just outside La Palud sur Verdon. It is the cheapest place to stay and a good one at that. There are rooms for 2-6 people, bunk beds and clean, shared bathrooms. There is a large communal kitchen with a refrigerator. They also allow a few tents in their grounds and campers can use the bathrooms and kitchen.

Directions:
The youth hostel lies on the left hand side of the road heading towards Le Chalet de la Malina. Follow the signs for this chalet and for the Hotel Les Gorges du Verdon.

Camping de Bourbon

Camping at the Auberge de Jeunesse

La Chalet de la Maline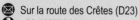

✉ Sur la route des Crêtes (D23)
📞 +33 492773805
@ ca.maline@ffcam.fr
🌐 www.ffcam.fr/fr/chalet

📱 N 43°44'46,6 E 06°20'42,1

Open   Mid March - end October

Price   between €24.50 and €36.65 per
              person per night for half pension

This beautifully situated chalet lies 8km from La
Palud sur Verdon along the route des Crêtes. They
have two rooms that accommodate 6 people, two
rooms for 8, one for 12 and another for 20 people.

Directions:
In La Palud sur Verdon follow the signs for Le
Chalet de la Maline along la route des Crêtes
(D23). The quickest way there is from the west.

Le Perroquet Vert

✉ 04120 La Palud sur Verdon
📞 +33492773339
@ perroquetvert@ifrance.com

📱 N 43°46'48,3 E 06°20'29,5

Open   April 1 - November 1

Price   €58 per person per night
              or €69 for two people per night
              including breakfast

The friendly Sabine and Michel Jourdan offer two
rooms with bathrooms for rent. They also have an
excellent restaurant and are the owners of the only
climbing shop in the Verdon.

Directions:
You'll find it along the main road through La Palud
sur Verdon.

La Palud sur Verdon

Gîte Arc-en-Ciel

📧 04120 La Palud sur Verdon

📱 N 43°46'48,1 E 06°20'32,0

Open   Year round except for Christmas
and New Year

Price   €10.15 per person per night,
breakfast is €5,
dinner is €8.50 - €14.50 and
half pension is €23 - €29

*This gîte in the centre of La Palud sur Verdon has
one big dormitory with 6 double beds. Reservations
can be made per person or on a group basis.*

Directions:
The gîte is located at the small square near the
post office in the centre of La Palud sur Verdon.

Gîte L'Escales

📧 04120 La Palud sur Verdon
📞 +33 492773002
@ mataedlinger@wanadoo.fr

📱 N 43°46'43,5 E 06°20'19,9

Open   from Easter to end of October

Price   20 p.p.p.n.;
€25 including breakfast
and €40 for half pension

*This gîte has 5 double rooms and a room for 3
people, one for 4 people, and one for 5 people.
Bathroom facilities are shared.*

Directions:
The gîte is just before the centre of La Palud
sur Verdon on the right hand side coming from
Moustiers.

*The 8a Séance Tenante is a locals' favourite,
Sector Séance*

Hôtel des Gorges du Verdon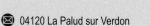

✉ 04120 La Palud sur Verdon
☎ +33 492773826
@ bog@worldonline.fr
🌐 www.hotel-des-gorges-du-verdon.fr

📱 N 43°46'30,7 E 06°20'42,9

Open   April 6 - October 21

Price   Double rooms start at €95
             in low season and go up to €365
             in high season

This is the best hotel in La Palud sur Verdon with 30 comfortable rooms, a beautiful terrace with a panoramic view, a swimming pool, a tennis court, table tennis, and a great restaurant.

Directions:
The hotel is signposted from La Palud sur Verdon. The hotel is located just past the youth hostel (Auberge de Jeunesse).

Hotel des Gorges du Verdon

Markus Durrer enjoying the nice route Je suis une légende (7a), Sector Carelle

Biking is very popular in the Verdon too

The new topo is for sale for €33 at the climbing shop Le Perroquet Vert in the centre of La Palud sur Verdon. They also sell the detailed hiking map of the Verdon.

Where to buy groceries?

There is a small supermarket in La Palud sur Verdon that sells all you need. It is open from 8am to 8pm daily. There is also a bakery, a couple of bars and a few small restaurants.

Where to find the local climbing guidebook

"Escalade au Verdon" is a new guidebook and uses photos exclusively. Unfortunately it is not comprehensive and it is still rather difficult to find the right route. If you happen to have an old topo of this area it might be wise to bring it along and compare the two for the most complete information.

What else is there to see & do

Canyoning
The Verdon is widely known for its great canyoning and this is a fantastic way to explore the rocks and waterfalls. The average price for half a day of adventure is €45 per person and €70 for a full day. There are a few agencies based in La Palud sur Verdon that offer guided trips.

Rafting / canoe / hydrospeed
All agencies also offer guided rafting, canoe, or hydrospeed trips. Prices are similar to canyoning, around €45 per person for a half day and €70 for a full day.

Hiking
It goes without saying that the whole Verdon area is great for hiking with several grand routes to choose from.

Watersports at the Lake de Ste Croix
Besides swimming it is also possible to rent a waterbike or go windsurfing at the lake. It is a great place to spend a day, especially if you have children.

In summer most sectors have shade in the late afternoon

Gorges du Verdon

At most inland crags, you normally first make a long walk to the start of the route, climb up and, once at the top, either abseil down or risk your life scrambling down some vague descent path. It is exactly the opposite here at the Verdon! Here you can conveniently park your car at the top of a route, abseil down, while gaining a bit of beta, and climb back up again. This is the most common way to do both the shorter and longer routes. As you might guess, this makes climbing in the Gorges du Verdon an exceptional experience.

The big walls aside, there are also a handful of smaller crags in the surrounding area that are perfect for single pitch routes. The total number of routes of all flavours exceeds 1500. The grades are quite equally spread and there is something for everyone.

For short routes you will just need a 70 metres rope and quickdraws but for the long multi pitch routes we advise using a double rope and taking extra gear, such as some friends, nuts, and slings because some of the routes can feel very exposed.

A good place for getting used to the climbing in the Verdon is the sectors at the parking at Du Belvedere de la Carelle. Here you can find easier single and multi pitch routes and also some harder single pitches that are well bolted.

Wynand on the 12th pitch of the classic La Demande

Those who have just started climbing and want to gain some experience on longer routes may wish to consider doing a guided climb. There are several agencies offering guided long climbs for around €125 per day (possible with two people per guide). It is also possible to take climbing courses in the Verdon with one of the agencies, which costs on average €40 per person for half a day. Check *www.escalade-verdon.com* or contact Alan Carne, an experienced and very friendly British guide, via *alanduverdon@yahoo.com.*

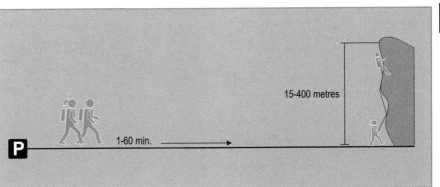

15-400 metres

1-60 min.

P

Type of rock

Limestone

Protection

1   2   3   4

Depends per route

Family friendly

The Verdon area in general is very family friendly but it is not possible to take young children climbing.

Climbing angle

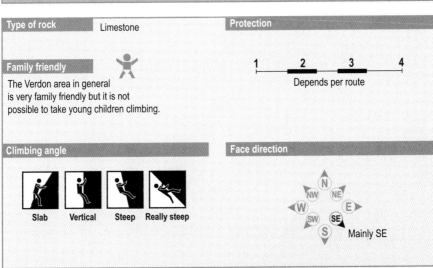

Slab   Vertical   Steep   Really steep

Face direction

Mainly SE

Number of routes & Grade range

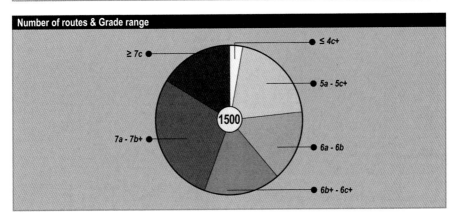

≥ 7c

≤ 4c+

5a - 5c+

7a - 7b+

1500

6a - 6b

6b+ - 6c+

Alan Carne balancing through on L'ange

Gorges du Verdon

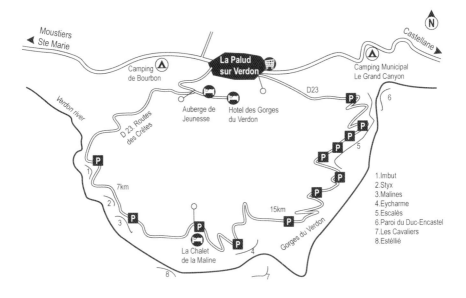

Moustiers
Ste Marie

Castellane

La Palud
sur Verdon

Camping
de Bourbon

Camping Municipal
Le Grand Canyon

D23

Verdon river

D 23. Routes
des Crêtes

Auberge de
Jeunesse

Hotel des Gorges
du Verdon

6

5

7km

1.Imbut
2.Styx
3.Malines
4.Eycharme
5.Escalès
6.Paroi du Duc-Encastel
7.Les Cavaliers
8.Estéllié

2

3

15km

Gorges du Verdon

La Chalet
de la Maline

4

8

7

Alan Carne on Graphique (8a)

Climbing area Les Calanques

The Calanques is one of France's most famous natural beauties. Situated in the far south on the Mediterranean coast, this limestone mountain range spans all the way from Marseille to the pretty little town of Cassis, 20km to the east. This is one of the largest rock climbing areas in the country and one of the most stunning too. The area is marked by a rough coastline with hidden coves, large cliffs, and deep green bays that is not only wonderful to look at but tempting to swim in too!

The climbing is enormously varied with technical slabs looking directly out over the Mediterranean, steep overhangs in caves, multi-pitch delights in a mountain setting, and steep single pitches right on the sea's edge. There are many different sectors with a total of circa 2500 bolted routes and 1000 trad routes. Each sector has its own characteristics but all are picturesque and the setting feels somewhat wild.

| Spring | Summer | Autumn | Winter |

The Calanques is truly an exceptional climbing destination, especially at those times of year when the rest of Europe is cold and rainy.

When to go

Being right on the south coast the climate is Mediterranean with very mild winters and extremely hot summers. It is one of the driest regions in France and recorded temperatures in summer are often the highest in the country. This, together with

Les Calanques

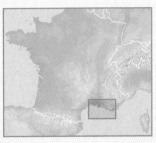

road access restrictions for fire protection, makes summer an unsuitable period to go climbing here. On the other hand spring, autumn and winter are great but in these periods the Mistral, a cold dry northwesterly wind, can blow extremely cold - on average it blows 107 days per year. Fortunately the Calanques possesses an exceptionally warm microclimate on its south-facing slopes due to marine thermal regulation, the glare of the sun, and the sheltered aspect (from the Mistral). This does make it a perfect winter destination.

Crag

Ⓐ Les Calanques

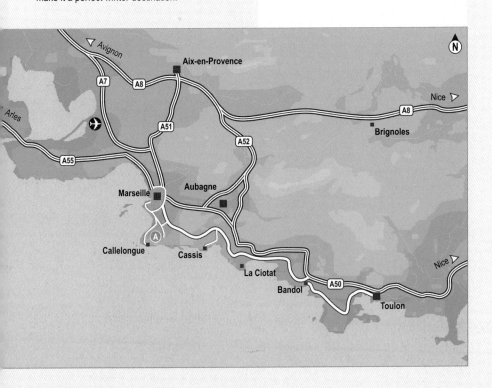

How to get to the area & how to move around

You will need a car to get to the climbing in the Calanques.

 By public transport

Hop on one of the low cost airlines to Marseille. There are car rental agencies based at the airport.

Marseille is also connected by railway to Paris. See the 'Moving around' section in the beginning of this chapter for information on websites of rail companies.

 By car

Take the Autoroute du Soleil from Paris to Marseille, via Lyon. From Marseille take the D559 east towards Cassis and then bear off this main road to find the individual crags.

Climbing at Les Goudes, photo by Fred van Nijnatten

Where to stay

The problem in the Calanques is finding accommodation near the crags. The closest accommodation is in Marseille and in Cassis. As Marseille is a large city and is not particularly attractive we fully recommend basing yourself in Cassis. It is both a popular and pretty town just east of the Calanques. The nearest campsites are located in La Ciotat and Ceyreste.

The time it will take you to get to the crags will vary quite a bit depending on the season, access restrictions on roads, and the time of the day (and thus the traffic!). In general you can get to most crags in something like 35 to 60 minutes by car from La Ciotat.

Bivouacs under the crags are not allowed.

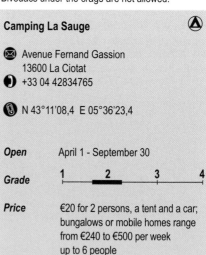

Camping La Sauge

✉ Avenue Fernand Gassion
13600 La Ciotat
☎ +33 04 42834765

⊚ N 43°11'08,4 E 05°36'23,4

| *Open* | April 1 - September 30 |

Grade 1 ——— 2 ——— 3 ——— 4

Price €20 for 2 persons, a tent and a car; bungalows or mobile homes range from €240 to €500 per week up to 6 people

A two star campsite but not a particularly attractive one due to its location next to a busy road. They also rent 4 to 6 person bungalows and mobile homes.

Directions:
Coming from the A50 motorway take the exit for La Ciotat. After the toll (peage) you come to a roundabout. Go straight to the second roundabout and turn right. At the third roundabout turn left and the campsite is just here.

The traverse Face au Large at the Cap Morgiou

Camping Hôtel de Plein Air

✉ Avenue Eugène Julien
   13600 Ceyreste
☎ +33 04 42830768
@ campingceyreste@yahoo.fr
🖰 www.campingceyreste.com

🌐 N 43°13'12,7 E 05°37'42,6

Open   April 1 - November 11

Grade

1	2	3	4

Price   Price €18 for 2 people, a tent and a car; prices per week for a bungalow or a mobile home are between €260 and €510 for up to 6 people

This is definitely the better campsite of the two closest to the Calanques. It is quietly located in a pine grove that provides a lot of shade. There is a small shop. Bungalows and mobile homes are also for rent.

Directions:
Coming from the A50 take the exit for La Ciotat. Follow the directions for Ceyreste in La Ciotat. The campsite is clearly signposted.

Hôtel Laurence

✉ 8, rue de L'arène
   13260 Cassis
☎ +33 04 42018878
@ contact@cassis-hotel-laurence.com
🖰 www.cassis-hotel-laurence.com

🌐 N 43°12'49,3 E 05°32'22,4

Open   February 1 - October 31

Price   €42 - €85 for a double room without breakfast

Nice and warmly decorated hotel. All rooms have en suite bathrooms.

Directions:
Drive towards the harbour in Cassis. The hotel is in one of the side streets just off the harbour, less than two hundred metres from the boules court. This is on the left side of the harbour when facing the sea.

Hôtel Cassitel

✉ Place Clémenceau
   13260 Cassis
☎ +33 04 42018344
@ cassitel@hotel-cassis.com
🖰 www.hotel-cassis.com

🌐 N 43°12'49,6 E 05°32'20,6

Open   Year round

Price   €60 - €90 for a double room without beakfast

Attractive hotel at the port in Cassis.

Directions:
The hotel is located at the port at the end of the same street as the Hôtel Laurence.

Robert van den Broek on Une Mort tres douce (6b),
Aiguille de Sugiton, photo by Fred van Nijnatten

Hôtel Liautaud

✉ 2, rue Victor-Hugo
13260 Cassis

☎ +33 04 42017537

📱 N 43°12'50,3 E 05°32'18,5

Open   April 1 - December 1

Price   €69 - €79 for a double room
                without breakfast

One of the largest of the hotels located at the port.

Directions:
The hotel is located at the left side of the port, when facing the sea, in the middle.

Sea cliff climbing at Cap Morgiou, La Triperie,
photo by Fred van Nijnatten

Hôtel Le Provencal

✉ 7, avenue Victor Hugo
13260 Cassis

☎ +33 04 42017213

@ le-provençal@aliceadsl.fr

🌐 www.cassis-le-provencal.com

📱 N 43°12'51,3 E 05°32'19,3

Open   Year round

Price   €40 - €66 for a double room
                without breakfast

One of the more basic hotels in Cassis. The rooms are small and the cheapest don't have bathrooms.

Directions:
The hotel is located in one of the shopping streets in Cassis just off the port.

L'Abri Côtier, Morgiou, photo by Thomas Rijniers

Hôtel Le Commerce

 12, rue Saint Clair
13260 Cassis
📞 +33 04 42010910
🌐 www.hotel-lecommerce.com

📍 N 43°12'53,1 E 05°32'07,2

Open	February 15 - November 15
Price	€35 - €66 for a double room without breakfast

Basic hotel with inexpensive rooms without bathrooms and more expensive ones with bathrooms and sea-views.

Directions:
The hotel is one street in from the port. Standing at the port facing the sea, the hotel is on the right hand side.

After a good day of climbing a beautiful sunset awaits you, photo by Adam van Eekeren

Where to buy groceries?

There are supermarkets in Cassis and the villages surrounding the Calanques, such as Mazargues and Madraque de Montredon.

Where to find the local climbing guidebook

The topo is called Escalade Les Calanques. It is for sale for €30 at the bookshops in Cassis and also at the climbing wall in Marseille (Salle Grimper Marseille - 73 Bd de St Marcel). It can also be ordered directly via *www. topo-calanques.com.*

What else is there to see & do

There are lots of things to do on your days off - walking, boat-trips, a trip to the Camargue (Western Europe's largest river delta), shopping in Marseille or at one of the massive Decathlons and Hypermarkets.

Alternatively, Aix-en-Provence has a fantastic collection of antique shops and there are many pretty cities, such as Nîmes, Arles, or Avignon, to visit, all of which have their own unique style and beauty. If you are not staying in Cassis, make sure to come here for a coffee at the harbour or spend some hours relaxing on the beach at the very least.

The port of Cassis

Les Calanques

The range is divided into 8 main areas and each has its own distinct atmosphere.

1. Les Goudes

Situated at the far west side of the Calanques above the charming village of Callelongue lies the superb area of Les Goudes, where climbing is possible on both north and south faces; the south faces are simply perfect in winter. The walk up from the parking takes about 45 minutes and, once you get around the back of the crag, some stunning views await you. There are bolted routes here in all grades (with a lot 5th and easy 6th grade routes) and even some easier grade multi-pitch routes on either side of the main sport climbing area.

Les Goudes

2. Marseilleveyre

This is the universal name for a group of different sectors that are spread out south of Marseille. Each sector has its own parking. Climbing here is possible both in winter and also on hot summer days as many sectors face north or northeast. There are lots of easier climbs averaging 30m in length and it's well worth spending a day here ticking them off.

3. La Melette

Some ten different crags form La Melette. It is ideal in autumn and winter. The majority of the routes are on slabs or pocketed vertical grey limestone walls. There is one crag with easier routes although this area is best suited to those who can climb around 6c.

Morgiou in the early morning, photo by Adam van Eekeren

4. Sormiou

This is one of the prettiest places in the Calanques - there are many different sectors with well-equipped climbs, some of which are directly above the sea. The majority of the routes are in the easier grades, with many in the 3rd and 4th grades. Another plus is the short walk-in and it goes without saying that a welcoming dip into the sea at the end of the day is a must!

5. Morgiou

A diverse area with fantastic sea cliff climbing - abseil descents to the starts of the routes are required. On Cap Morgiou there are two interesting traverses of seven and eight rope pitches.

Cap Morgiou, photo by Fred van Nijnatten

6. Luminy

This is a very diverse area with something for everyone's taste. The Grotte de L'Ours has some great powerful routes in the 8th grade in a cave. At the Paroi des Toits there are even a few tufa routes in the 6's. The Le Socle de la Candella and La Candelle offer some fantastic multi pitch climbs.

Toon van Gerwen on the traverse Le Couloir Suspendu, La Candelle, photo by Thomas Rijniers

7. Gardiole

Despite the long walk-ins, the climbing, mainly multi pitch with both sport and trad, is very worthwhile. There is enough to choose from across the grade range and the mountainous setting is very pleasant.

8. En Vau

En Vau is a must-visit, not just for its fantastic routes but also for its sheer beauty. Great cliffs form both sides of a little bay and, when you start to tire, the beach is very nearby. Again, this area consist of many smaller sectors each one of them with its own style of climbing. There are both easier and more difficult sport routes to be found as well as some superb multi pitch lines. This is a great place for families too as the children can play on the beach.

Paroie des toits, photo by Fred van Nijnatten

Les Goudes offers great conditions on fine winter days, photo by Fred van Nijnatten

Les Calanques

1. Les Goudes
2. Marseilleveyre
3. Melette
4. Sormiou
5. Morgiou
6. Luminy
7. Gardiole
8. En Vau

Directions

Having lunch on a beautiful winter day at Paroie des Toits, photo by Fred van Nijnatten

▶ *By Car*

The D599 connects Marseille and Cassis. From this road head to the location of your choice. Les Goudes can be reached year round by car but Sormiou and Morgiou have restricted access. The road, named "La Route du Feu", is closed from June till the second week of September due to a high fire risk. If you happen to be here during this time of the year, park the car as close as you can and walk for about an hour.

The entire Calanques region is extremely fragile and most of the climbing here is in a protected environment. Please respect the flora and fauna, stay on the marked paths, and take all litter away. Be aware that in summer many roads are closed and access to certain areas is restricted in order to minimize the fire risk. Please respect the current access situation available at *www.topo-calanques.com*.

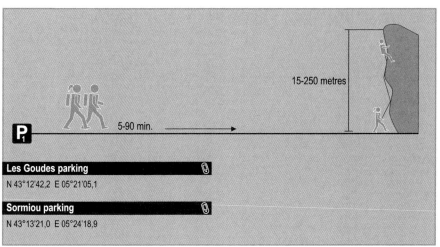

15-250 metres

5-90 min.

Les Goudes parking

N 43°12'42,2 E 05°21'05,1

Sormiou parking

N 43°13'21,0 E 05°24'18,9

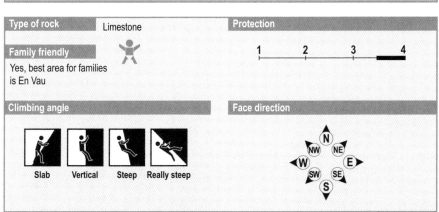

Type of rock   Limestone

Protection

1   2   3   4

Family friendly

Yes, best area for families is En Vau

Climbing angle

Slab   Vertical   Steep   Really steep

Face direction

N
NW NE
W   E
SW SE
S

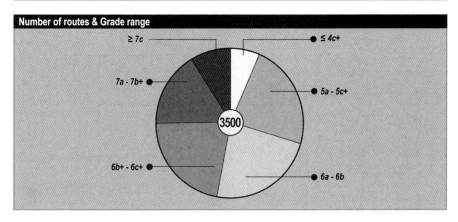

Number of routes & Grade range

≥ 7c

≤ 4c+

7a - 7b+

5a - 5c+

3500

6b+ - 6c+

6a - 6b

Climbing area Corsica

Spring   Summer   Autumn   Winter

Corsica, a wonderfully diverse island in the Mediterranean, is a great destination for a climbing trip. Even though Corsica is a French island, it is in many ways a separate nation. Actually, it has only been French for 200 of its 4000 years of history and, luckily, many aspects of its unique culture have survived. With many natural and historical gems, Corsica is one of the most fascinating islands of the Mediterranean. It is the fourth largest after Sardinia, Sicily, and Cyprus. Inland Corsica is surprisingly wild and mountainous - Monte Cinto is the highest peak at 2706m. The east side of the island is mainly flat while the western coast is rocky and steep. In July and August the island gets terribly overrun by tourists but at any other time of year it is a peaceful get-away.

The climbing on Corsica is well developed with many different areas and styles. The island actually has it all: sport and trad climbing, bouldering and deep water soloing, plus some mountaineering thrown in for good measure! The rock is mainly granite but limestone and sandstone can also be found. Most of the crags are situated inland. In general, Corsica lacks good routes above 7b so don't come here if that is what you're after. Otherwise there is a lot of choice for intermediate climbers!

The best crags on Corsica are Rocher des Gozzi, Bavella, and Restonica. Rocher des Gozzi is close to Ajaccio, the most important city on the island on the west coast and birthplace of Napoleon Bonaparte. The other two are situated inland.

When to go

Corsica has a true Mediterranean climate with very hot summers and mild and rainy winters. In winter it can also snow in the mountains and, since this is where most of the climbing takes place, it is not the best season to go. Spring and autumn will see you happy here. Summers are way too hot.

Sector Sorbellu at Restonica breaths out a fantastic atmosphere, photo by Agnès Donnet

Crag

Ⓐ Rocher des Gozzi
Ⓑ Col de Bavella
Ⓒ Restonica

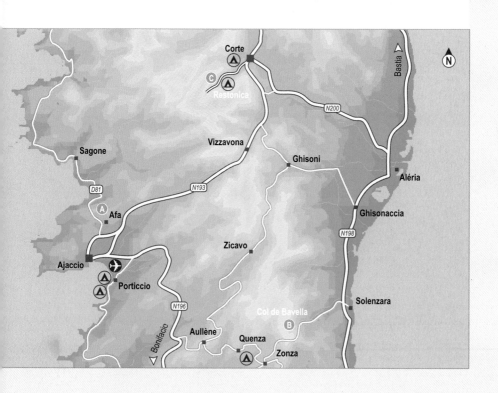

Sector Frassetta at Restonica offers a collection of difficult routes, photo by Bertrand Maurin

How to get to the area & how to move around

A car is an absolute necessity!

 By public transport

Corsica has four airports - Ajaccio, Bastia, Calvi and Figari. Ajaccio has the main airport and is most convenient for the climbing areas. The airport sees many Air France flights but until now not those of any low-cost airlines. TUIfly offers good budget deals but only flies to Calvi, in the north.
There are shuttle buses that operate frequently between the airports and the city centers.

 By (car) ferry from France / Italy

Corsica is well connected by (car) ferry from France and Italy. The ferries depart from Marseille, Toulon, and Nice in France and from Savona, Livorno, Piombino, and Civita Vecchia in Italy. There are routes to several ports on the island - Ajaccio, Bastia, Ile Rousse, Calvi, and Porto-Vecchio. The cost for a single trip for 2 adults plus a normal car is between €175 and €350 depending on the on-board services, season, and route. Check out the following websites for information and bookings: *www.sncm.fr*, *www.corsicaferries.com* and *www.cmn.fr*.

Where to stay

Corsica has many campsites spread over the island. The only problem is that they are generally only open between April 1st and October 15th. Fortunately there are plenty of hotels and gîtes to choose from too. Rates for a double room start at €35 / €50 depending on the season. Camping rates are between €17 and €25 for 2 people, a car and a tent.

If you choose to climb at Rocher des Gozzi there are two campsites near Porticcio, a 10 minutes drive from Ajaccio. For Bavella you can either stay in Zonza or at the Col de Bavella directly. Those heading to Restonica can either stay in the Restonica valley itself or in Corte.

Rocher des Gozzi

Camping U Prunelli

✉ Pont du Prunelli
   20166 Porticcio
☎ +33 04 95251923
@ camping-prunelli@wanadoo.fr
🕸 www.camping-prunelli.com

📍 N 41°54'41,5 E 08°49'30,7

Open   April 1 - October 15

Grade   1 —— 2 —— 3 —— 4

Price   €25.50 for 2 people, a tent and a car;
   €268 to €649 for a 2 to 4 person
   cottage per week

Sector Sorbellu at Restonica, photo by Bertrand Maurin

This very nice campsite has large shady places to pitch your tent. There is a swimming pool, a shop, and a basic restaurant. Nice wooden cottages are also for rent.

Directions:
From Ajaccio follow the road to Bonifacio. Take the exit for Porticcio. Be careful not to miss the campsite which comes straight after a roundabout.

Camping Benista

✉ Bvd Rive Sud
   20166 Porticcio
☎ +33 04 95251930
@ benista20@club-internet.fr
🕸 http://benista.free.fr

📍 N 41°54'25,0 E 08°49'19,9

Open   April 1 - October 31

Grade   1 —— 2 —— 3 —— 4

Price   €25.30 for 2 people, a tent and a car;
   €310 to €800 for a 4 to 6 person
   cottage per week

This four star campsite offers the same facilities as U Prunelli.

Directions:
From Ajaccio follow the road to Bonifacio. Take the exit for Porticcio. The campsite lies a few hundred metres on the right after U Prunelli.

The beach offers a good escape from the heat in summer

Bavella

Camping U Fuconu

 20124 Zonza

 N 41°45'50,2 E 09°10'29,1

| Open | May - September |

Grade

1   2   3   4

| Price | €12 for 2 people, a car and a tent |

A basic and very quiet campsite with lots of shady spots.

Directions:
From Zonza follow the road in the direction of Quenza for 1.5km.

Auberge du Col de Bavella

 20124 Bavella - Zonza
 33 04 95720987
@ auberge-bavella@wanadoo.fr
 www.auberge-bavella.com

 N 41°47'42,5 E 09°13'43,9

| Open | April - November |

| Price | €64 for a double room including half pension |

Nice inn with a restaurant and rooms that can sleep up to 6 people. It is a 15 minutes walk from the lodgings to the climbing.

Directions:
The inn is located a few hundred metres from the Col de Bavella.

Gîte Les Aiguilles

Gîte Les Aiguilles de Bavella

 20124 Bavella - Zonza
 +33 04 95720188

| Open | Year round |

| Price | €75 for a double room including half pension |

A good gîte that only gets really busy during the weekends. It is a charming place with a friendly atmosphere.

Directions:
The gîte is located directly on the Col. From here it is only 10 minutes to get to the first sector.

Hôtel L'Alcudina

 20124 Zonza
 +33 04 95786771
@ hotel.incudine@wanadoo.fr

 N 41°45'00,0 E 09°10'16,8

| Open | April 15 - October 15 |

| Price | €54 for a double room (half board is compulsory in August for €68 p.p.) |

A very tastefully decorated hotel where each room has its own unique color.

Directions:
The hotel is located along the road to Porto Vecchio, between the roundabout and the church.

Hôtel Chiar di Luna

✉ 20124 Zonza
☎ +33 04 95785679
🏠 www.hotelclairdelune.com

📍 N 41°44'54,4 E 09°10'12,6

Open	Year round
Price	€61 - €68 for a double room without breakfast

A good two-star hotel a few minutes from the centre on foot.

Directions:
The hotel is 250m after the roundabout along the road to Levie.

Restonica

Camping de Tuani

✉ 20250 Corte
☎ +33 04 95461165

📍 N 42°16'31,5 E 09°06'25,5

Open	April 1 - October 10
Grade	1 2 3 4
Price	€20.50 for 2 people, a car and a tent

This campsite with a restaurant is nicely located right in the Restonica valley and is ideal as a base to explore the nearby climbing on foot. The pine trees provide a lot of shade. Be aware that the campsite gets very packed at the weekends during summer!

Directions:
From Corte take the D623 into the Restonica Valley. The campsite is 5.5km after the turn for the valley.

Picturesque Corte

Camping Usognu

✉ 20250 Corte

📍 N 42°18'00,9 E 09°08'52,3

Open	March 28 - October 15
Grade	1 2 3 4
Price	€18 for 2 people, a car and a tent

A very basic campsite without much shade.

Directions:
The campsite is 200m after the turn for the Restonica Valley along the D623.

Camping de Tuani

Camping L'Alivetu

- ✉ 20250 Corte
- 📞 +33 04 95461109
- @ camping-alivetu@laposte.net
- 🏠 www.camping-alivetu.com

🧭 N 42°17'53,9 E 09°08'58,0

Open April 1 - October 15

Price €21.10 for 2 people, a car and a tent;
2 to 6 person bungalows are
€271 - €586 per week

*This quiet campsite has shady pitches and a bar.
Bungalows are also for rent. It is only 10 minutes
on foot away from the centre of Corte.*

Directions:
Coming from Aleria follow the signs for the
Restonica Valley. Before you cross the bridge turn
left for the campsite.

Hôtel De La Poste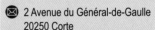

- ✉ 2, Place Padoue
  20250 Corte
- 📞 +33 04 95460137

🧭 N 42°18'30,0 E 09°09'02,7

Open Year round

Price €53 for a double room without
breakfast

*This is a reasonable two-star hotel conveniently
located in the centre of Corte.*

Directions:
Head for the centre of Corte where the hotel is
signposted.

Corsican products

Hôtel De La Paix

- ✉ 2 Avenue du Général-de-Gaulle
  20250 Corte
- 📞 +33 04 95460672
- 🏠 socoget@wanadoo.fr

🧭 N 42°18'31,0 E 09°09'07,2

Open January - November

Price €45 - €53 for a double room
without breakfast

*A basic but clean hotel in a quiet location in the
centre of Corte.*

Directions:
Once in the centre you'll see signs for the hotel.

The impressive statue at Col De Bavella

Where to buy groceries?

As the crags are situated near cities or larger villages there are always big supermarkets around. Be aware that smaller shops in the villages close from noon to around 4pm.

Where to find the local climbing guidebook

There is a very colourful guide to Corsica called Falaises de Corse (€30) written by the enthusiastic Bertrand Maurin and Thierry Souchard. It has clear drawings and is written in English and French. It is for sale at the climbing shop Alti Monti, 46, Avenue Noêl Franchini in Ajaccio (+33-0495100437) and at Le Monde Vertical,12, Boulevard Auguste Gaudin in Bastia. Camping de Tuani near Corte also sells it.

Sector Murzella in Bavella, photo by Bertrand Maurin

Hiking
Corsica has a huge national park and a famous long-distance path leading through it, the GR20. The park has many huts (refuges) where you can spend the night. The refuges are open year round and cost €9.50 per person per night.

Water sports
The island offers many water sports such as sailing, wind surfing, and scuba diving. Most campsites or hotels rent gear but you'll also find surf schools based on the beaches.

What else is there to see & do

Canyoing
There are a few canyons around Zonza that can be visited. Most trips take 4 to 5 hours. Have a chat to the people in 'Corsica Madness' for more information - they are based opposite the tourist office in Zonza.

Archaeological sites
Corsica has several archaeological sites which can be visited, such as Cauria and Aleria. The Roman city of Aleria which used to be the capital of the island in ancient times is still being excavated.

Corsica offers numerous water sports

Rocher des Gozzi

This crag lies just north of Ajaccio and is a popular place with those living in the capital. The superb red rock not only offers good quality climbing but also a magnificent view! Rocher des Gozzi has single pitch sport routes as well as a range of things for trad climbers, like the multi pitch routes at The Couloir that are up to 250 metres long.

The sectors have a huge range of routes on solid granite with long cracks, interesting corners, and pumpy overhangs. It is also a good place to escape the heat as there is always shade to be found. As there is a large number of 6th grade routes, Rocher des Gozzi is a welcoming destination for intermediate climbers. The approach of 50 minutes is a bit long, but don't let this put you off!

As the sun sets the rock turns red at Rocher des Gozzi, photo by Bertrand Maurin

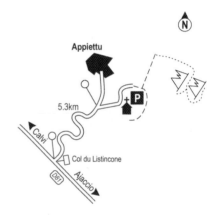

Directions

Thierry Souchard trying hard at Rocher des Gozzi, photo by Bertrand Maurin

▶ *By Car*

Take the N194 from Ajaccio in the direction of Corte. Soon the D81 towards Calvi will be signposted. Follow the D81 until the roundabout and the exit for Afà. Don't take the exit but continue straight on for another 3.1km where there is a sign for Appiettu. Take this road and follow it for 5.3km. At the junction turn right and drive for another 500m. Park near the church.

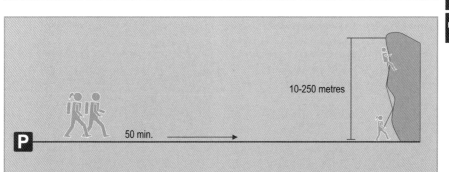

Parking

N 42°00'37,0 E 08°46'06,8

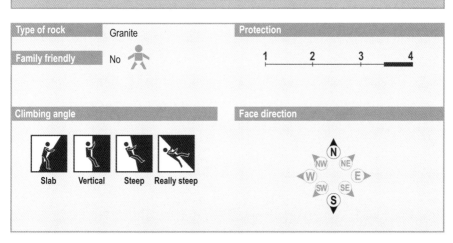

Type of rock — Granite

Family friendly — No

Protection

1 2 3 4

Climbing angle

Slab   Vertical   Steep   Really steep

Face direction

N   NW   NE   W   E   SW   SE   S

Number of routes & Grade range

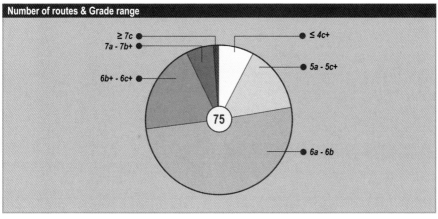

≥ 7c
7a - 7b+
6b+ - 6c+
≤ 4c+
5a - 5c+
6a - 6b

75

Col de Bavella

Bavella is a truly beautiful mountain massif, north east of Zonza. The granite walls of these mountains are technical challenges, mainly in the 5th and 6th grade. On the mainly slabby and vertical rock good footwork instead of muscle power is the key to success. It used to be a traditional crag but many climbers have now bolted some fantastic lines. Most bolted routes are single pitch.

It is a 10 minute walk from the obvious parking to the first sectors. Be aware that the wind can blow very strongly at the Col de Bavella and sudden downpours can occur as well. It is a 95km drive from Ajaccio so it is best to stay either in Zonza or at any of the gîtes at the Col de Bavella itself.

Bavella

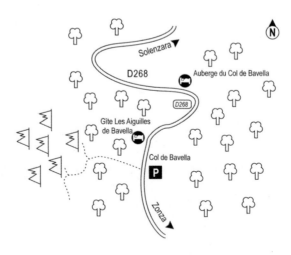

Solenzara

D268

Auberge du Col de Bavella

D268

Gîte Les Aiguilles de Bavella

Col de Bavella

P

Zonza

N

Directions

► *By Car*

Coming from Ajaccio follow the N196 towards Bonifacio. In Petreto-Bicchisano take the D420 to Aullène and continue to Zonza. The Col de Bavella is signposted in Zonza (D268).

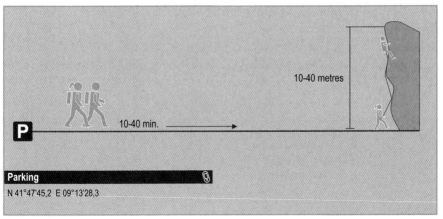

Parking

N 41°47'45,2 E 09°13'28,3

Type of rock

Granite

Family friendly

Yes, but only at the picnic area near the parking.

Protection

1   2   3   4

Climbing angle

Slab   Vertical   Steep   Really steep

Face direction

N
NW   NE
W   E
SW   SE
S

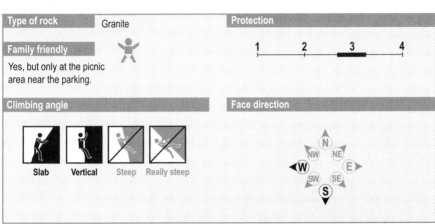

Number of routes & Grade range

7a - 7b+
6b+ - 6c+
≤ 4c+
5a - 5c+
6a - 6b
104

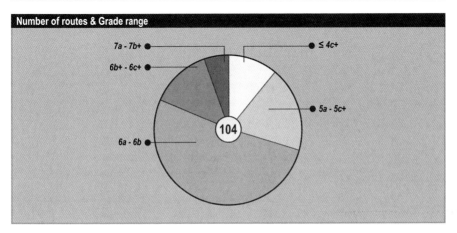

Superb climbing at Bavella, photo by Betrand Maurin

The 'Vallée de la Restonica' is one of Corsica's most important crags. The climbing is situated in the Restonica valley south west of Corte. This stunning mountain setting is a highlight for many outdoor lovers - both hikers as climbers - and the pine forest creates a wonderful landscape.

The seven sectors are situated in the valley north west of the D623. There are routes for beginners, such as at Sector L'Ortale, as well as some in the 8th grade at Sector Frassetta. However the majority of the routes are 5th and 6th grade. Almost all sectors face south.

The easy access and the inviting scenery will make this trip very memorable!

Sector PGHM offers a great set of routes in the low 6's, photo by Bertrand Maurin

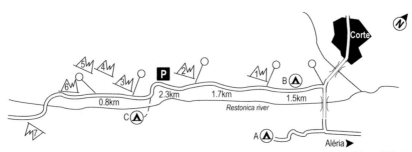

A.Camping L' Alivetu
B.Camping Usognu
C.Camping de Tuani

1.Sector L' Ortale
2.Sector Picellu
3.Sector Tuani
4.Sector PGHM
5.Sector Sorbellu
6.Sector Frassetta
7.Sector A Tomba

Directions

Sector Picellu at Restonica has some very technical
climbing, photo by Bertrand Maurin

▶ By Car
Coming from Ajaccio follow the N193 to Corte.
The Restonica valley is signposted in Corte and is
reached by taking the D623.

France | Corsica | Restonica

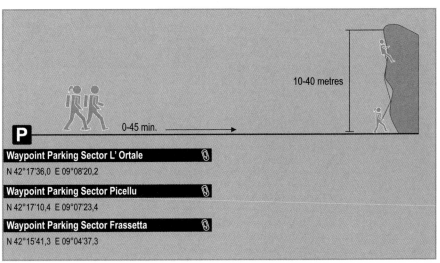

10-40 metres

0-45 min.

Waypoint Parking Sector L' Ortale
N 42°17'36,0 E 09°08'20,2

Waypoint Parking Sector Picellu
N 42°17'10,4 E 09°07'23,4

Waypoint Parking Sector Frassetta
N 42°15'41,3 E 09°04'37,3

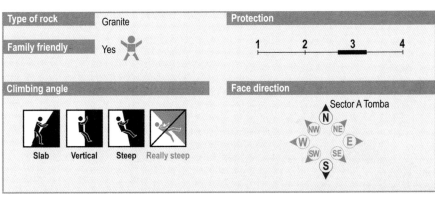

| Type of rock | Granite |
| Family friendly | Yes |

Protection

1   2   3   4

Climbing angle

Slab   Vertical   Steep   Really steep

Face direction

Sector A Tomba

N
NW   NE
W   E
SW   SE
S

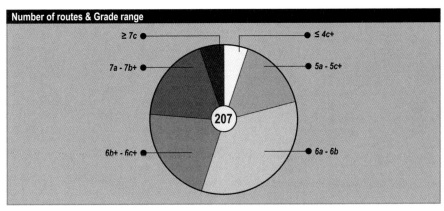

Number of routes & Grade range

≥ 7c

≤ 4c+

7a - 7b+

5a - 5c+

207

6b+ - 6c+

6a - 6b

...all that Europe has to offer...

Italy

Nympha Stassen on Nutella (6b+) in Arco, photo by Paul Lahaye

Italy really is Europe's treasure box. It has it all! You name it, spectacular mountain ranges, beautiful lakes, idyllic islands, splendid cities with a wealth of culture, a perfect climate, amazing cuisine, and warm and friendly people. Plus it offers sun-drenched limestone and granite crags in glorious mountain and beach settings. A climbing trip here will be unforgettable!

What can we say about Italy that hasn't already been said?! Well, it speaks volumes that Italy is considered the best place in Europe for so many things. Italian cuisine ranks among the finest in the world, as does its wine - people come here on holiday just to eat and drink. Italy's affair with cars and motor-sport needs no introduction and the country is the home of so many famous marques. Football too: if there's one country more passionate about the sport than Brazil, it's Italy. Then there's the culture. The Roman Empire profoundly influenced the western world and its legacy can still be seen and felt, not only in most European languages, and legal and political systems, but also in contemporary and classical architecture, the remains of which can still be found in the country. Italy in the middle ages was the home of the Renaissance movement, which is still so fundamental to our present-day culture and influences everything from music and art, to scientific and philosophical thought. And then, of course, Rome is the centre of the Roman Catholic Church, which alone attracts millions of visitors each year.

So, it should come as no great surprise that Italy is a major destination for climbers too! The Alps and the Dolomites, which form the northern border, are home to many great mountains, including the Matterhorn and Mont Blanc, and a number of significant pure rock-climbing areas. The great lakes of Como, Maggiore, Iseo, and Garda - themselves great outdoor-activity hubs - mark a transition to an altogether flatter landscape. The rest of the Italian boot-shaped peninsula is characterised by rolling hills although the Apennine mountain range, which forms the backbone of the country, is reasonably significant. However, climbers should look to the islands for more climbing action. Sardinia, the second largest island in the Mediterranean, is distinctly rocky. So, read on, and find out why climbers rank Italy among the best destinations in Europe.

Climbing information

Italy has many good crags but the best are to be found in the northern part of the country and on the islands. The high quality limestone and granite have since long attracted climbers from all over the world and there's everything from short single-pitch routes to major big-walls. But it's not just about roped climbing - there's some truly world-class bouldering here as well. The areas described in this chapter offer a huge variety of routes and climbing styles. Those wanting to escape the cold have, in Sardinia, a top winter destination with some great climbing, as well as a super family venue. The whole island seems to be one big rock and there are not only a huge number of developed routes but also the potential for thousands more.

Climbing area Finale

Finale Ligure is one of the top spots in Italy. There are over 2000 routes spread over several sectors around gorgeous Finale Ligure. The climbing, the pretty environment and the vicinity of the sea will make you want to come back here again!

Climbing area Val di Mello

This gem is hidden high up in the mountains and is perfect for big-wall adventures on solid granite. If you like cracks or slabs, you'll be in heaven here! There's also some superb bouldering in the valley and the setting is spectacularly beautiful.

Climbing area Arco

Arco is famous around the world for being one of Europe's best climbing destinations. Judge for yourself! One thing is for sure - it will take you a lifetime to do all the routes.

Climbing area Sardinia

The island of Sardinia has an abundance of magnificent limestone crags. It is a great destination for families and has a huge range of climbing. The crags covered are Domusnovas, Isili, Jerzu, Baunèi and Cala Gonone.

Unknown climber on Rombo di Vento (6c), Sulla Ovest di Rocca di Corno, photo by Paul Lahaye

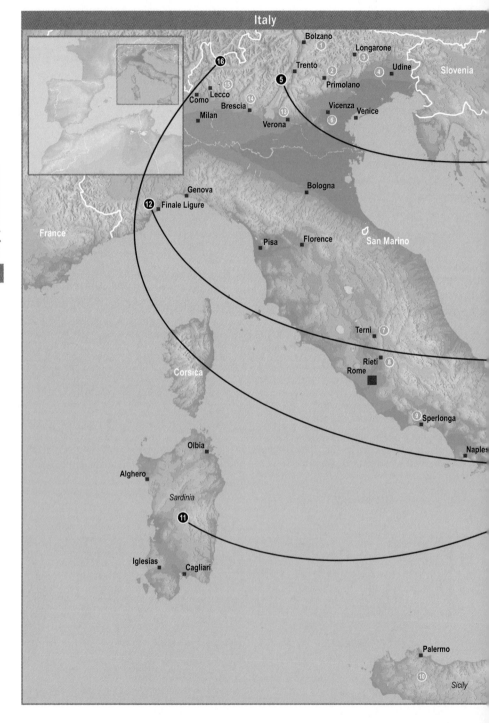

	Climbing area	Routes	
①	Sella	700	
②	Covolo	150	
③	Erto	250	
④	Val Colvera	225	
⑤	**Arco**		
	Arco	2247	
⑥	Lumignano	500	
⑦	Ferentillo	400	
⑧	Grotti	250	
⑨	Sperlonga	270	
⑩	Sicily	930	
⑪	**Sardinia**		
	Dosmusnovas	667	
	Isili	252	
	Jerzu	215	
	Baunèi	132	
	Cala Gonone	450	
⑫	**Finale**		
	Finale Ligure	2000	
⑬	Ceredo	200	
⑭	Madonna della Rota	80	
⑮	Cornalba	210	
⑯	**Val di Mello**		
	Val di Mello	371	

Note: This list only shows
the major climbing areas in Italy.

Climate

Italy's climate has a general pattern of warm, dry summers and mild winters. However, there are variations ranging from the more moderate north to the typically Mediterranean climate of the south. In general the summers are hot and dry along the coastal areas, especially in the south, and cool in the mountains. Winters are mild in the south of the country, but in the north they can be at least as cold as anywhere in the Northern Hemisphere.

The lowest number of rainy days and the highest number of hours of sunshine occur in the extreme south of the mainland, and in Sicily and Sardinia. Here sunshine averages from four to five hours a day in winter and up to ten or eleven hours in summer. Generally, the hottest month is July (where temperatures can reach 32°C/34°C); the coldest month is January; the wettest month is November, with an average rainfall of 129mm; while the driest month is July, with an average rainfall of 15mm.

The months to visit Italy to enjoy the best weather (and lack of crowds) are April to June, and September to October.

Month	Average temperature (°C)	Average rainfall (mm)
Jan	3	44
Feb	5	59
March	9	77
April	14	95
May	18	75
June	22	115
July	25	65
Aug	23	91
Sept	20	69
Oct	14	124
Nov	8	122
Dec	4	76

Climate table Milan

View of Lake Garda from one of the sectors near Arco

Getting there

 By plane

Italy is well served by the regular budget airlines and Alitalia (*www.alitalia.com*), the national carrier, also has good deals. As the majority of the climbing is situated in the north of Italy buy a ticket either to Milan, Génova, or Venice. Another option is to fly to Nice in France, which is close to the Italian border.

To get to Sardinia fly to Cagliari, the nearest airport to the crags described in this guide. The two other airports, Alghero and Olbia, are less convenient, being further from the climbing, but are still a viable option if you rent a car. Some of the budget airlines operating flights to Sardinia include Tuifly, Ryanair, EasyJet, and Meridiana.

From the USA, Canada, or any other country outside Europe, you will most likely fly to Milan (better if heading for the climbing in the north) or Rome. If Sardinia is your destination book an onward flight from either city. Meridiana (*www.meridiana.it*) operates inexpensive flights from Milan or Rome to Cagliari.

 By train

Milan is well connected to the rest of Europe by train. Check *www.reiseauskunft.bahn.de* for international timetables.

By bus

There are a number of bus companies connecting Rome, Milan and Venice to the rest of Europe. See *www.eurolines.com* for more information.

 By car

Italy can be reached by car from its neighbours: France, Switzerland, Austria, and Slovenia. Some of the border crossings are via high passes, such as the well known Brennerpass connecting Austria and Italy.

Moving around

Even though virtually all the climbing areas can be reached in theory by public transport, a car makes your life much easier as a lot of the climbing is well spread out. The Val di Mello is the exception: it's well connected to the public transport system and the climbing is all within walking distance of the main accommodation.

 Milan Bergamo airport information

The company named Terravision operates buses between the airport and the Milan railway station. Car rental agencies are based at the airport.

 Cagliari airport information

Cagliari's Elmas airport is the biggest on Sardinia. There are buses operating between the airport and Cagliari's bus station in the centre. The airport has car rental agencies.

 By public transport

The train network is an efficient way to get around Italy and *www.trenitalia.com* provides information on times and prices, and can be used for bookings. There are different types of trains operated by the railway company, Ferrovie dello Stato: slower trains can be a lot cheaper than faster and more comfortable ones.

Italy also has a decent bus network. There are hundreds of different companies operating in different regions. However trains and buses do not always reach smaller villages.

 By car

The road system is well developed. The only problem might be the hectic and passionate driving style of the locals! If you have never driven in the country before it might take some time to get used to the local road attitude. Everyone always seems to be in a hurry; take your time and don't let anyone rush you.

It is obligatory to drive with your lights on in Italy. Don't forget this, as police checks are common, even on Sardinia. On many roads, particularly motorways, you have to pay a toll.

Almost every Italian airport has car rental agencies. There is a lot of competition so check prices carefully before booking. Car rental on Sardinia is unfortunately rather expensive. Generally it is best to book a car in advance via the internet, as this can save a lot of money.

Italian shop sign

Diarmuid Duggan on Corvo Solitario at Isili, Sardinia, photo by Eoin Lawless

Accommodation

The huge popularity of Italy as a holiday destination for tourists from all over the world has resulted in a well developed tourist infrastructure. Put it another way, there is no shortage of accommodation! Campsites are scattered around the country, as are hotels and apartments. However many campsites and hotels only open during the tourist season which normally runs from Easter to mid October. This is something to bear in mind as spring and autumn are usually the best seasons for climbing and you might find yourself a little limited and having to look around.

Prices vary heavily according to season. On a campsite, expect to pay €20 to €30 for 2 people, a car and a tent. Prices for budget hotels range between €40 and €70 for a double room including breakfast. Many of the cheaper hotels will call themselves an Albergo.

Even though it is not legal, the locals are fine with you wild camping in Sardinia, as long as you leave no trace.

Italian cuisine is delicious

Food & drinks

The art of Italian cuisine is in its balance. Never heavy, never over-complicated, just fine and fresh and absolutely delicious! Dishes are always made with high-quality ingredients, simply prepared, retaining their original taste and freshness. The food has a history of rich inventiveness making Italian cuisine one of the world's most famous.

Nympha Stassen on Topless (5b), Capo Noli, Finale, photo by Paul Lahaye

Besides food, the coffees served are the best you can get. A cappuccino is taken for breakfast but an espresso is taken after lunch and dinner. The main meal of the day is normally lunch. A meal consists of antipasti (a starter) a primo piatto (pasta, rice or soup), a secondo piatto (meat or fish) with contorno (vegetables or salad), and fresh fruit is often served as a desert but gelato (ice cream) is also possible. Finally the meal is finished with espresso and maybe a grappa or amaro (a strong digestive liqueur). Ordering a cappuccino after dinner is considered to be impolite!

Then there's the wine - no surprise, given this is the land of the Romans! Italian wine is among the best in the world, sumptuous and varied. Virtually every corner of the whole country has some kind of wine production, even if this takes the form of Nonno (Granddad!) turning out a few bottles from a single row of vines on his land!

There is no place in Italy where you cannot find a ristorante or pizzeria. Eating out is still relatively cheap. Simple meals start at €8 per person and for a complete meal you would normally pay about €20. An espresso would normally go for €2 and a beer on a terrace would also be about €2.

Climbing guidebook

There are guidebooks of all the areas described in this chapter. See the 'Climbing area' sections for detailed information.

Finalborgo is one of the prettiest villages in Italy

Facts about Italy

Facts & figures

Population:	59 million
Religion:	Roman Catholic
Capital:	Rome
Time zone:	GMT+1
Telephone code:	+39

Money

Currency:	Euro
ATM machines:	widespread

Language

The official language of Italy is Italian.

Goodmorning	*Buon giorno*
Thank you	*Grazie*
Goodbye	*Arrivederci*
Yes / No	*Si / No*
Right / Left / Straight	*Destra / Sinistra / Dritto*
Rock climbing	*Arrampicare*

Visas & formalities

EU	Other European nationalities	USA / Canada	All other nationalities
No visa required for a period of up to 90 days.			Most other nationalities do not require a visa for a period of up to 90 days. Check *www.esteri.it* for more information.

Safety

Italy has a relatively low rate of violent crime. However, petty crime is, as everywhere, something to be aware of. Take the normal precautions and don't leave any valuables inside your car.

Emergency numbers

General:	112

Use of mobile phone

Several mobile operators cover the whole country.

Internet access

Available in most towns for around €3 per hour.

Water

It is not advisable to drink tap water in Italy - it is better to use bottled water. The price for six 1.5l bottles of water is around €2.

Climbing area Finale

The Finale climbing area is a cluster of different sectors all situated around three marvellous old towns - Finale Marina, Finalpia, and Finalborgo. Together these towns form Finale Ligure, along the Gulf of Génova. The area offers a staggering 2000 routes to choose from! However, it is not only the amount of routes and their excellent quality that makes this destination so popular; there is also massive scope for other activities. Finale Ligure lies right on the sea and there are superb water sports and great beaches. Furthermore the area is also excellent for biking and hiking. Rest days can happily be spent in Finalborgo, 2km inland. This is a fantastic 15th century walled town. Inside the walls you can wander through the tiny streets and enjoy the beautiful buildings. There are many small shops and on the Piazza Garibaldi the locals serve great espresso. But Finale Marina and Finalpia too, the latter with fine sandy beaches, prove to be very pleasant places to spend the day.

Spring   Summer   Autumn   Winter

The great bonus of this area is the well developed tourism infrastructure, which makes it easy to find decent accommodation and easy to get to, with low cost flights operating to nearby Génova and Nice (France). Simply put, the huge choice of crags and routes, and the diverse and accessible area guarantees an unforgettable climbing holiday!

Wonderful Finale Ligure

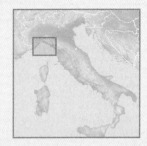

When to go

The best periods for climbing are spring and autumn. Summers are normally too hot: you can climb in the late afternoon on shady sectors but you'll have to spend the bulk of the day swimming in the sea. From November onwards the Tramontana, a cold wind from the north, picks up and can get really strong, making climbing less comfortable. This is something to take into account when planning your trip.

Crag

Ⓐ Finale Ligure

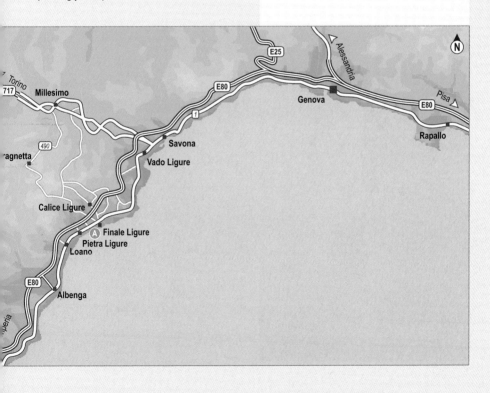

How to get to the area & how to move around

You're best off renting a car to get to the different sectors. Some climbers have been known to hire bikes - not altogether a bad idea but this will eat into your climbing time.

 By public transport

The closest airports to Finale Ligure are Génova (also spelt Genoa) and Nice (France) and are served by budget airlines. Cars are available to rent at both airports.

A train line links Finale Ligure and Génova [45min - 1h30, €3.95]. The airport bus, the Volabus, runs every 20 minutes between the airport and Stazione Principe FS, Génova's main railway station.

 By car

Take the E80 / A10 from Génova in the direction of Savona and Nice (France). Exit at Finale Ligure. If you're coming from Nice, the same motorway takes you (in the opposite direction!) to Génova.

Climbers at Falesia del Silenzio, photo by Alberto De Giuli

Monte Cucco

Where to stay

The most convenient place to stay is in Finale Ligure itself, as it is closest to the climbing action. There are a few campsites and a large selection of very decent 2-star hotels. At Sector Monte Cucco you can camp for free and it even has a toilet block. There is a bunch of 2-star hotels along Via Brunenghi, the road from Finale Ligure to Finalborgo. You need a car to get to the sectors.

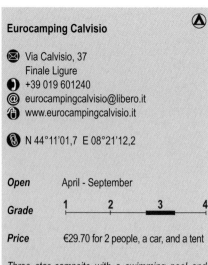

Eurocamping Calvisio

✉ Via Calvisio, 37
 Finale Ligure
☎ +39 019 601240
@ eurocampingcalvisio@libero.it
🌐 www.eurocampingcalvisio.it

📍 N 44°11'01,7 E 08°21'12,2

Open	April - September

Grade	1 — 2 — 3 — 4

Price	€29.70 for 2 people, a car, and a tent

Three star campsite with a swimming pool and restaurant.

Directions:
There are signs for the campsite in the village.

Camping Mulino

✉ Via Castelli
   Finale Ligure
☎ +39 019 601669
@ info@laterrazzahotel.com
🏠 www.campingmulino.com

📍 N 44°10'24,3 E 08°20'59,9

Open   April - September

Grade   1 ——— 2 ——— **3** ——— 4

Price   €27 for 2 people, a car, and a tent;
              two to four person bungalows cost
              between €47 and €93 per night

*Pretty and quiet campsite situated on a hill. They
rent bungalows and there is a bar.*

Directions:
You'll find signs for the camping in the village.

*Niels van Veen on Another Day in Paradise (6c+),
photo by Frank Koppens*

Albergo il Faro

✉ Via San Francesco 5
   Finale Ligure
☎ +39 019 692369
@ info@albergoilfaro.it
🏠 www.albergoilfaro.it

📍 N 44°10'11,0 E 08°20'21,5

Open   Year round

Price   a double with bathroom costs
              €55 including breakfast

*This two star hotel is close to the beach. The rooms
are fine but nothing special.*

Directions:
In Finale Ligure take the turn for FinalBorgo,
along the Via Brunenghi. Go under the railway
bridge. The hotel is a few hundred metres further
on the left.

Albergo Giardino

✉ Via T.Pertica 49
   Finale Ligure
☎ +39 019 692815
@ giardinofi@libero.it

📍 N 44°10'06,1 E 08°20'35,4

Open   May - September

Price   a double with bathroom costs
              €53 to €68 including breakfast

*Nice hotel right in the centre of Finale Ligure. It has
a back entrance directly onto the boulevard.*

Directions:
The hotel is located on the main shopping street in
Finale Ligure, which runs parallel to the boulevard.

Giardino delle Rose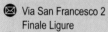

✉ Via San Francesco 2
Finale Ligure
☎ +39 019 692534
@ giardinodellerose@giardinodellerose.com
🌐 www.giardinodellerose.com

📱 N 44°10'11,0 E 08°20'22,7

Open   Year round

Price   a double with bathroom costs
€50 including breakfast

The hotel offers about the same quality as its neighbour, the Albergo il Faro.

Directions:
In Finale Ligure take the turn for FinalBorgo, along the Via Brunenghi. Go under the railway bridge. The hotel is a few hundred metres further on the left.

Hotel Medusa

✉ Lungomare di Via Concezione
Finale Ligure
☎ +39 019 692545
@ giardinofi@libero.it

📱 N 44°10'07,1 E 08°20'41,0

Open   Year round

Price   half board from €50 p.p.p.n.

This comfortable three star hotel offers nice rooms right on the beach.

Directions:
The hotel is on the boulevard in Finale Ligure.

Michel Dickhaut on Finale Y2K

Rosso Antico (6a+), Rocca di Corno,
Finale, photo by Alberto De Giuli

Where to buy groceries?

There is a large Coop supermarket along the river between Finale Ligure and Finalborgo.

Where to find the local climbing guidebook

The local guide is called 'Finale by Thomas' and covers the 9 sectors around the village of Finale Ligure (€16). It is in full colour and has English and German translations. The proceeds of the guidebook sales go directly into the local bolt-fund, helping sustain development of the area. It is sold at the Mountain shop, Via Nicoteria 6, in Finalborgo, just off the main square. There is another climbing shop in Finalborgo called Rockstore, located on the central square, Piazza Garibaldi 14. Although it does not stock the 'Finale by Thomas' guide, it has a wide range of guidebooks covering the rest of Italy.

You may also come across another guide, 'Finale Y2K', written by Andrea Gallo (€26). However it is a few years old and is pretty outdated.

Rocca di Perti

What else is there to see & do

Mountain biking
This region is very popular with mountain bikers and there is even a comprehensive guide that describes the best routes (on sale at Rockstore in Finalborgo). On a bike, the hills in this area become a great playground! Mountain-bikes can be rented at two different shops in Finalborgo.

Windsurfing
The warm water along this part of the Italian coast along with good winds gives rise to excellent conditions for windsurfers. There are several windsurf schools based along the coast. Expect to pay around €9 per hour to rent a board. If you are a beginner, go during summer when conditions are not so challenging. From November the Tramontana wind peps things up and more experienced windsurfers come out.

The central square in Finalborgo

Finale Ligure

The sectors situated inland from Finale Ligure are good quality limestone; the routes are mainly single pitch although there are some up to four pitches long. The variety is simply huge - slabs, smooth and pocketed vertical walls, and pump-inducing overhangs can all be found. There are 9 sectors in total, of which Rocca di Perti, Monte Cucco, and Rian Cornei are (justifiably) the most visited.

Rocca di Perti is an extensive place and has around 300 routes, the majority being in the 6th and 7th grade. Monte Cucco offers around 250 routes at around the same level. Technique is your best friend here but you will need a lot of stamina too: fingery small holds sap a lot of energy. Rian Cornei really is enormous, with 450 routes to choose from, single pitch 6th grade being the name of the game here.

Don't leave any valuables inside your car. Most of the sectors are a little away from the main roads and break-ins are not uncommon here, unfortunately. Take care and employ some common sense!

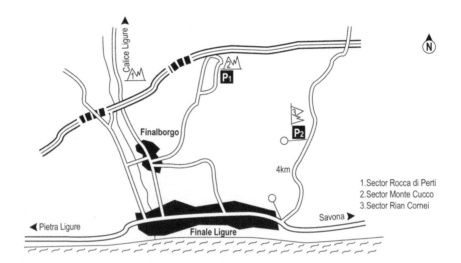

1. Sector Rocca di Perti
2. Sector Monte Cucco
3. Sector Rian Cornei

Directions

▶ For Rocca di Perti take the road from Finale Ligure in the direction of Finalborgo. Cross the bridge and continue on to Calice Ligure. The small turning for Rocca di Perti is signposted and comes after passing under the motorway.

For Monte Cucco also take the road from Finale Ligure to Finalborgo. From there continue driving towards Feglino. After 3.1km turn right towards Feglino Orco and continue for another 2.2km until you see the Ristorante Il Rifugio. Turn right onto a small road until you come to the free campsite after a few hundred metres.

To get to Rian Cornei, cross the medieval bridge in Finale Ligure and turn left towards Calvisio / Vezzi Portio. Continue for 4km and park at the Pizzeria Cornei on the left hand side of the road.

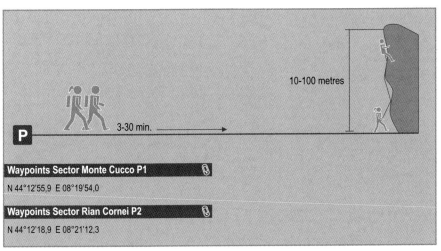

10-100 metres

3-30 min.

P

Waypoints Sector Monte Cucco P1

N 44°12'55,9 E 08°19'54,0

Waypoints Sector Rian Cornei P2

N 44°12'18,9 E 08°21'12,3

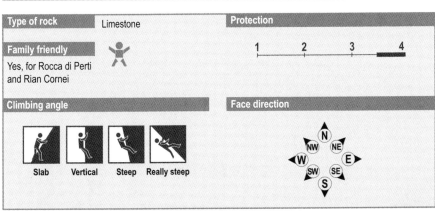

Type of rock Limestone

Family friendly
Yes, for Rocca di Perti and Rian Cornei

Climbing angle

Slab Vertical Steep Really steep

Protection

1   2   3   4

Face direction

N
NW NE
W   E
SW SE
S

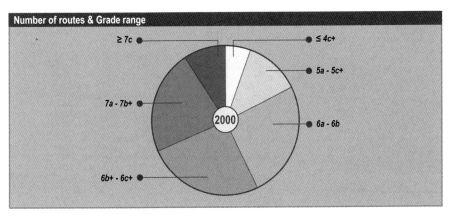

Number of routes & Grade range

≥ 7c

≤ 4c+

5a - 5c+

7a - 7b+

2000

6a - 6b

6b+ - 6c+

Climbing area Val di Mello

Europe's Yosemite? Well, that's the claim, and it's not just the Italians making it. You simply have to come here once in your life and check it out for yourself - there's a very special atmosphere, the scenery is stunning, and the climbing is just great. It may turn out to be love at first sight, in which case this is one place you'll be coming back to, time and time again!

The Val di Mello is a gorgeous valley in northern Italy, close to the Swiss border. It was a centre of free climbing development in the 80's due mainly to the enormous quantity of high quality rock in the valley and the trend for freeing and putting up big routes. The huge granite walls - up to 800 metres high - rising up from the lush pastures of the valley still attract a large number of climbers of both trad and sport persuasions. Boulderers too are not forgotten, and there is a serious quantity of hard granite problems to tackle. Further, the Bregaglia

| Spring | Summer | Autumn | Winter |

Alps, for which the Val di Mello provides the southern border, has an outstanding range of alpine rock routes, Piz Badile being the most famous peak.

The Val di Mello stretches out behind the small village of San Martino. Although the village gets a lot of people passing through it - mainly Italian day-trippers - it remains a peaceful place and is a great springboard from which to discover the rest of the valley. There is a fair range of accommodation and the locals warmly welcome any newcomers. Apart from climbers, the area also attracts a lot of hikers and there are many excellent trails.

The valley is also home to "Melloblocco". This annual international bouldering competition attracts a large number of serious boulderers who come to really push

Val di Mello has fantastic trad climbing opportunities, photo by Adrian Berry

the boundaries. If this appeals, make sure you book well in advance as accommodation fills up quickly. See *www.melloblocco.it* for more information.

When to go

The best period for climbing is during late spring and early autumn. As the valley is high up in the mountains summers can work as well (especially if you are flexible and want to mix in some alpine routes too) although some of the valley routes can get quite hot. The valley is in the rain shadow of the Bregaglia Alps so the weather is more reliable than some other Alpine venues. If you're coming to do the longer routes, May and June are your best bets so as to maximise your daylight hours!

Crag

Ⓐ **Val di Mello**

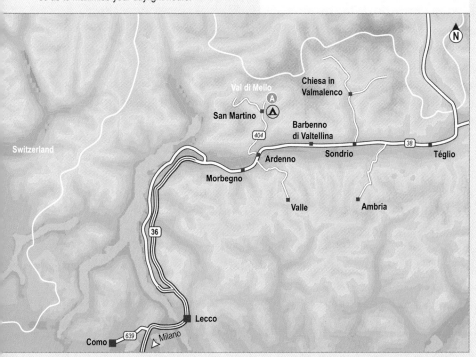

How to get to the area & how to move around

You don't need a car to get to any of the climbing.

 By public transport

The best airport is Milan Bergamo (also called Orio al Serio) - it is not far away from the Val di Mello and is served by budget airlines, such as Ryanair, Easyjet, and Tuifly. Car rental agencies are based at the airport.

Getting to the Val di Mello from Bergamo airport by public transport involves a combination of buses and trains (but the journey is quite straightforward). First, take a local bus to Bergamo train station [frequent service, €1.65]. From here, trains run every hour to Morbegno, via Lecco. The train takes about 1hr50 and a single ticket costs €7.50 (if you find yourself in central Milan for whatever reason, there's also a connection to Morbegno via Lecco running every 2 hours and taking a similar length of time). The final stage from Morbegno to San Martino is by bus, which runs three to five times a day, depending on the season. Be careful, the last bus leaves Morbegno at something like 6pm and there is neither much to do nor many places to stay there! If your connection looks tight, you might be best off stopping over in Lecco and catching the first train in the morning.

By car

From Milan Bergamo follow the directions for Lecco. After Lecco drive through an endless number of

Climber on Luna Nascente, photo by Sjaak de Visser

tunnels on the east side of Lago di Lecco and Lago di Como. After the tunnels follow the directions for Morbegno which is the N38. On the N38 San Martino is signposted. The last section, going up into the mountains, is 13.7km long.

Where to stay

The small mountain village of San Martino lies at the start of the Val di Mello. It's a very pretty village and is a convenient place to stay as it offers a good choice of accommodation and is close to all the climbing.

Camping Sasso Remenno

✉ St. Sasso Remenno 2
  23010 San Martino
☎ +39 034 2640059
@ info@campingsassoremenno.com
🌐 www.campingsassoremenno.com

Open   Year round

Grade   1 ——— 2 ——— **3** ——— 4

Price   €18 for 2 persons, a car and a tent

The campsite is in a very beautiful and peaceful setting a couple of kilometres below San Martino. It is small, family friendly and clean with a good and popular restaurant just next to a river. As it is the nearest campsite to the village - and right next to the bolt clipping on Sasso Remenno - this is where most climbers stay. From the campsite it is 4km on foot to the entrance of the valley.

Directions:
The campsite is 2km before San Martino, just after the huge "boulder" of Sasso Remenno, and can't be missed. If arriving by bus, ask the bus driver to drop you off at the entrance.

Camping Sasso Remenno is wonderfully located

The Val di mello is 2km from San Martino

Albergo Badile

✉ 23010 San Martino
☎ +39 034 2641140

📍 N 46°14'26,2 E 09°37'52,6

Open   June - September

Price   a double with bathroom costs
€37 including breakfast

The Albergo Badile is a basic but friendly hotel which only opens during the summer.

Directions:
You'll find signs for the hotel in the village.

Albergo Genzianella

✉ Via Vanoni 19
23010 San Martino
☎ +39 034 2641040
@ info@ genzianellavalmasino.com
🌐 www.genzianellavalmasino.com

📍 N 46°14'26,5 E 09°37'44,5

Open   Year round except for November

Price   a double with bathroom costs
€48 including breakfast;
full pension is €40 p.p.p.n.

This very calm and friendly place is a good place to stay if you don't speak Italian since the owner speaks English.

Directions:
You'll find signs for the hotel in the village.

The boulders are in a beautiful setting

Albergo Bucaneve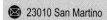

✉ 23010 San Martino
☎ +39 034 2641166

📍 N 46°14'25,3 E 09°37'41,4

Open   Year round

Price   a double with bathroom costs
             €42 including breakfast;
             full pension is €42 p.p.p.n.

The hotel offers fine rooms for the price and it has a very chilled-out terrace.

Directions:
This is the first house on the left when entering the village.

Hotel Le Cime

✉ 23010 San Martino

📍 N 46°14'24,1 E 09°37'33,3

Open   April - September

Price   a double with bathroom costs
             €25 to €30 including breakfast

The hotel has passable rooms but less character than the albergi in the village.

Directions:
The hotel lies along the main road passing through San Martino.

Where to buy groceries?

There is a small and rather expensive supermarket in San Martino, although it's pretty well stocked and sells fresh bread. If you have a car, you're best off doing the bulk of your shopping in one of many supermarkets along the N38 before heading up the valley.

The Albergo Bucaneve in San Martino

Where to find the local climbing guidebook

The best guide is called Solo Granito, published by Versante Sud and written by Mario Sertori and Guido Iisignoli. It is written in Italian (there is also a German edition called Nichts als Granit) and not only covers the Val di Mello but also many other crags in the region, including some across the Swiss border. While comprehensive, the quality of the topos for some of the more esoteric crags can be variable, so their inclusion only adds marginal value to the guide. Finding the starts of some of the routes can be hard. It is sold at the climbing shop or the newsagent/postcard shop in San Martino. Camping Sasso Remenno also sells the guide.

There's also a very quirky and humourous guide (in Italian only), the reprinted 1985 classic 'Val di Mello - 9000 Metri Sopra I Prati', written by Paolo Masa and Jacopo Merizzi, who were two of the leading activists at that time. This book contains around 100 routes in the Val di Mello itself, including all the classics. It's full of great photos - the guide is worth it for the photos themselves! - and it perfectly captures the unique atmosphere of the era, and wild nature of both the valley and the climbing itself.

The boulder problems are described in a topo: 'iBloc, Bouldertopo Italia' by Ulrich and Harald Röker. There are English, German and Italian versions. It can be ordered via *www.gebro-verlag.de* for €29.90.

Sonja Brambati on Poesia di una squow della riserva on the Alkekengi, photo by Paolo Vitali

What else is there to see & do

Hiking

If you have active family members who love walking, or don't mind a bit yourself, the Val di Mello valley is a great place to be. There are countless walking trails and the mountain scenery is just spectacular. The newsagent/postcard shop in San Martino sells hiking guides and maps of the area (if you can find them, the Swiss maps are far superior to the Italian versions). The mountain huts (Rifugi) in the area are great, and it's possible to spend a few days up high, linking them by means of some spectacular alpine passes.

Mountaineering

The Bregaglia has one of the finest collections of high-mountain rock routes in the Alps. Certainly you shouldn't come to the Val di Mello without bringing your mountain gear - a hot day in the valley will make for perfect conditions higher up. Routes on the Piz Badile (including the Cassin, Molteni, and N Ridge), Punto Allievi (Gervasutti) or Pizzo Cengalo are absolute classics and should not be missed by any competent party. They are all easily accessible from the Val di Mello via the Gianetti or Allievi huts.

San Martino

The enormous granite walls of Val di Mello mainly offer slab and crack climbing on big walls. The area was long known for its bold and exposed slab routes, with free crack climbing development occurring later. If any of these two styles suit you, you will be in absolute heaven here! There are a huge number of cracks that are long and sustained, and are of exceptional quality and situation (Oceano Irrazionale, splitting the headwall of the Precipizio degli Asteroidi, has to be seen to be believed - and, not allowing for the "interesting" approach and descent, goes at the relatively accessible grade of VII). The slabs are technical, long, and demand both balance and a cool head. The local climbing ethic is quite unusual for this corner of Europe, with the emphasis on adventure - there are bolts on routes, and belays are almost always bolted, but the majority of the big routes will tend to be psychological as well as physical tests! Mega-classic routes include Luna Nascente, Il Risveglio di Kundalini, Patabang, Polimago. Then there is the massive 950m Il Paradiso Puo' Attendere (VIII A3) - a serious granite big-wall in the heart of Europe!

Overall, the Val di Mello is a very good destination for the more experienced climber and those with a lot of stamina. The majority of the routes are high 6th grade and 7th grade routes and there are even some very good harder challenges. It's worth noting that, because of the historical emphasis on slab climbing, slab routes tend to feel slightly overgraded (this is, in part, due to the boldness!),

while crack climbs appear undergraded. Also, the bigger routes tend to require a certain amount of experience, which comes in handy in route finding, and in negotiating the sometimes exciting and involved descents.

There are some pure bolted sport routes in the area, notably on Sasso Remenno (technically a boulder and, at 50m high, the biggest in the Alps!), covering the entire grade range. You'll also find mountain routes masquerading as sport routes, most up around the Rifugio Allievi. These are multi-pitch (but relatively short) and bolted to a good standard. While still requiring care, they can be tackled in "cragging" rather than "mountain" mode, and make a good alternative when the valley gets too hot.

As far as boulders go, the valley is literally littered with boulders of all shapes and sizes! A good place to start is next to the river at the big parking lot where the boulders are still small. You won't be the only one there as this is a favourite local picnic spot.

The place to be to hook up with other climbers is Bar Monica in the centre of San Martino. The bar has internet access and there are lots of climbing books and magazines to enjoy on rainy days.

If you come by car be aware that there is no petrol station at San Martino. The village does have a cash machine.

Crack climbing techniques required for Qualido Qualifalaise, photo by Paolo Vitali

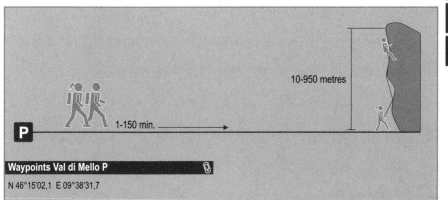

10-950 metres

1-150 min.

P

Waypoints Val di Mello P

N 46°15'02,1 E 09°38'31,7

Type of rock	Granite

Protection

1 ——— 2 ——— **3** ——— 4

The fixed protection varies per route

Family friendly

Yes, but only
for the bouldering.

Climbing angle

Slab   Vertical   Steep   Really steep

Face direction

N
NW NE
W   E
SW SE
S

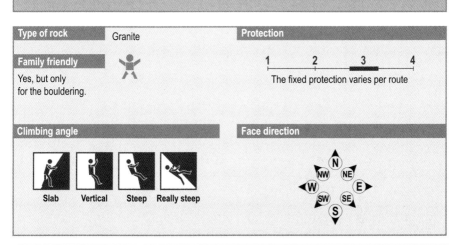

Number of routes & Grade range

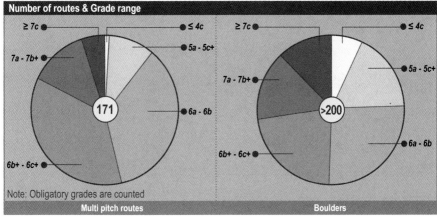

≥ 7c
7a - 7b+
171
6a - 6b
6b+ - 6c+
≤ 4c
5a - 5c+

≥ 7c
7a - 7b+
>200
6a - 6b
6b+ - 6c+
≤ 4c
5a - 5c+

Note: Obligatory grades are counted

Multi pitch routes   Boulders

Val di Mello

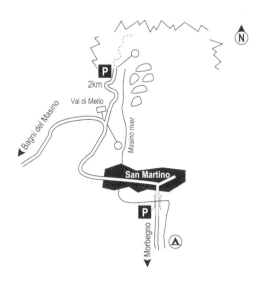

Directions

Climbing on Lo Scivolo, photo by Sjaak de Visser

► In the months of June and July, when the access road is closed to regular traffic, there is a taxi service running up and down from San Martino to the entrance of Val di Mello [2km, €1]. Don't try to park up in the valley during these months - you will get a ticket!

Climbing area Arco

Spring   Summer   Autumn   Winter

Welcome to Europe's top spot for outdoor adventurers!

Arco is the best-known climbing destination in Italy and among the best in SW Europe. The area encompasses a staggering 80 sectors with more than 2000 routes! You can spend a lifetime climbing here. The magnitude of this area is hard to sum up in words and so is the quality of the climbing. However, the area is not just a magnet for climbing's sake alone - Arco stands for outdoor life in general and there are many other sports going on.

Arco itself is a town located in northern Italy, just north of Lake Garda. The setting is magnificent and the area exudes a relaxed but also very active atmosphere. Nowhere in Italy are there so many outdoor shops located so close to each other. Well known climbing brands have opened up their own dedicated shops and, due to the competition, it is cheap to by your gear here. From shoes to ropes or rucksacks, this is the place to do your shopping!

The tourism industry here is well developed, not just on account of the outdoor types that descend on the area, but also because of the range of people who come to enjoy the beautiful setting. Accommodation is plenty and there is no lack of nice bars and restaurants. The flip side to this success story is that climbing at Arco has become enormously popular and busy, but thankfully the area is big enough to avoid succumbing to polished routes and crowds.

Torbole - Lake Garda, photo by Paul Lahaye

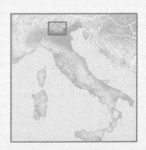

When to go

Climbing at Arco is possible for most of the year. However spring and autumn are the best periods. Summers are hot, especially August, and if you come at this time of year, you'll be forced to seek out shady sectors.

Crag

Ⓐ Arco

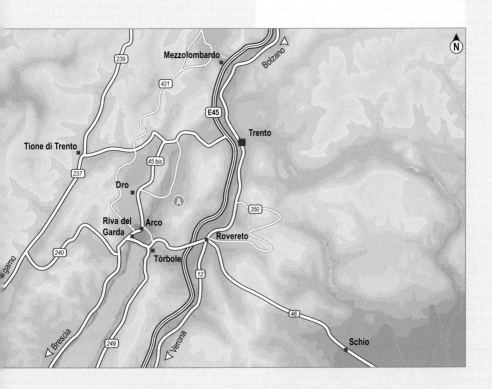

How to get to the area & how to move around

The sectors are a little spread around. If you have a car you can reach most sectors within a half an hour drive from Arco.

 By public transport

The quickest and cheapest way to get to Arco by plane is to fly to either Milan or Verona. Low cost airlines operate to both cities. Take the train from either Milan [2h35, €17.50] or Verona [1h, €4] to Rovereto. There are daily buses from Rovereto to Arco.

By car

Coming from Innsbruck in Austria follow the A22/E45 highway to Trento. Leave the highway at Trento and continue to Arco / Riva del Garda on the 45 bis.

Where to stay

Despite the spread out nature of the area, it is best to stay in Arco itself, even if you fancy climbing at some of the further off sectors. This outdoor minded village is the centre of the climbing scene and the majority of the climbers stay here. There are a few campsites and most hotels rent out separate apartments as well.

Camping Arco

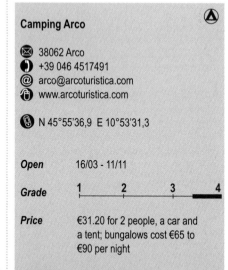

- 38062 Arco
- +39 046 4517491
- arco@arcoturistica.com
- www.arcoturistica.com

N 45°55'36,9 E 10°53'31,3

Open	16/03 - 11/11
Grade	1 2 3 4
Price	€31.20 for 2 people, a car and a tent; bungalows cost €65 to €90 per night

This quiet campsite lies along the river that runs through Arco. It has all the facilities you might want and the overall standard is very high. There is even an indoor bouldering wall for use on rainy days! There are also nice wooden bungalows which sleep 4 people.

Directions:
In Arco, turn right after crossing the bridge. The campsite is signposted.

Helmut Größling on the classique Titanic (7a+), Nago, photo Paul Lahaye

Camping Arco rents nice wooden cottages

Camping Zoo

 38062 Arco
 +39 046 4516232
@ zoo@camping.it
 www.camping.it/trentino/zoo

 N 45°55'57,9 E 10°53'33,7

Open   15/02 - 15/11

Grade   1   2   3   4

Price   €23.50 for 2 people, a car and a tent

This is Camping Arco's neighbour and equal in terms of quality. It is a friendly place with a large swimming pool.

Directions:
In Arco, turn right after crossing the bridge. The campsite is signposted.

Camping Arco Lido

38062 Arco
+39 046 4505077
@ lido@arcoturistica.com
www.arcoturistica.com

Open   April - November

Grade   1   2   3   4

Price   €25.60 for 2 people, a car and a tent

The campsite is very nicely situated along the bank of Lake Garda. Unsurprisingly, it attracts a lot of windsurfers!

Directions:
Camping Arco Lido is situated 700m from the centre of Torbole.

Centre of Arco, photo by Paul Lahaye

Hotel & Apartments Marchi

Via Ferrera 22
38062 Arco
+39 046 4517171
@ info@hotelmarchisnc.it
www.hotelmarchisnc.it

Open   April - January

Price   a double with bathroom costs €78 including breakfast; a 2 to 6 person apartment costs €60 to €150 per night

The three-star hotel is situated in one of Arco's older buildings. It is run by a friendly family and offers clean rooms. They can open the hotel on request in February and March. They also rent out apartments, which are separate from the hotel.

Directions:
Via Ferrera is the street that runs parallel to the shopping street (the one with all the outdoor shops!) in the old part of Arco.

Hotel & Apartments Pace

✉ Via Vergolano 50
   38062 Arco
☎ +39 046 4516398
@ info@hotelpace.net
🖱 www.hotelpace.net

📎 N 45°55'11,1 E 10°52'59,8

Open   Year round

Price   a double with bathroom costs €80
            including breakfast; half pension
            €57 p.p.p.n; three to four person
            apartments are €490 to €790
            per week

*Modern three star hotel. They also rent out good
apartments.*

Directions:
The hotel is situated in the old part of Arco at the
end of the main shopping street.

Hotel & Apartments Al Sole

✉ Piazza S. Anna
   38062 Arco
☎ +39 046 4516676
@ info@soleholiday.com
🖱 www. soleholiday.com

📎 N 45°55'06,1 E 10°53'11,5

Open   Year round

Price   a double with bathroom costs
            €90 including breakfast;
            two person apartments are €85
            to €160 per night

*Modern hotel with a small bouldering wall. They
also rent out apartments.*

Directions:
The hotel is situated next to the big car park in the
old part of Arco.

Third pitch of Zanzara e Labbradoro, Sector Colodri in Arco, photo by Alberto De Giuli

Berghaus is a brand that is synonymous with exploration and adventure since it formed in 1966. That spirit is reflected in its diverse and outstanding team of sponsored athletes, who push themselves to the limit in the outdoors, testing Berghaus products in the most challenging and extreme environments around the world.

Over the last decade, Leo Houlding has set the climbing scene alight with bold ascents, audacious stunts and ambitious firsts around the world. Packing adrenaline and confidence into each fresh challenge, whether he's climbing up a route or base jumping triumphantly off its top. Now taking his approach to the Himalaya and other great ranges, Leo's impact and influence has already been huge, and he has only just started.

Anniken Binz is a new breed of model, with a passion for extreme sport. The 29 year old has been a base jumper for seven years and joined the Berghaus team in 2006. Rather than spending her time applying makeup, or seeking out the latest designer handbag, Anniken prefers diving out of planes, off buildings or leaping from mountain tops. She is Beautiful, daring and stylish, with a high flying career in more ways than one.

Next there are the masters of big wall climbing, Alex and Thomas Huber. The Huber brothers test themselves in the most gruelling climbs imaginable. They have scaled some of the world's highest peaks and between them have forged a status as two of the best and most committed climbers on the planet. Their reputation is formidable and for several years they have been key members of the Berghaus team.

Leo Houlding

Anniken Binz

Rob Jarman

berghaus

www.berghaus.com

Rob Jarman is an outstanding mountain bike free rider with an insatiable appetite for adventure. Rob has tested his Berghaus kit to the extreme in his pursuit of the next mountain biking challenge, whether on a bob sled run, competing in the gruelling Himalayan Yak Attack race or in any number of other perilous locations.

Spanish climber Carlos Suarez has taken on big wall climbs in some of the world's most dramatic massifs such as Patagonia, Yosemite, and Andes. Not afraid of taking on a challenge, Carlos has climbed more than twenty routes in solo in the Alps alone, sometimes climbing with no rope or harness, only a chalk bag and climbing shoes holding him to the rock. Always seeking new adrenaline packed action, Carlos is also an experienced base jumper.

Kristen Reagan is a climber and base jumper who dedicates his time to making waves in the extreme sports world. Specialising in extreme ice, alpine and big wall climbing, Kristen likes to take the 'easy' route down by base jumping. Often pushing boundaries by climbing without ropes, he has made groundbreaking ascents of some of the world harshest walls, sometimes in challenging winter conditions.

Berghaus sponsored athletes will only use kit that performs and helps them achieve their demanding goals. They work closely with the design team at Berghaus to develop even better products every year. They can't afford to use products that let them down, which is why they choose to work with Berghaus. In turn, these athletes embody the Berghaus spirit in a way that inspires the brand and the people around the world who wear its products.

Berghaus® have been awarded both CoolBrands and SuperBrands status for 2007/08

Win €500 of Berghaus® product or one of 50 Huber Yosemite Books

Simply answer the question below by logging onto our website at **www.berghaus.com/comp/rca**

Q. Which athletes are associated with the following activities?

1. **Climbing**
2. **Base Jumping**
3. **Mountain Biking**

berghaus®

www.berghaus.com

NO PURCHASE NECESSARY. Competition is open to residents of the United Kingdom, Germany and the Netherlands only. Entrants must be 16 years or over to enter. By participating all entrants agree to the Terms and Conditions which are available at: www.berghaus.com/comp/rca. The promoter for this competition is: Berghaus Ltd, 12 Colima Avenue, Sunderland Enterprise Park, Sunderland, SR5 3XB, UK. Start Date: 01/12/2007. End Date: 01/12/2008. The winners will be picked at random on 02/12/2008. They will be contacted by either phone, email or letter by no later than 19/12/2008. BERGHAUS and ☐ are registered trade marks of Berghaus Limited. © Berghaus Limited 2007.

Where to buy groceries?

There are several supermarkets in Arco.

Where to find the local climbing guidebook

The topo for Arco is quite a substantial booklet - no wonder given the quantity of routes! It is called 'Arco Rock' and is for sale in English, German and Italian (€24.90). It is written by Manica, Cicogna, and Negretti and is published by Versante Sud. It describes 80 sectors and has some colour photos. It's only bad feature is its simple drawings, which can make it hard to find the starts of some of the routes. The topo is for sale just about everywhere in Arco.

The imposing walls of Arco

What else is there to see & do

Mountain biking & hiking
The area around Arco - and also to the west and east of Lake Garda - is full of superb mountain bike and hiking trails. The area is very hilly though, be warned! The bookshop close to the central square in Arco has trail information.

Bike shops in Arco rent out mountain bikes. Expect to pay between €16 and €24 for a half-day or full-day rental. Recommended shops are Giuliani on Via Bruno Galas 29A (*www.bikegiuliani.com*) and Bikbike on Via S.Caterina 9 (*www.bikbike.com*).

Other outdoor sports
If it is canyoning, via ferrata, windsurfing, or paragliding, the Arco area is the place to be. If gear rental or guiding services are required for any of these sports, a good starting point is the company 'Friends of Arco'. They are located at Via Segantini 16, the main shopping street in the old part of the town. The company specialises in a large number of outdoor sports and can also provide general information on the area.

Venice
If you have the time then a trip to Venice, Italy's most romantic city, is a must. It is a good 200km drive. Yes, it's touristy and busy, and beware of rip-off merchants at every corner - don't get on a gondola without agreeing a price! - but it's an amazing place. It's particularly worth heading away from the touristy areas and wandering around the small and charming neighbourhoods, where you'll catch a fascinating glimpse of local life.

Arco

Arco

The 80 sectors which together have turned Arco into a real climbing paradise offer every style and climbing technique one could possible want. Sector Massone, close to the campsites in Arco, is probably the most popular and best known and climbers can choose from one of the 147 routes. Most of the single pitch routes are in the 6th and 7th grade and they are seriously sustained. A little further to the right, Massone II Pueblo also has many overhanging 8th grade routes and, if that is not enough, there is even a 9a 'Underground'.

One of the other top sectors is Nago, 7.5km from Arco. This sector has less serious routes compared to Sector Massone. There are some 130 routes and 4th and 5th grade climbers will enjoy it.

The majority of the routes at Arco are single pitch but there are routes up to 300 metres long too. There is also a little bit of bouldering, but this is really minimal compared to the sport climbing.

*Patrick Coenen on Gameboy (7b) at the tough
Sector Massone, photo by Paul Lahaye*

Directions

▶ The Arco topo uses clear drawings and has descriptions on how to get to the 80 different sectors.

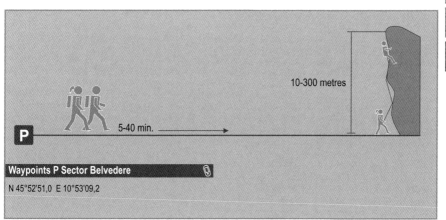

10-300 metres

5-40 min.

P

Waypoints P Sector Belvedere

N 45°52'51,0 E 10°53'09,2

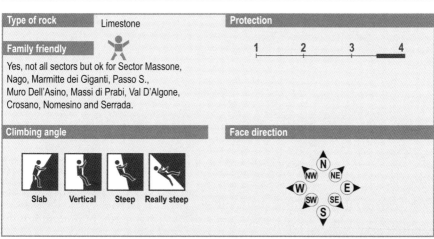

Type of rock

Limestone

Protection

1   2   3   4

Family friendly

Yes, not all sectors but ok for Sector Massone,
Nago, Marmitte dei Giganti, Passo S.,
Muro Dell'Asino, Massi di Prabi, Val D'Algone,
Crosano, Nomesino and Serrada.

Climbing angle

Slab   Vertical   Steep   Really steep

Face direction

N   NW   NE   W   E   SW   SE   S

Number of routes & Grade range

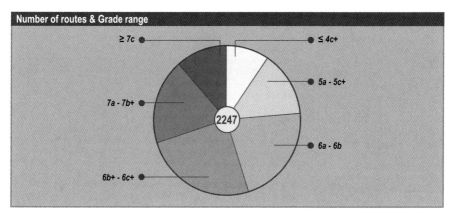

≥ 7c

≤ 4c+

5a - 5c+

7a - 7b+

2247

6a - 6b

6b+ - 6c+

Climbing area Sardinia

Small enough to be classified as an island but big enough to be it's own world, Sardinia lies about 200 kilometres west of the Italian peninsula. With 24.090 square kilometres of land it is the second largest island in the Mediterranean after Sicily. There are nearly 1.7 million inhabitants, most living in and around Cagliari in the south. The rugged, mountainous interior is littered with historic remains, sheep, small vineyards, and many producers of fruit and vegetables. However, most of the tourists stay on the coast with its brilliant sandy beaches and crystal clear water.

A Sardinian legend says that after completing his creation of the rest of the world, God had some rocks left over that he decided to drop in the Mediterranean. Some crags boast developed routes up to 500 metres in length but the undeveloped potential is even larger. The spectacular, wild coastline is also home to many sea cliffs. Most of the rock is compact

| Spring | Summer | Autumn | Winter |

limestone but there are granite boulders in the north. One thing is for sure - you will use up a lot of your holiday allowance visiting all the crags the island has to offer! To make life easier, we describe the best crags in this section. Each one has its own unique character and style of climbing, so there is something for everyone's taste: from very technical slab climbing to very sustained moves through big overhangs.

If you enjoy single pitch climbing in a pretty setting with a mass of routes to choose from go to Domusnovas. Isili is the place to be for short but very powerful steep wall and roof climbing. If technique is your thing, head for Jerzu. Baunèi is great for a variety of climbing styles in a very quiet setting not far from the sea. Cala Gonone is

Baunèi

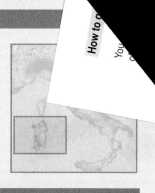

probably the most visited crag and for good reason. There is a lot of variety and there are even multi pitch routes, with some sectors lying right on the beach. Lots of nearby accommodation and a decent nightlife tops the package!

When to go

Sardinia is an all year round destination. However the best periods run from March to May and from September to December. In summer it gets unbearably hot but places like Isili and Jerzu, which are up in the mountains, are generally fine if you stick to the shady sectors. During the winter any of the crags along the coastline, like Cala Gonone, will be great venues. It could rain in winter but wet weather rarely lasts more than a couple of days.

Crag

Ⓐ Dosmusnovas

Ⓑ Isili

Ⓒ Jerzu

Ⓓ Baunèi

Ⓔ Cala Gonone

Italy | Sardinia

137

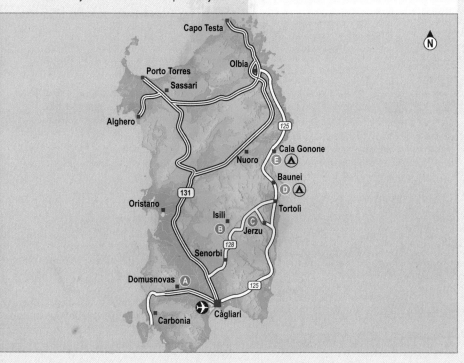

definitely need a car to get to the crags as most them can't even be reached by bus. Besides, getting from one village to another takes ages as public transport connections tend not to be that good. Also, many of the inland roads are very windy and even with a car it takes a while to travel around.

 By (car) ferry from France / Italy

Several ferry companies operate services between Sardinia and mainland Italy and France. For 2 adults and a normal car expect to pay between €200 and €350 depending on the company, season, exact route, and your requirements for onboard facilities. Some good websites to check prices and availability are *www.sncm.fr*, *www.corsicaferries.com* and *www.aferry.to*.

 By car

Main road numbers in Sardinia start with SS followed by the road number. Road signs are very clear. On SS roads it is compulsory to drive with your lights on, even in the day, but it is better to do this on any road. Always carry your ID and license as police checks are very common.

There are numerous car rental agencies located at the airports, each charging different rates, so it is worth shopping around and it's even better to book ahead via the internet. Prices start at €200 per week or €40 per day during winter with unlimited mileage. However it costs another €100 to purchase a collision damage waiver, limiting your risk to €300. In summer

Robert Nancy on Creuza de Ma (6b+) at Baunèi

prices go up 20% to 50% and reservations are essential. Try *www.autoeuropa.it* for the best deals.

Where to stay

Depending on your interests there are several places that could make a good base for exploring the region. You can either choose to stay in one town and visit other crags on daytrips or you could spend a few days at one place and then move on to another. A range of possibilities is given below.

Domusnovas
There is no accommodation in Domusnovas but if you love wild camping or are on a tight budget there are a few places to pitch a tent. There is some sheltered ground just after the small church of San Giovanni or, even better, a bit further uphill towards Sector Cartoonia. Take water with you from the town.

A better bet might be to stay in Cagliari as there is not much to do in the evening in Domusnovas. Cagliari is a lively town, 40 minutes by car from Domusnovas, with lots of restaurants and bars.

Cala Gonone harbour

Albergo Aurora

✉ Salita S.Chiara, 19
Cagliari
☎ +39 070 658625
🏠 www.hotelcagliariaurora.it

📍 N 39°13'05,2 E 09°06'51,1

Price   a double room with bathroom
costs €60 to €68 including
breakfast; a shared bathroom
makes it 20% cheaper

This one-star inn is in a fantastic location in a quiet street right in the centre, not far from Piazza Matteotti. It is nothing fancy but it has a great atmosphere. The coffee bars are around the corner and it only takes a few minutes to walk down to the pleasant harbour.

Diarmuid Duggan on no pain no gain, Isili, Sardinia, photo by Eoin Lawless

A taxi boat takes you to more remote crags

Hotel La Terrazza

✉ Via S.Margherita, 21
Cagliari
☎ +39 070 668652
@ info@laterrazzahotel.com
🏠 www.laterrazzahotel.com

📍 N 39°13'07,0 E 09°06'49,5

Price   a double room with bathroom costs
€65 including breakfast

Clean two star hotel in the street parallel to Albergo Aurora. Try to get a room on the top floor as these offer the best views.

Domu de Jaja

✉ Via Giotto, 19
Cagliari
☎ +39 070 541919
@ domudejaja@yahoo.it
🏠 www.domudejaja.org

Price   single €25, double €55 including
breakfast; 10% off in the low season

The B&B is located in the west of Cagliari, about 10 minutes from the centre by car. It has two rooms. Either the grandmother or her daughter will serve breakfast.

Isili

At Sector Urania there are some very idyllic wild camping spots on both sides of the brook. Buy water in Isili as the brook is not safe to drink from.

Hotel Il Pioppo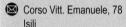

 Corso Vitt. Emanuele, 78
Isili
📞 +39 0782 802117
@ ilpioppo@ilpioppo.com
🖰 www.ilpioppo.com

🧭 N 39°44'24,6 E 09°06'34,1

Price a double with bathroom costs
€34 including breakfast

This is a favourite place to stay among climbers. They give discounts to climbers so make sure to let them know what you are in town for! The rooms are basic and the bathroom could be cleaner - depending on what you are used to - but it is a nice and friendly place. There is a pizzeria and a bar downstairs.

Directions:
The hotel is located on the main road on the right coming into town from the south.

Hotel Il Pioppo

Hotel Del Sol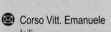

📧 Corso Vitt. Emanuele
Isili
@ hoteldelsol@tiscali.it

🧭 N 39°44'31,0 E 09°06'21,6

Price a double with bathroom costs
€46.50 including breakfast

Hotel Del Sol is a bit fancier than Il Pioppo.

Directions:
It is located on the same street as Il Pioppo, a bit further up.

Jerzu & Baunèi

If you are heading for Jerzu, or any of the crags around Baunèi, try to base yourself on the east coast around Tortoli. The coastline is very pretty and there are some picturesque villages in this area with small idyllic harbours.

The Lemon House

📧 Via Dante, 19
Lotzorai
📞 +39 0782 669507 / 339 7146496
@ peteranne@peteranne.it
🖰 www.peteranne.it

🧭 N 39°58'19,9 E 09°39'56,3

Open Year round

Price €30 to €35 p.p.p.n. including
breakfast; €300 to €600 for
the apartment, depending on
the time of the year

The Lemon House is a centre for climbers and bikers. It is run by Peter and Anne, a very friendly and welcoming couple from the UK. They can help out with everything, including showing you the crags. The house has big and very clean rooms and, on request, dinner can be cooked for you. The couple also owns an apartment close to the beach in Arbatax.

Camping Telis

✉ Porto Frailis
Arbatax
📞 +39 0782 667140
@ info@campingtelis.com
🖱 www.campingtelis.com

📍 N 39°55'29,5 E 09°42'25,6

Open	Year round
Grade	1 — 2 — 3 — 4
Price	€18 for 2 people, a car and a tent; a 2 person bungalow ranges from €420 to €770 per week

Camping Telis is located in a pretty spot in the small bay of Arbatax. Bungalows and caravans can be rented. There is a small supermarket.

Directions:
The campsite is well signposted within the village.

Hotel Agugliastra 🛏

✉ Piazza Principessa di Navarra
Santa Maria Navaresse
📞 +39 0782 615005
@ agugliastra@tiscali.it
🖱 www.hotelagugliastra.it

📍 N 39°59'19,7 E 09°41'23,3

Open	Year round
Price	€38 to €75 for a double, depending on the season

This smart hotel lies in the small and charming village of Santa Maria Navaresse, and is a nice place to stay if you are after a bit more luxury.

Cala Gonone

As Cala Gonone attracts many tourists throughout the year, especially in summer, there are numerous hotels and apartments. However most hotels only open from April to October! For apartments check out *www.sardiniapoint.it* or *www.sardegna-costaorientale.com* - both list several available apartments in town.

Camping Villagio

✉ Cala Gonone, Dorgali
📞 +39 0784 93165
@ info@campingcalagonone.it
🖱 www.campingcalagonone.it

📍 N 40°17'03,7 E 09°38'01,5

Open	1/4 - 2/11
Grade	1 — 2 — 3 — 4
Price	€26 to €37 for 2 people, a car and a tent, depending on the season; a 2 person chalet ranges from €47 to €100 per week

This somewhat overpriced campsite lies along the main road on the east side of the village. It has a swimming pool and a pizzeria. They also rent bungalows and chalets.

Curious audience at Jerzu

Richard Bailey pushing it on Sixteen (6a), Sector Cala Fuili

Hotel Miramare

✉ Piazza Giardini, 12
Cala Gonone
@ miramare@tiscali.it
🖰 www.htlmiramare.it

Open   end of March - end of October

Price   a double with bathroom costs
€30 to €70 including breakfast

Good three-star hotel with a great view over the sea.

Directions:
The hotel is located along the main road a few metres from the beach.

Where to buy groceries?

Even the smaller towns will have a supermarket although the range of products may be a little limited, compared to larger places. Most supermarkets are open Monday to Saturday but close from noon until 4 or 5pm.

The lush inland of Sardinia

Rent a kayak at Cala Gonone

Where to find the local climbing guidebook

The topo for the whole of Sardinia is called 'Pietra di Luna' and is written by Maurizio Oviglia. There are English, French, Italian and German versions. The topo gives a good overview of the climbing on the island but not all routes are included.

The topo is hard to get on the island itself. It is sold in Cala Gonone at the scuba diving and climbing shop, Lapia Leonardo on Via C.Colombo 36, which is close to the small harbour on the main road that goes through the village. However you are best off getting the book before arriving - Cordee distributes the book and it can be ordered through their website (*www.cordee.co.uk*).

What else is there to see & do

Gorroppu Gorge
The Gorroppu Gorge is located close to Dorgali and Cala Gonone and is a really great place to visit on a rest day. The gorge is the deepest in the world! From either side of the road (SS125), the gorge is well signposted. It is a pleasant walk of around 1½ hours along the river in the valley before you reach the gorge. To get to the prettiest part you have to cross a field full of white boulders. It is a pity there are no good landings as it would have been a nice bouldering spot!

The locals have bolted a few routes inside the gorge but those are very hard and strenuous. One of the best known routes here is 'Hotel Supramonte'. It is completely bolted and has pitches from 7c to 8b following 400 metres of overhanging rock!

Mountain biking & hiking
The island boasts endless biking and hiking opportunities. In the more touristy places mountain bikes can be rented for about €16 per day.

Kayaking
In Cala Gonone kayaks can be rented for €24 per day. If you want go wind surfing, find out where this is permitted. The area around Cala Gonone is a nature reserve and surfing or jet skiing is prohibited.

In the Gorroppu Gorge

Domusnovas is one of the best-known crags in Sardinia as it is the biggest with over 650 single pitch routes. The whole setting is very quiet and the surroundings are just beautiful. Also, most of the sectors here are very easily accessible. They are all located around a stunning cave, the Grotta di San Giovanni. Make sure you take a peek deeper inside the cave – it's illuminated and it makes a very nice walk as the road is now car-free.

There is quite a range of climbing to be found at Domusnovas. One of the best known sectors is Canneland which marks the entrance of the cave and has some very steep routes. The only bummer is the pigeons inside. Sector Chinatown has mainly 6th and 7th grade routes on vertical and overhanging rock. If you are up for 7th and 8th grade routes head for Sector Ruota del Tempo at the other side of the cave. Sector Catoonia has several 6a's and 6b's and requires slab climbing technique.

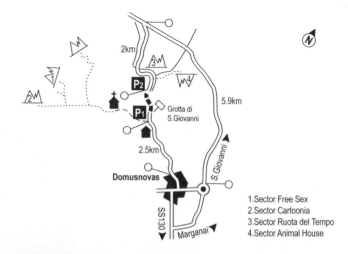

1. Sector Free Sex
2. Sector Cartoonia
3. Sector Ruota del Tempo
4. Sector Animal House

Directions

Sector Chinatown, Domusnovas

▶ Coming from Cagliari along the SS130 follow the signs to Domusnovas. Head into the village and follow the signs for S.Giovanni. After the last building it is another 2.5km to the end of the road where there is a car parking in front of the entrance of the cave (Sector Canneland). To reach the sectors on the other side of the cave either walk through it - about ½km - or drive around. The latter involves following the sign for Marganai immediately after turning off the SS130. Follow this road to the roundabout and continue straight for another 5.9km. A sharp turn to the left, signposted S.Giovanni, leads to the entrance at the other side of the cave. Either park there or 350 metres further back, opposite Sector Ruota del Tempo.

Don't leave any valuables inside the car!

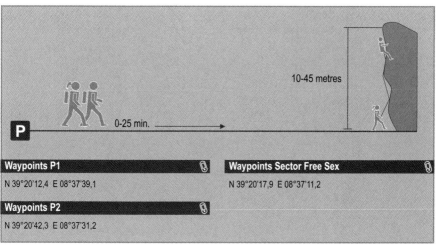

10-45 metres

0-25 min.

P

Waypoints P1

N 39°20'12,4 E 08°37'39,1

Waypoints P2

N 39°20'42,3 E 08°37'31,2

Waypoints Sector Free Sex

N 39°20'17,9 E 08°37'11,2

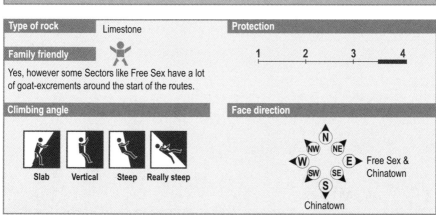

Type of rock   Limestone

Family friendly

Yes, however some Sectors like Free Sex have a lot of goat-excrements around the start of the routes.

Climbing angle

Slab   Vertical   Steep   Really steep

Protection

1   2   3   4

Face direction

N
NW   NE
W   E ► Free Sex &
SW   SE   Chinatown
S

Chinatown

Number of routes & Grade range

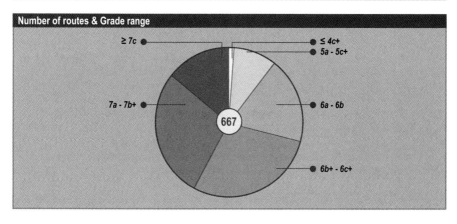

≥ 7c

≤ 4c+

5a - 5c+

7a - 7b+

6a - 6b

667

6b+ - 6c+

The village of Isili is inland, high up in a mountainous region - it's very peaceful and the views are simply great. In general it is a place for stronger climbers as the single pitch routes mainly are in the 6th, 7th and 8th grade. The most important sector, and definitely the reason to come here, is Isili Classica. The routes here demand the maximum from your arms and fingers! If you like big overhangs and roofs make sure to check out Sector Urania too. The routes are not that long, about 20 metres, but this is definitely enough to get you wasted!

The rock is characterized by many small and big pockets and most route names are written at the bottom. The routes at Sectors San Sebastiano and La Mansarda are shorter and not really recommended, although they are in a very pretty setting.

Sector S.Sebatiano lies in the middle of the lake

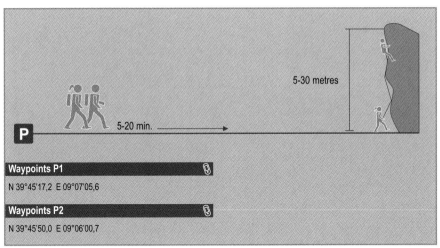

Waypoints P1

N 39°45'17,2 E 09°07'05,6

Waypoints P2

N 39°45'50,0 E 09°06'00,7

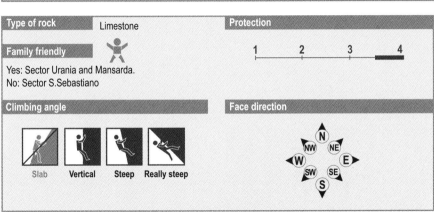

Type of rock	Limestone

Family friendly

Yes: Sector Urania and Mansarda.
No: Sector S.Sebastiano

Protection

1   2   3   4

Climbing angle

Slab   Vertical   Steep   Really steep

Face direction

N
NW NE
W   E
SW SE
S

Number of routes & Grade range

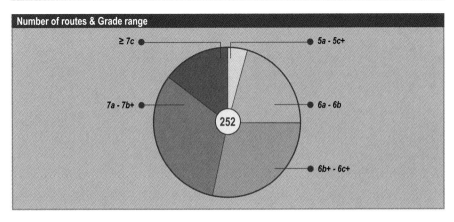

≥ 7c

7a - 7b+

5a - 5c+

6a - 6b

6b+ - 6c+

252

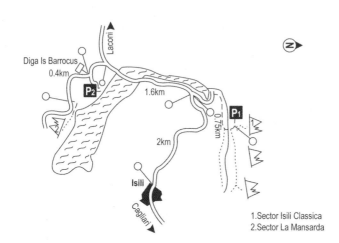

1.Sector Isili Classica
2.Sector La Mansarda

Directions

► From Cagliari first follow the SS131 in the direction of Oristano. Take the SS128 to Senorbi and onwards to Isili which is well signposted. Continue driving through the village in the direction of Laconi. For Sector Isili Classica take a sharp right onto a small road. This is 2km after the last house in the village. By now you will be able to see the overhanging rocks of Urania on your right. Drive down the road, which turns into a dirt track, and park below Urania.

For Sector San Sebastiano and Mansarda continue on the main road towards Laconi. After 1.6km from the turn-off for Sector Isili Classica, a turning to the left takes you down to the lake.

Sector Classica, Urania

Jerzu equals: very technical climbing on mainly vertical limestone. The routes require a lot of finger strength. Of the three sectors, Il Castello is the most technical. This section has more pockets than Il Palazzo but with many slopers too. Actually, the climbing here is all about balance and trusting your feet!

The setting itself is very attractive and it is a good place to climb during the summer due to the altitude. Jerzu has routes at a variety of levels but the majority are in the 6th and 7th grade. Most of the route names can be found conveniently written on the rock.

Italy | *Sardinia* | Jerzu

149

Sector Il Castello

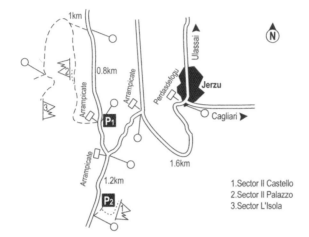

1km

Ulassai

Jerzu

0.8km

Arrampicate

Arrampicate

Perdasdefogu

Cagliari ▶

P₁

3

N

Arrampicate

1.6km

1.2km

Arrampicate

P₂

1. Sector Il Castello
2. Sector Il Palazzo
3. Sector L'Isola

Directions

ARRAMPICATE

AREA PICNIC

AREA PICNIC

The paths to the crags are well indicated in Jerzu

▶ Jerzu lies close to the coast just south west of Tortoli. From Tortoli head south towards Cagliari on the SS125. Jerzu is signposted. Just when you enter the village take the turn left for Perdasdefogu. After 1.6km you'll see signs for the climbing saying 'Arrampicate'. Sector Il Palazzo has an abandoned mini-golf course at the bottom!

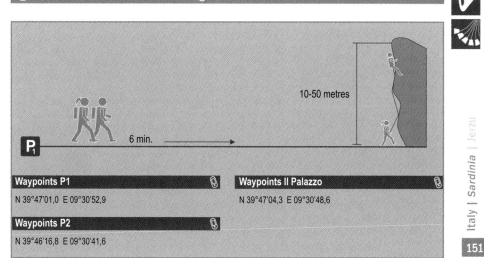

Waypoints P1	Waypoints Il Palazzo
N 39°47'01,0 E 09°30'52,9	N 39°47'04,3 E 09°30'48,6

Waypoints P2
N 39°46'16,8 E 09°30'41,6

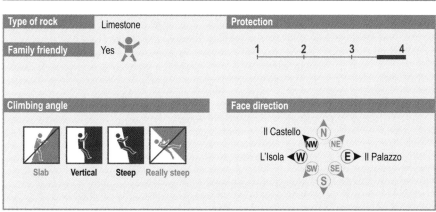

Type of rock Limestone

Family friendly Yes

Protection
1 ——— 2 ——— 3 ——— 4

Climbing angle
Slab Vertical Steep Really steep

Face direction
Il Castello N NE
L'Isola ◀W   E▶ Il Palazzo
NW SW SE S

Number of routes & Grade range

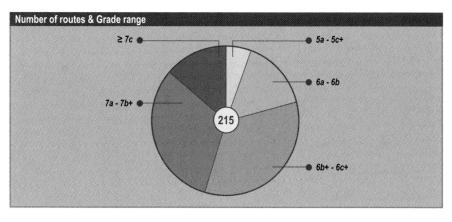

≥ 7c
5a - 5c+
6a - 6b
7a - 7b+
215
6b+ - 6c+

If climbing in a picturesque spot, where the only sounds you'll hear are the gentle clatter of goat-bells and the rustling of wild pigs, sounds like heaven, then you should definitely head for Baunèi! Between Lotzorai and the village of Baunèi a small road winds its way down a valley to the sea. A few beautiful sectors lie along this road, which hardly gets any traffic because it comes to a dead end.

Sector Creuza de Ma has sharp routes on excellent limestone with lots of pockmarks. The rock is mainly vertical but leans slightly to the top. This sector has the longest routes, up to 35 metres. A bit further down the road there is Sector Ichnusa, which is slabby. There is little to put your feet on and the tiny cracks require good technique; most of the routes are graded 6a or 6b.

There are also some fantastic fully bolted multi pitch climbs on the sectors north and northeast of Baunèi. The longest route here is 390 metres (max 7a, 6b obligatory)! In total there are 42 multi pitch climbs on different sectors. When you've finished climbing, head down to the sea for a dip in the crystal clear waters!

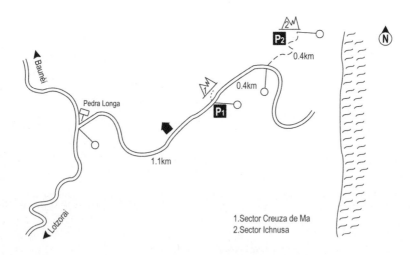

1. Sector Creuza de Ma
2. Sector Ichnusa

Directions

▶ From Lotzorai head towards Baunèi. After 7.5km turn right onto a road signposted Pedra Longa. Continue for 1.1km and, if you're heading for Sector Creuza de Ma, park on the right side of the road. For Sector Ichnusa continue a further 400 metres down the road and turn left onto the gravel track. From here it is another 400 metres to the obvious parking.

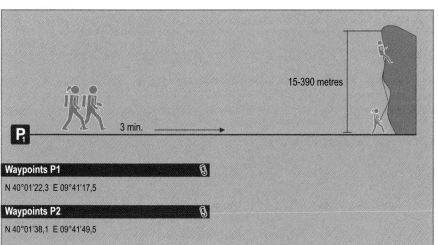

Waypoints P1

N 40°01'22,3 E 09°41'17,5

Waypoints P2

N 40°01'38,1 E 09°41'49,5

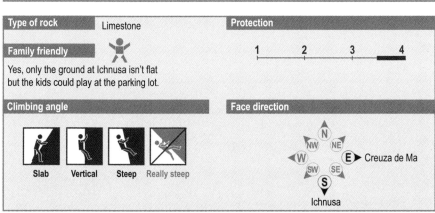

Type of rock Limestone

Protection

1   2   3   4

Family friendly

Yes, only the ground at Ichnusa isn't flat but the kids could play at the parking lot.

Climbing angle

Slab   Vertical   Steep   Really steep

Face direction

N
NW NE
W   E ► Creuza de Ma
SW SE
S
Ichnusa

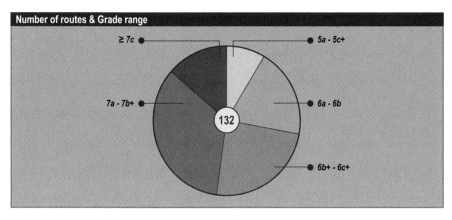

Number of routes & Grade range

≥ 7c
7a - 7b+
132
5a - 5c+
6a - 6b
6b+ - 6c+

154

Cala Gonone is the best known climbing spot in Sardinia and it has been promoted intensively over the past few years. This is not without reason as the setting is very attractive, with several sectors being right at the beach. However, there are many more sectors to be discovered and, due to the huge variety in style of climbing and type of rock, you could easily spend two weeks here.

There's not enough space to give you a comprehensive run-down of all the sectors, but some of the best are La Poltrona, Budinetto, and Cala Fuili, in terms of quality and setting. Some of the longest routes can be found on La Poltrona, where good technique is a firm requirement. Budinetto has many easier routes on a slabby wall. Cala Fuili is very nicely situated at either end of a river gorge near the beach but it gets overrun by tourists during summer.

The downside of the popularity of Cala Gonone is the number of routes that are getting polished. Try to avoid coming here during summer - not only does the village attract lots of tourists sending accommodation prices sky-high, but it will also be unbearable hot.

To get to any of the crags along the coast you can get a taxi boat at the small port of Cala Gonone. One of the companies, Malu, charges €25 p.p. return from the port to Cala Goloritze, for example. They will pick you up at the end of the day. Call (+39) 348 7653503 to make a reservation.

Monica Raho enjoys the easy climbing at Cala Gonone

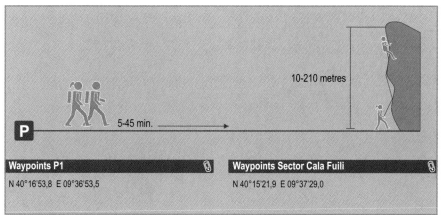

Waypoints P1

N 40°16'53,8 E 09°36'53,5

Waypoints Sector Cala Fuili

N 40°15'21,9 E 09°37'29,0

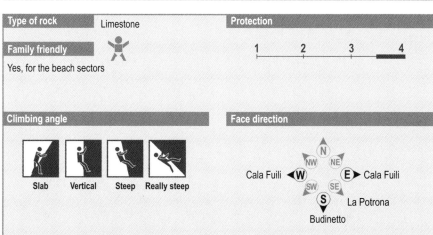

Type of rock Limestone

Family friendly

Yes, for the beach sectors

Protection

1　　　2　　　3　　　4

Climbing angle

Slab　Vertical　Steep　Really steep

Face direction

N
NW　NE
Cala Fuili ◄ W　　E ► Cala Fuili
SW　SE
S　La Potrona
Budinetto

Number of routes & Grade range

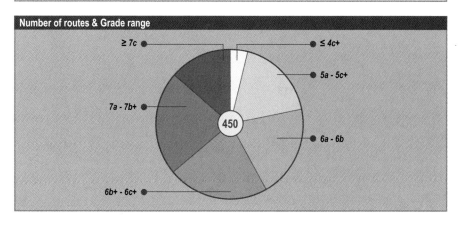

≥ 7c

≤ 4c+

5a - 5c+

7a - 7b+

450

6a - 6b

6b+ - 6c+

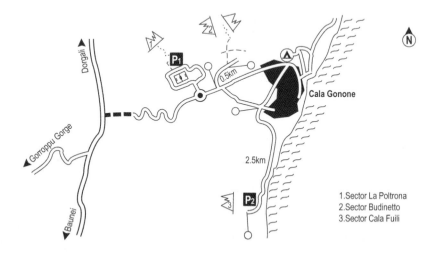

1. Sector La Poltrona
2. Sector Budinetto
3. Sector Cala Fuili

Directions

Sector La Poltrona

▶ Cala Gonone lies at the east coast near Dorgali. It is well signposted coming from the SS125.

Sector Cala Fuili

...the romantic heart of the Mediterranean...

Malta

If you're looking for a "romantic" destination to go climbing with your partner, Malta could be a first choice! Not only is there good climbing and deep water soloing, there's lots of sun, sea, and culture – all the ingredients for a special climbing trip!

The Maltese archipelago lies virtually in the middle of the Mediterranean; the biggest island, with the capital Valetta, is called Malta. The other islands are Gozo, Comino, and the uninhabited Cominotto and Fifla. The Islands are a feast for the senses, and are a popular holiday destination for newly-weds with supremely sunny weather, beautiful beaches, and, above all, fascinating culture.

Malta gained independence from Great Britain in 1964, and the influence of the British is still very obvious – cars drive on the left, you order a "pint of beer", and English is one of the two official languages spoken. Malta joined the EU in 2004 and the Euro will be introduced in 2008.

Malta has 7,000 years of history and is literally saturated with places of interest that really can't be missed. There are wonderful excavated temples from the Neolithic period, very well preserved Baroque palaces, Renaissance cathedrals, ancient forts, and many museums. The clear waters of the Maltese archipelago are also a real treat for beach bums, scuba divers, and wind surfers. And then there is lots of limestone (although it must be said that it will never beat the quality of climbing in France or Greece). So if it's not only the climbing you're after but a rich culture and fantastic water sports too, then make sure to put Malta on your hit-list!

Alexia Chapman at home on some of the great routes Malta has to offer, photo by Matthew Mirabelli

Climbing information

The first walking guide for Malta was published in 1949 but it was Commander John Graham of the British army who produced the first real rock climbing guide for the island in 1971. In keeping with British climbing ethics, the Commander only described traditional climbing and hiking routes and this set the trend for further development. Then, in 1986, the Italian army suddenly started bolting routes for their training programs, without any discussion with the local climbing community. This resulted in a furious reaction from local climbers who removed all the bolts. The Italians, not to be outdone, replaced them again! However, this time both parties agreed to leave them in place.

Andrew Warrington enjoying the climbs at one of his favourite crags - Wied Babu

Thus Malta boasts a mixture of climbing styles (there being far more trad routes than sport) and there is a small but active group of local climbers (about 35 in total!). There are about 1300 routes on the Maltese archipelago of which 15% is sport. The majority of the trad routes are to be found on Malta itself but the best sport climbing is on Gozo. Also, there's a fair bit of deep water soloing on Malta, Comino, and Gozo, the best being on Comino.

There is so much traditional sea-cliff climbing on the islands it is hard to pick where to go. To make your choice easier, we only describe the more well-trodden crags, which will generally be equipped with lower-offs and be easily accessible.

Make sure you bring all your own gear – it's very hard to buy climbing equipment on Malta. There is one Scout shop (E.S. Tonna Square, Floriana) that has a few ropes, harnesses, and some other items but the selection is both limited and expensive. They open on Tuesday and Thursday in the late afternoon, and on Saturday morning.

Climbing area Malta

Most of the crags are situated along the southwest coast directly above the sea. An abseil approach is required for most routes. Of the crags that are (partly) bolted the most interesting ones are Wied Babu and Blue Grotto. Some local climbers also recommend Victoria Lines in the northwest of the island but, as most of the traditional routes only are 10 to 15 metres in length, it is not that worthwhile.

Climbing area Gozo

Gozo is Malta's little sister and it has some of the better climbing the islands have to offer. The climbing on Gozo is more scattered but the main crag - Mġarr ix-Xini - has 120 routes of which 50 are bolted. On the west side of the island the beautifully situated crag of Dwejra offers some great climbing in an extraordinary position.

As the bolting of routes still is a very sensitive matter there is a ban on bolting at designated crags with traditional climbing. However, no such restrictions apply at designated sport crags. If you are here with your drill, please contact the Malta Rock Climbing Club (*www.climbalta.com*) or Andrew Warrington (*climbmalta@onvol.com* / +356 99 470377) to check the situation. If you bolt, make sure you use 316 stainless steel bolts – in the salty, sea-cliff environment lower quality steel rusts quickly.

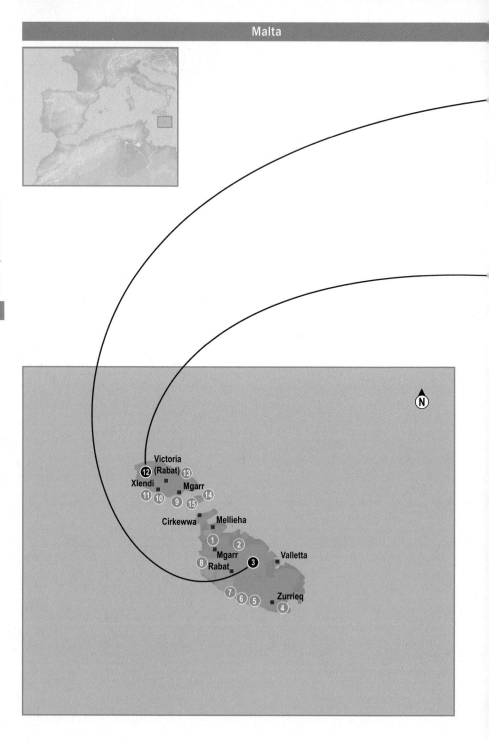

Climbing area	Routes	
① Ta'l Argentier	40	🅿
② Victoria Lines	45	🅿 🖼
❸ Malta		
Wied Babu	79	🅿 🖼
Blue Grotto	12	🅿
④ Ghar Hasser	45	🖼
⑤ Ras il-Hamrija	85	🖼
⑥ Ghar Lapsi	120	🅿
⑦ Ix-Xaqqa	150	🅿
⑧ Ras ir-Raheb	145	🅿
⑨ Tac-Cawla	5	DWS
⑩ Xlendi Bay	15	🅿 🖼
⑪ Black Slabs	14	🅿 🖼
⑫ Gozo		
Mġarr ix-Xini	120	🅿 🖼 DWS
Dwejra	44	🖼 DWS
⑬ San Blas	30	🅿 ▢
⑭ Lantern Point	8	DWS
⑮ Comino Caves	6	DWS

Gozo, clear water and sunshine

Sea-cliff climbing involving an abseil descent is an inherently committing activity. Please make sure you have the skills (aid-climbing) or means (abseil rope and ascenders) to reach the top of the crag in the event of not being able to free climb your chosen route (especially if you are unfamiliar with the route/crag). Also, there is an increased risk of loose rock, especially on routes that see less traffic – if in doubt, treat the rock with caution and wear a helmet!

Climate

Malta has a Mediterranean climate – a long and hot summer with an average temperature of 26°C and a very mild winter. The temperature in summer can go over 40°C, especially when the Sirocco, a hot wind from Africa, blows over the islands. The average temperature in winter is 12°C but it cools down in the evening, so always bring warm clothes. The rainy season lasts from September to April but rain tends to come in short and heavy bursts.

The best time to climb is spring and autumn, but winter is generally fine as well because it never gets really cold. The islands are at their greenest at the end of the rainy season. If you're coming for the deep water soloing, summer or early autumn is the time, when the water temperature will be around 25°C.

Month	Average temperature (°C)	Average rainfall (mm)
Jan	12	88
Feb	12	61
March	13	45
April	15	25
May	19	9
June	23	4
July	25	1
Aug	26	9
Sept	24	40
Oct	20	123
Nov	17	77
Dec	14	100

Climate table Malta

DWS on Comino

Getting there

 By plane

Air Malta (*www.airmalta.com*) is the national carrier. This airline handles flights to most major destinations within Europe and also to Morocco, Turkey, Russia, and Australia (via London). However you often can find better deals with Alitalia or one of the budget airlines, such as German Wings, Air Berlin, or Tuifly. Tickets from a European city start at €230 in winter and are often double that price during summer.

If you are coming from the USA or Canada there's no direct route, so you'll probably end up flying via London.

 By boat

Virtu ferries sail from Sicily (Pozzallo and Catania) to Malta. A return ticket from Pozzallo or Catania to Valetta for one person costs €81, rising to €99 in August. The fare for a passenger car from Pozzallo is €81 (€110 in August) and from Catania €137 (€155 in August). Check *www.virtuferries.com* for schedules.

Moving around

Buses will get you pretty close to most crags, so a car is not really necessary.

 Malta airport information

The Malta International Airport is conveniently located 11km from the capital. The airport is small but modern. Bus number 8 operates twice per hour between the airport and Valetta [30 min, €0.46]

There is a prepaid taxi stand in the arrivals hall where you can purchase a ticket. Taxis are somewhat expensive in Malta, especially compared to the bus. It costs €15.70 to get from the airport to Valetta

St.John's Cathedral, photo from Malta Tourism Authority

and, for example, €20.30 to Sliema or St. Julian's. The large international car rental agencies are located in the arrivals hall as well.

 By public transport

There are no railways but the bus network is well organized. It is the most convenient and by far the cheapest way of getting around. The main starting and stopping point for most buses on Malta is the Triton Fountain in Valetta. If you find this you won't get lost! Some of the yellow buses are really slow but they make for a fun ride and are a very good way to see island life calmly going about its day.

A bus ride will never take more than one hour and a ticket will never cost more than €1.40, with prices starting at €0.46. Sometimes an extra luggage fee of €0.35 is charged if your luggage takes up additional seat in the bus. Tickets are purchased on the bus. If you are planning on seeing a lot of Malta it is even better value to buy a day ticket or multi-day ticket: a 1-day ticket costs €3.50; 3-day €9.30; 5-day €11.60; 7-day €13.90.

In Gozo all buses originate from and return to the main Victoria bus terminal. Even though the buses don't run as frequently as on Malta, they are still a convenient way to get to the crags.

By car

Despite the decent bus system, cars are still convenient. Watch out for the chaotic driving of the locals and the road conditions, which are not very good (lots of potholes!). The road signs are in English but not every junction has a sign, making navigation a challenge. The locals, however, are always very willing to point you in the right direction. Fuel is slightly cheaper compared to most other western European countries.

Cars can be rented at the airport, with prices starting at €23 per day and €150 per week for the smallest type and unlimited mileage during winter. Prices are 25% higher in the summer season. Slightly better deals can be found with one of the several agencies in the cities but it really doesn't save you much. The minimum age for car rentals is 25 years.

Valetta, photo from Malta Tourism Authority

⚓ By ferry

Gozo Channel Line ferries operate one to two times per hour each day between Cirkewwa on Malta and Mgarr on Gozo. The trip takes approximately 25 minutes and a return ticket costs €4.65 per person. A car plus one passenger is €15.70. Tickets are only sold as returns, as this is the only way to get to and from Gozo by public transport. They are purchased at the harbour of Cirkewwa. There isn't even a ticket office on the Gozo side!

The same company also runs a ferry on weekdays between Sa Maison (southwest of Valetta) and Mgarr, which takes 1½ hours. However it is cheaper to take the bus to Cirkewwa and make the crossing between the two islands over there.

Accommodation

As Malta sees a lot of tourists, especially during summer, it offers a wide range of accommodation. The winter season is the cheaper period of the year. Expect to pay €16 for a double room in a guest house in Valetta and €25 for a budget hotel. These prices can double during peak season (July and August).

Malta has one official campsite. But it is in a very inconvenient spot, in the northwest corner of the island and away from the main crags, so we haven't included it here.

Maltese food

Food & drinks

Malta has a wide variety of restaurants and bars – from deluxe to fast-food, including fish and beachside restaurants. The food is a true blend of Mediterranean cuisine with a splash of Italian and North African influences. National specialties are the lampuki pie (fish pie), bragoli (beef olives) and fenek (rabbit cooked in wine).

A complete meal in a good restaurant costs around €15 per person. A beer in a bar would normally go for €2 and a cappuccino for €2. Supermarket prices are comparable to other European countries.

Climbing guidebook

The guidebook of the island, `Malta rock climbing', is written by Andrew Warrington, Richie Abela, and John Codling. The guide covers both the traditional and sport routes on Malta, Gozo, and Comino. It is on sale via *www.climbmalta.com*. The sport routes in the guidebook have French grades and the trad ones British grades.

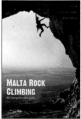

There also is a smaller climbing guide for the Gozo crags. This fine little volume not only covers the rock climbing on Gozo but also the scuba diving, biking, and hiking trails, and explains what coasteering is all about. It can be ordered via the author, Xavier Hancock: *info@gozoadventures.com*, Tel. +356 21564592 / +356 99241171. Xavier is also the man to ask to find the best deep water solo spots. He also has climbing gear to rent. Make sure you contact him!

Facts about Malta

Facts & figures

Population:	0.4 million
Religion:	Roman Catholic (98%)
Capital:	Valetta
Time zone:	GMT+1
Telephone code:	+356

Money

Currency:	Euro (€)
ATM machines:	widespread

Language

The official languages of Malta are Maltese and English.

Goodmorning
Bonġu

Thank you
Grazzi

Goodbye
Saħħa

Yes / No
Iva / Le

Right / Left / Straight
Lemin / Xellug / Dritt

Rock climbing
Climbing

Visas & formalities

EU	Other European nationalities	USA / Canada	All other nationalities
No visa required for a period of up to 90 days.			Most other nationalities do not require a visa for a period of up to 90 days. Check www.gov.mt for more information.

Safety

Malta is a safe place to travel around. However, make sure you lock your car when going climbing and don't leave any valuables inside.

Use of mobile phone

There is wide GSM coverage on both Malta and Gozo.

Internet access

Internet cafés are found in most towns. The costs are €1.15 to €2.30 per hour.

Emergency numbers

General:	112
Police:	191
Fire brigade:	199
Ambulance:	196

Water

Tap water is safe to drink on the islands. A pack of six 2l bottles of water costs around €2.

Climbing area Malta

Malta boasts most of the documented trad routes in the Maltese archipelago. The range is huge – from 3-4 pitch sea cliffs to easily accessible inland crags with single pitch routes. Malta is very small: it is easy to go climbing at one crag in the morning and head for another in the afternoon.

Much of the limestone is very solid and let's just say that the Maltese love climbing pockets! These pockets not only provide the ingredients for some very nice routes but are also useful thread protection. Threads are commonly used as anchors at the top of a sea cliff.

The most visited crags, Wied Babu and Blue Grotto, are situated close to each other in the south. For sport climbing Wied Babu is king. If you are looking for traditional sea cliff climbing with some equipped lower offs then head for the Blue Grotto.

Spring   Summer   Autumn   Winter

When to go

The best periods to visit the crags are spring and autumn. Most of the sea cliff climbing is situated to the south and southwest which makes climbing them during the summer unbearable. Winter can be a good period although the rain expectancy is a bit higher. However it never rains for long and the sun always comes out shining soon after.

Sunset...time to call it a day!

Crag

A Wied Babu

B Blue Grotto

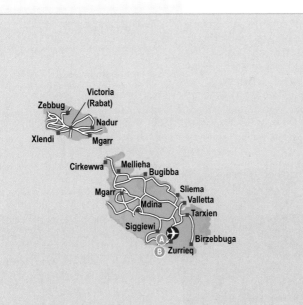

How to get to the area & how to move around

The bus network is perfect and you don't need to have a car.

 By public transport

Make sure you pick up a bus map at any of the hotels or at the bus terminal at the Triton Fountain in Valetta. Bus 45 operates between Valetta and the harbour at Cirkewwa [60 min, €0.60]. Number 645 goes to Cirkewwa from Sliema and St. Julian's [50 min]. The last service back is at 6.45pm.

By car

From Valetta it is around 20km to Wied Babu and the Blue Grotto.

Where to stay

The majority of the tourists stay on the north coast where there is a lot of accommodation, ranging from basic guest houses up to five star hotels. St. Julian's is the place to be for a good night out and most teenagers stay there. If wandering around narrow meandering streets and enjoying true culture is more your thing, then stay in Valetta.

Many people also stay in Sliema as it is a bit more spacious compared to Valetta. In Sliema and St. Julian's, in particular, many hotels are nicely located along the waterfront. It doesn't really matter where you chose to stay - any of these places are not far away from the climbing.

If you are staying outside the peak season make sure to ask for a discount, especially if you are staying for a period of one week or longer.

Asti Guesthouse

18, St. Ursula Street, Valetta
+356 21 239506/227483

N 35°53'44,6 E 14°30'45,0

Price   Bed & breakfast: single €17
and double €30 per room

Very charming and clean guesthouse situated in one of the quieter streets in southwest Valetta. The old lady who owns the place is quite a character! There are communal bathrooms.

British Hotel

40, Battery Street, Valetta
+356 21 224730
info@britishhotel.com
www.britishhotel.com

N 35°53'44,7 E 14°30'47,9

Price   Bed & breakfast: single €35
and double €50 per room

The British is a justifiably popular hotel in Valetta because the view from the rooms is simply superb, and it's at a reasonable price. It is nothing fancy but for a two star hotel it is a very nice place to stay. The rooms with a sea view are slightly more expensive. Make sure you book ahead!

Guesthouses in the narrow streets in Valetta

Andrew Warrington on the east face of Wied Babu

Soleado Guesthouse

✉ 15, Ghar id-Dud Street, Sliema
☎ +356 99450388/99840795
@ info@soleadomalta.com
🌐 www.soleadomalta.com

📎 N 35°54'46,1 E 14°30'22,6

Price   Bed & breakfast: a double with
bathroom €26 in winter and €31
in summer

Basic guesthouse in Sliema with a very convenient location near the beach. The cheaper rooms don't have an en suite bathroom.

Europe Hotel

✉ 138 Tower Road, Sliema
☎ +356 21 334070
@ getaroom@europahotelmalta.com
🌐 www.europahotel-malta.com

📎 N 35°54'52,6 E 14°30'22,3

Price   Bed & breakfast: a double with
bathroom €25 in winter and €49
in summer.

This two star hotel is nicely situated along the sea front. The rooms are basic but perfectly fine, and have an en suite bathroom. Some have a balcony and a nice view over the sea. In the lobby there is internet access. Try to get a room high up as the adjacent bar can get noisy at night.

Where to buy groceries?

Many small supermarkets are scattered around the island as well as some large ones. The price level is comparable to the rest of western Europe.

Mdina

Where to find the local climbing guidebook

See the 'Climbing guidebook' section in the beginning of this chapter.

What else is there to see & do

Visit the ancient cities & sights
Just walking around beautiful Valetta, the three cities (Vittoriosa, Cospicua, Senglea) or a trip around medieval Mdina makes for a wonderful rest day. During the summer you'll invariably find big street parties being thrown somewhere or other! Valetta is very touristy; Mdina receives less visitors and has tremendous views over the island. It is also believed Malta has the oldest freestanding temple in the world called Ggantija, which is even older than the pyramids of Egypt.

Marsamxett, photo from Malta Tourism

Water sports
Malta has plenty of water sport facilities, including scuba diving, sailing, and windsurfing. The island has 24 dive clubs, and many hotels and beach clubs offer sailing or windsurfing gear to rent. A PADI Scuba Diving Open Water course costs around €300.

Valetta exuds a long history

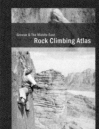

Also available

Rock Climbing Atlas - Greece & The Middle East

This edition covers the best climbing areas in:
Egypt, Greece, Jordan, Lebanon, Syria and Turkey

Wied Babu

The Babu Valley (Wied means valley) is the main sport climbing crag on Malta and has climbs at all grades. During the weekend it gets very popular with Maltese climbers but on weekdays you will most likely have the crag to yourself. The valley is also a popular picnic place and sometimes people even camp here, albeit illegally.

There are single pitch routes on both sides of the valley and the limestone is very pocketed, giving excellent hand and footholds. The routes on the west side are bolted and, although it is reasonably well equipped, there are some interesting run outs and not all climbs have top anchors. The routes are rather sustained on a vertical wall which gets rather steep at some parts. The east side boasts traditional climbing.

Although the rock is solid, always watch out for falling rock, especially on the traditional routes.

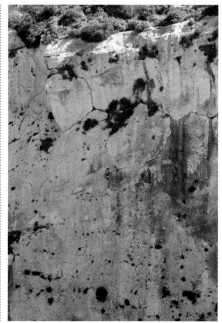
Wied Babu, Sector West Face

Directions

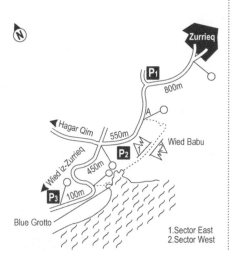

▶ *By car*
Head to Zurrieq and, once in the town, follow the signs for Wied iz-Zurrieq and Hagar Qim. After you have left Zurrieq look out for a small road on the right after a few hundred metres. Park your car at P1 and continue on foot for another 200 metres along the bigger road you arrived on. Jump the fence on the left side of the road (marked as A in the detailed drawing). A trail leads to the first routes on the west side which you should reach after only a couple of minutes.

▶ *By bus*
From Valetta take bus #38 or #138 [30min, €1.20] and get off at the junction to Wied iz-Zurrieq (better known as Blue Grotto). Walk back along the road you came from for 550 metres and cross the fence on the right side of the road.

A taxi from Valetta will cost around €22.

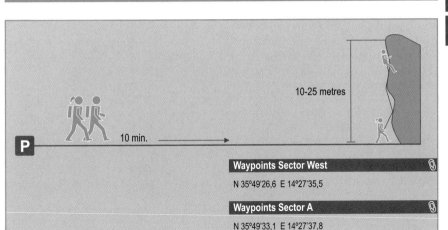

Waypoints Sector West

N 35°49'26,6 E 14°27'35,5

Waypoints Sector A

N 35°49'33,1 E 14°27'37,8

Type of rock

Limestone

Family friendly

Yes, but the track gets pretty narrow at certain points.

Climbing angle

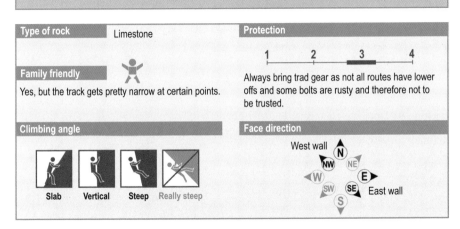

Slab   Vertical   Steep   Really steep

Protection

1   2   3   4

Always bring trad gear as not all routes have lower offs and some bolts are rusty and therefore not to be trusted.

Face direction

West wall

East wall

Number of routes & Grade range

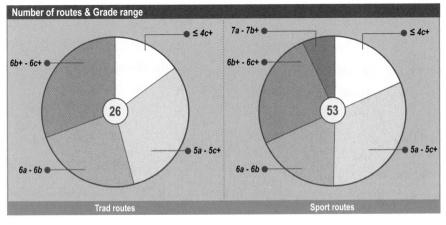

Trad routes   Sport routes

DWS

Blue Grotto

This crag is named after the cave which is on the tourist trail and which is only accessible by boat. Don't be surprised to have a big audience watching you as boats visiting the Blue Grotto cave pass by! The climbing at both sides of the crag, named the Blue and the Red walls, requires trad gear. The Red Wall has five routes and has some bolts (but to describe it as a sport climbing crag is stretching the imagination!). If you walk towards the furthest point of the crag you will find some lower offs for which a seventy meter rope is required. The Red wall, the side closest to the Blue Grotto cave, has a small plateau at the bottom where the belayer can comfortably stand.

On hot days the Blue Grotto is also a good place for deep water soloing. Watch out for the boats passing through!

Directions

▶ *By car*
From Zurrieq follow the directions for Wied iz-Zurrieq and park at the big parking spot at the end of the road. Follow the road back up for 100 metres and on a bend in the road there is a path leading to the right. Follow the path for about 300 metres along the coastline, with the sea on your right, until you find the bolted lower offs.

▶ *By bus*
If you are coming by bus follow the same directions as Wied Babu. When you get off at the junction, walk down towards Wied iz-Zurrieq. After 450 metres the trail starts on the left side of the road.

A taxi from Valetta to the Blue Grotto shouldn't cost more than €22.

Blue Grotto

DWS

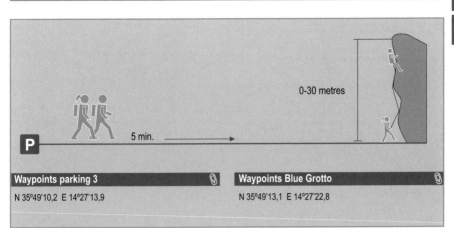

0-30 metres

5 min.

P

Waypoints parking 3

N 35°49'10,2 E 14°27'13,9

Waypoints Blue Grotto

N 35°49'13,1 E 14°27'22,8

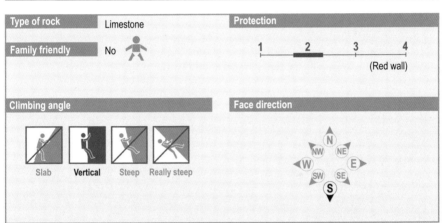

Type of rock	Limestone
Family friendly	No

Protection

1   2   3   4

(Red wall)

Climbing angle

Slab   **Vertical**   Steep   Really steep

Face direction

N   NE   NW   W   E   SW   SE   S

Number of routes & Grade range

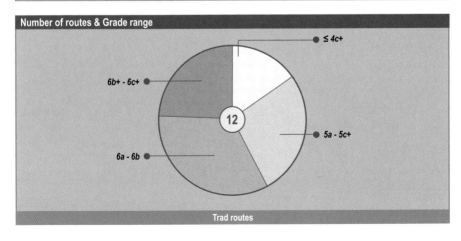

≤ 4c+

6b+ - 6c+

5a - 5c+

12

6a - 6b

Trad routes

Climbing area Gozo

Gozo is a wonderfully relaxed tiny island – the second largest in the Maltese Archipelago but containing only one-twelfth of the overall population of Malta. Gozo has a varied geology and larger relief contrasts and it is certainly greener and quite more peaceful than its big sister. It covers an area of 67 square kilometres, it is 14km long, and 7km wide, and it has a beautiful rocky coastline 43km long.

The climbing here is in nice surroundings and, as Gozo only has 5 climbers, you'll most probably have the crags to yourself. The rock is pretty good – all limestone, sharp and unpolished, and there are many impressive sea cliffs of over 120 metres high. The northwest has the best sea cliff climbing. This side of the island also has truly remarkable beach structures making it an ideal place to relax after a hard day. Additionally, the many small bays around Gozo give fantastic deep water soloing potential.

| Spring | Summer | Autumn | Winter |

When to go

Spring and autumn are the best periods but winter can be a great season too. Even though most routes on the sea cliffs face northwest try to avoid doing them in summer. In summer it is simply best to go deep water soloing around the island or at Comino.

Port of Gozo

Crag

A Mġarr ix-Xini

B Dwejra

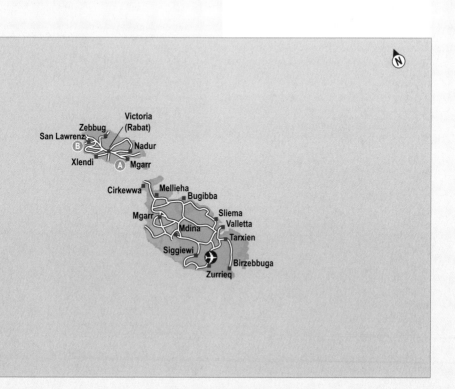

How to get to the area & how to move around

You won't need a car as long as you are up for a bit of walking.

 By public transport

See the 'Moving around' section in the beginning of this chapter how to get to Gozo.

 By car

The drive from Valetta to Cirkewwa where the ferry crosses over to Gozo takes a bit less than an hour.

Where to stay

Gozo is so small it doesn't really matter where you stay. Most people choose Victoria or Xlendi, the latter being very nicely and calmly situated around a small bay. Here you can rent farmhouses built by the locals. The houses are rather luxurious with swimming pools and they lie peacefully in the countryside. It is an excellent choice for groups. See *www.gozofarmhouses.com* for more information.

Gozo coastline

Downtown Hotel

✉ Triq l-Ewropa, Victoria
☎ +356 22108000
@ info@downtown.com.mt
🖥 www.downtown.com.mt

📍 N 36°02'42,5 E 14°14'45,8

Price   Bed & breakfast: double with bathroom ranging from €22 to €38 depending on the time of year

The Downtown Hotel is the only hotel in the centre of Victoria. The hotel is located opposite of the Gozo Sports Complex (where you'll also find a small bouldering wall!). Make sure you book ahead if you want to stay in the centre of town!

Xavier Hancock enjoys yet another beautiful day in March

Local fishermen

Where to buy groceries

Gozo has several small supermarkets and there is a daily market on the main square in Victoria.

Where to find the local climbing guidebook

See the 'Climbing guidebook' section in the beginning of this country chapter.

What else is there to see & do

Visit Victoria
Victoria is the capital of Gozo and embraces both the citadel, the ancient city of the island, as well as Rabat, the old suburb of the citadel. The cobweb of narrow streets is definitely worth a walk around. Simply enjoy the good atmosphere, the small markets and the great terraces.

Charter a boat
Why not spend your rest day on the water and do some deep water soloing? The daily rate for a boat which can handle 18 people is around €350 including lunch and water. Ask around at the Mgarr harbour. Alternatively contact the very friendly Xavier Hancock, the author of the Gozo topo. He has a boat and knows all the best deep water solo and climbing spots on the island. He even does sunset boat cruises including dinner. See the 'Climbing guidebook' section in the beginning of this chapter for his contact details.

Scuba diving
There are various scuba diving agencies based on Gozo. A recommended 5 star PADI diving school is Moby Dives based in Xlendi Bay (*www.mobydives-gozo.com*). An accompanied dive including gear costs €26 to €30.

Biking
A nice and fun way to explore the island is on bike. Daily rates are €5 in the low season and double the price in high season. Check with Xavier Hancock.

The island of Gozo

Mġarr ix-Xini

Mġarr ix-Xini, the harbour of the pirates, is a deep valley snaking into the sea with the best pick of the sport routes on the Maltese Archipelago. There are also plenty of trad routes - only a very small section has been bolted to date.

There are routes on both sides of the valley but (at present!) the best sectors are situated on the same side as the waterworks. Make sure to visit Sector Dream Walls, which will demand a lot of strength on the sustained and overhanging wall! The deeper you go into the valley the better and longer the routes get.

The majority of the routes are in the higher grades. However, the grading is a bit confusing due to retro bolting and on some routes the bolts are well spaced out. Nevertheless Mġarr ix-Xini has the potential to become the prime attraction of the Maltese Archipelago. The only, and serious, problem here is the brambles which need to be cut constantly to clear the paths. The valley could really do with more climbers developing more routes.

Roland Sultana on Bulk Order, Sector Dream Walls, Mgarr ix-Xini, photo by Reuben Sultana

Mgarr Ix-Xini

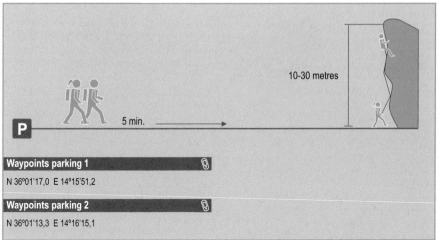

10-30 metres

5 min.

P

Waypoints parking 1

N 36°01'17,0 E 14°15'51,2

Waypoints parking 2

N 36°01'13,3 E 14°16'15,1

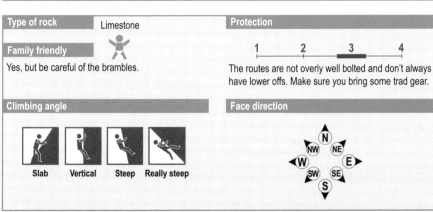

Type of rock   Limestone

Family friendly

Yes, but be careful of the brambles.

Protection

1   2   3   4

The routes are not overly well bolted and don't always have lower offs. Make sure you bring some trad gear.

Climbing angle

Slab   Vertical   Steep   Really steep

Face direction

N
NW NE
W E
SW SE
S

Number of routes & Grade range

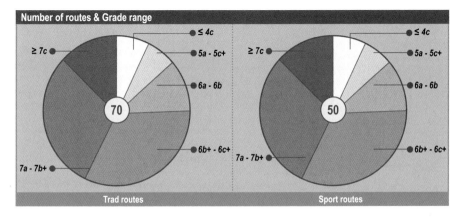

≤ 4c
≥ 7c
5a - 5c+
6a - 6b
70
6b+ - 6c+
7a - 7b+

≤ 4c
≥ 7c
5a - 5c+
6a - 6b
50
6b+ - 6c+
7a - 7b+

Trad routes   Sport routes

DWS

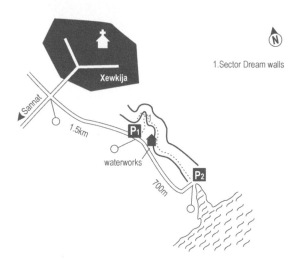

1.Sector Dream walls

Directions

Mgarr Ix-Xini, sector Dream Walls

► Coming from Victoria drive to Xewkija. This is the same way as Mġarr, where the ferry arrives. From the church at Xewkija you'll see clear signs for Mġarr ix-Xini. Either park close to the waterworks on the left side of the road or continue all the way towards the end. It is better to park near the waterworks as this gives you the easiest approach to the best sectors of the valley.

If you don't have a car, take any bus from Mġarr harbor to Victoria and ask the driver to drop you off at, or close to, Xewkija. Coming from Victoria, bus numbers 42 and 43 [6 min, €0.50] go to Xewkija. It will take you about 35 minutes to walk from the church in Xewkija to P1.

Alternatively a taxi from Victoria to the valley costs around €10.

Dwejra, Azure Window

Helga Cutajar on Whinger, Inland Slabs

DWS

Dwejra

Dwejra, with its incredible rock formations, is a miraculous place giving the potential for climbing, swimming in the spectacular deep-sea or in the Inland Sea, and the rare experience of diving into the so called "Blue-Hole" near the Azure Window.

It is the stunning environment that makes climbing at Dwejra to special. Dwejra is a traditional crag with routes up to three pitches long. The Inland Sea, which is connected by a tunnel to the sea, has a few routes originating from the water (approachable by boat or via a lower off). The hardest routes can be found directly above the tunnel. Some of the easier routes are located at a sector on the right side of the tunnel called the Inland Slabs. On the sea side, the Azure Window is a prime tourist spot and a great place for deep water soloing. Be aware that the Azure Window can't itself be climbed anymore as it is no longer structurally sound.

Please respect the plant and bird life and bear in mind that you are climbing at a World Heritage Site. Some of the plant species here are the only ones on the Maltese islands!

The trad bit of Dwejra, at the Inland Sea

Directions

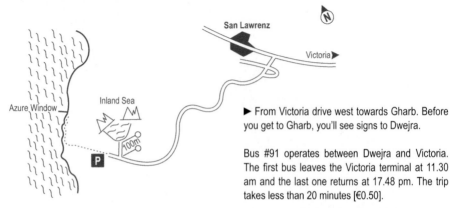

▶ From Victoria drive west towards Gharb. Before you get to Gharb, you'll see signs to Dwejra.

Bus #91 operates between Dwejra and Victoria. The first bus leaves the Victoria terminal at 11.30 am and the last one returns at 17.48 pm. The trip takes less than 20 minutes [€0.50].

A taxi from Victoria will charge around €12.

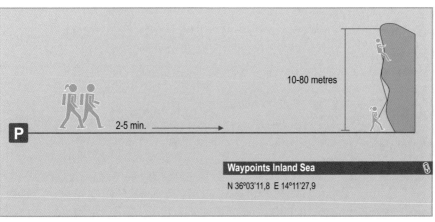

10-80 metres

2-5 min.

P

Waypoints Inland Sea

N 36°03'11,8 E 14°11'27,9

Malta | Gozo | Dwejra

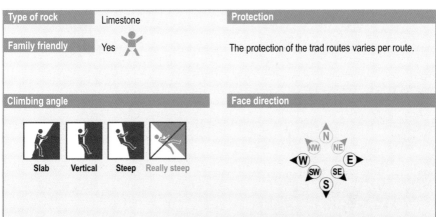

Type of rock	Limestone	Protection	

Family friendly Yes

The protection of the trad routes varies per route.

Climbing angle

Slab   Vertical   Steep   Really steep

Face direction

N
NW NE
W   E
SW SE
S

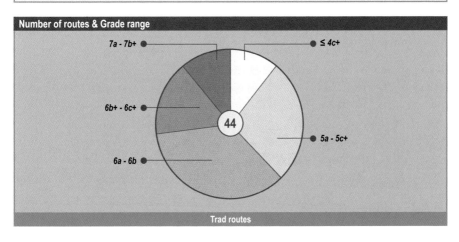

Number of routes & Grade range

7a - 7b+

≤ 4c+

6b+ - 6c+

44

5a - 5c+

6a - 6b

Trad routes

...an exceptional adventure
and mystery...

Morocco

Wynand enjoying perfect rock in Taghia

Just half an hour's ride on the ferry from Spain, Morocco seems at once to be much further from Europe, with its deeply traditional culture, Moorish cities, endless sands of the Sahara, and mountains inhabited by the indigenous Berbers. For many climbers, it's a place that's certainly not on the radar as a climbing destination. Yet, besides being an exceptionally interesting country to discover, Morocco boasts some exceptional climbing too!

Morocco gained independence from French and Spanish rule in 1956 and is essentially a safe and politically stable country to visit. A trip to Morocco (even without a rope!) will be a rewarding and intense experience. The country's geography itself is extraordinary: from a Mediterranean and Atlantic coast, through four different mountain ranges, to the beautiful Sahara covered with oases. It all offers something for every taste: walking, trekking or mountain biking in the mountains, with even a possible ascent of Mount Toubkal (4167m); four-wheel-driving or camel riding in the desert; wandering around the famous cities of Marrakesh and Fes; or simply enjoying the sea and the sun. Climbing at any of the areas we describe can easily be combined with other activities or a bit of sightseeing and, as a bonus, Morocco is cheap and easy to get to, the weather is good even in winter and the rock is extremely solid. This is, simply put, why Morocco is such an attractive climbing destination. So if you want to experience a different culture, see some amazing scenery and get some excellent climbing done as well, then you're in for a good time in Morocco!

Climbing information

The Todra Gorge is undeniably the most popular climbing area in Morocco. Unfortunately it has already lost most of its charm that attracted the adventurous climbers in the early days, and many regular tourists visit the Todra Gorge too. However, the infrastructure is very good and - in all honesty - the sport climbing remains truly wonderful. If you fancy more adventure and getting away from the touts then head to the beautiful Taghia Gorge. The multi pitch climbing here is still at its very early stage and, due to its remoteness, it will never become too crowded. A third area, Tafraoute, is also relatively unknown by climbers, though the normal tourists - attracted by the beautiful surroundings - are slowly finding their way here. Here there are thousands of granite boulders and kilometres of orange quartzite, which is perfect for trad climbing.

All three areas are completely different and where you choose to go really depends on your preferred climbing style.

However, there is one highly attractive option we would like to highlight: you can combine visits to the Taghia and Todra Gorges by making a three day trek between them on foot, with your equipment carried by a donkey. More details about this can be found in the Taghia section.

Climbing area Todra Gorge

This is the destination for you if you fancy bolt clipping in a truly special setting. The Todra Gorge is well developed – hundreds of bolted routes, plenty of hotels, and it is easy accessible. As well as equipped routes there are also many traditional lines to be found. This is definitely a place not to miss!

Climbing area Taghia Gorge

Hidden in the High Atlas far away from paved roads, hotels and carpet vendors lies the beautiful Berber village of Taghia. It is surrounded by soaring steep red walls of perfect limestone which have over 115 developed multi pitch routes. A great place!

Climbing area Tafraoute

This is the place to come for bouldering and trad climbing. There are literally thousands of granite boulders to explore (with a lot of potential for new problems) or there are great trad routes on solid quartzite. Either way the climbing will be an adventure!

The Taghia Gorge valley

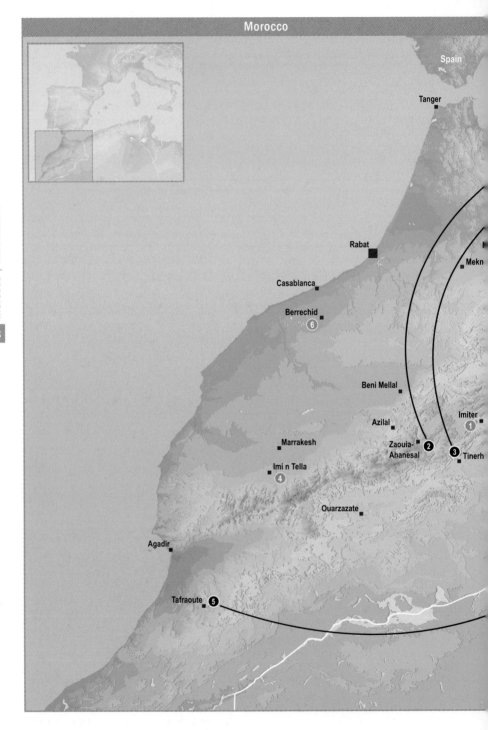

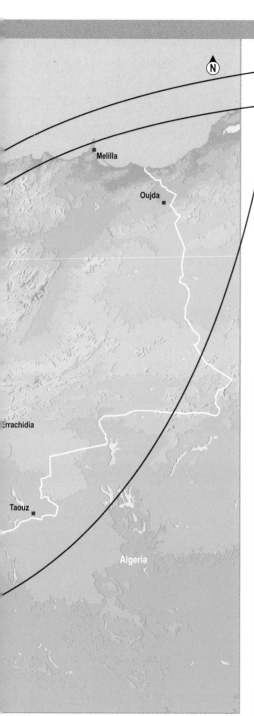

1 Imiter	100
2 Taghia Gorge	
Taghia Gorge	115
3 Todra Gorge	
Todra Gorge	420
4 Imi n Tella	35
5 Tafraoute	
Jebel el Kest massif	160
Tafraoute boulders	>5000
6 Ain Blmesk	25

Melilla

Oujda

Errachidia

Taouz

Algeria

Theo van Bokhoven getting pumped in Sector Petite Gorge in the Todra Gorge

Panoramic view from the top of La Cascada at the Taghia Gorge

The most famous square in Morocco - Djemaa el Fna in Marrakesh

Musicians at Djemaa el Fna in Marrakesh

Climate

The Moroccan climate varies greatly depending on the location. In summer it is incredibly hot in the southern and south eastern desert areas. On the other hand, the temperature drops considerably in the higher lying mountainous areas, even getting to freezing point at night. Generally the best time to visit Morocco for rock climbing is winter, spring and autumn, with the exception of the Taghia Gorge, which you should avoid in winter.

Month	Average temperature (°C)	Average rainfall (mm)
Jan	11	26
Feb	13	28
March	16	34
April	19	30
May	22	14
June	25	8
July	29	4
Aug	29	4
Sept	25	10
Oct	21	24
Nov	16	32
Dec	13	31

Climate table Marrakech

Getting there

 By plane

The best and cheapest entry point for the Todra Gorge and the Taghia Gorge is Marrakesh - most low cost airlines, such as Tuifly, Easyjet, Ryanair and Atlas Blue, operate flights here from many European cities. The Todra Gorge can also be reached by flying to Ouarzazate, which will save you a few hours on the bus, although your choice of airlines will be limited to Air France and Royal Air Maroc. This makes it a more expensive option. Casablanca could also be an option but you have to travel further overland to reach the climbing. If you're heading direct to Tafraoute, you are best advised to fly to Agadir, also served by many low cost airlines.

Another option is to pick up a bargain package deal from one of the tour operators in your home country for either Agadir or Marrakesh.

There are a few direct flights from the US and Canada to Casablanca, though it is generally better to travel via Europe. Check *www.fly-cheapo.com/flights/marrakech* for cheap flights from Europe to Marrakesh.

 By boat

There are many ways to reach Morocco by ferry. The following routes are possible from Spain:

Tarifa - Tanger
Algeciras - Tanger and Ceuta
Malaga - Melilla
Almeria - Melilla and Nador
Barcelona - Tanger

There are catamarans, slow ferries and fast ferries in operation. The journey time and price depends on the service you choose. Taking a vehicle on the ferry is possible but prices are easily two to three times the price of a foot-passenger ticket. The best website to start looking for schedules and fares is *www.cemar.it/dest/ferries_morocco.htm*. Other useful websites are *www.viamare.com* and *www.directferries.co.uk*.

There is also a ferry from Sète and Marseille in France to Tanger [36H] and from Genova in Italy to Tanger [48H].

Approach to the Lion's Face, Tafraoute

Morocco | Introduction

Wynand testing the granite at Tafraoute

Moving around

 Marrakesh airport information

The city's airport is only 4km southwest from the city centre. A bus runs every half hour from the airport to the Place Djemaa el Fna [20min, 20dh]. It's more convenient to take a taxi but you will definitely be overcharged! Try to arrange a fare of 60dh from the airport to the bus station or any other place in Marrakesh.

Poste Maroc

 Agadir airport information

Agadir's airport is 25km east of the city and there is no bus service between the city and the airport. If you don't rent a car at the airport then you can take a taxi to either Agadir or to Inezgane for onward bus services. Fares should be 200dh and 150dh respectively.

 By public transport

Moroccan public transport is, on the whole, pretty good. There is an efficient rail network linking the main towns and elsewhere it is fairly easy (and

Breakfast at Youssef's gîte in Taghia

most certainly cheap) to travel by bus. The fare for example from Marrakesh to Azilal, a 4 hours journey, is 55dh per person. In general, seats on popular buses fill up quickly, so book your ticket one day before departure if possible. You'll usually have to pay a baggage supplement of 5dh to 20dh.

Another way to get around is the collective grand taxis. These operate a wide variety of routes and are much quicker than buses while the fares remain reasonable. You don't have to worry about timetables: you just show up at the terminal and ask around for a seat to a specific destination. As soon as the taxi is full it sets off. However, make sure you ask for "a taxi collectif" as drivers often presume that a tourist will want to charter the whole taxi (...and pay for all the seats!). Most collective taxis leave from the bus stations.

In the mountains and desert local people maintain a network of market-day lorries for which you pay a small fare as locals do.

By car

There are no real problems driving in Morocco but be aware the accident rate is high. Treat pedestrians with suspicion - they can and will cross in front of you when you least expect it - and assume cyclists may well swerve into the middle of the road unexpectedly. Your fellow motorists may also be rather chaotic in their driving. However, despite these caveats, daytime driving and certainly long-distance driving can be as good as anywhere. Petrol and diesel prices are somewhat lower than in Western Europe.

The Taghia Gorge

Renting a car can be a good idea, at least for a part of your trip. Most major companies allow you to rent a car in one city and return it to another. Rates start around €30 per day for a small car. The major companies and also a few local ones will be open for business at the airports - shop around for the best deal. It may be worth booking in advance just to make sure that a small cheap car will be available. It can also be even cheaper to book in advance over the internet.

Hitchhiking

Hitchhiking is not very big in Morocco. However, it is often easy to get rides from other tourists, especially if you ask around at the campsites. Out on the road, hitchhiking is definitely not to be advised.

Accommodation

Accommodation in Morocco is cheap, good value, and easy to find. There is a lot of choice in the budget hotel range; the price for a double room with shared bathroom is normally around €10 including breakfast. For a bit more comfort you would pay around €25 for a double room with private bathroom. Outside the big cities you can often find hotels that offer dinner included in the price. In the mountains there are refuges and gîtes d'étape for fairly cheap rates.

Campsites are to be found at regular intervals along most of the developed coast, and also in towns or cities that attract a lot of tourists. Most sites are very cheap at around €3 per night for two people with a car and a tent. However, facilities are not up to European standards.

If you stay at one place for more than just a few nights make sure you ask for a discount. Remember that bargaining is part of life in Morocco!

Food & drinks

Food in Morocco falls into two basic categories: true Moroccan meals served in local restaurants or at food stalls, and French-influenced tourist menus in up-market restaurants. A classic Moroccan meal begins with a harira soup. This is a thick, very filling soup, and is often spicy and contains beans. The soup is followed by tajine, couscous, or kebab. A tajine is a stew, steam-cooked slowly in an earthenware dish over a charcoal fire. Classic tajines include lamb/mutton with prunes and almonds, or chicken with olives and lemon. They are absolutely delicious! Couscous is perhaps the most famous Moroccan dish and a good couscous is ordered two to three hours in advance. It comes with vegetables, mutton, chicken, or occasionally with fish. Vegetarians should ask for a tajine of couscous without meat - "sans viande" in French. Harira soup may be served with or without meat - ask to be sure. A complete dinner in a basic restaurant would be between €6 and €10 per person.

A cola or coffee in a normal café would be around €0.75.

Climbing guidebook

There is no single guidebook covering the whole of Morocco. However you'll find one for the Todra Gorge and the traditional climbing in Tafraoute. The bouldering in Tafraoute is not yet documented. Route information for the Taghia Gorge can be found on the internet. See the different climbing area descriptions for detailed information.

Moroccan tea

Bouldering in Morocco

View from one of the restaurants at Djemaa el Fna

Facts & figures

Population:	33 million
Religion:	Islam
Capital:	Rabat
Time zone:	GMT
Telephone code:	+212

Money

Currency:	Moroccan Dirham (dh)
Exchange rate:	€1 = 11.24 dh
ATM machines:	widespread in major towns and cities

Language

The official language is Arabic but French is the dominant business language. Spanish is often spoken in the north. English is fairly widely spoken. Then there are three distinct Berber languages; Tashelhaït is spoken in the High Atlas. Below we give Moroccan Arabic and Tashelhaït translations.

Goodmorning
Salam - Salame

Thank you
Shokran - Saha

Goodbye
Bslemah – Akayaoon Arbee

Yes / No
Na'am / La – Eyeh / Oho

Right / Left / Straight
Leemin / Leeser / Neeshan - Fofaseenik / Fozelmad / Neeshan

Rock climbing
Altalir arouluid

Visas & formalities

EU	Other European nationalities	USA / Canada	All other nationalities
No visa is required for a period no longer than 3 months.	Most other nationalities do not require a visa for a period no longer than 3 months.	No visa is required for a period no longer than 3 months.	Most other nationalities do not require a visa for a period no longer than 3 months.

Safety

Violent crime is still quite rare in Morocco but getting harassed by "guides" is common and petty theft can happen. Keeping your luggage and money secure is an important consideration in Morocco, but the situation is not necessarily worse than in any other country.

Use of mobile phone

There is reasonable GSM coverage in most towns and along the main roads. In the mountains coverage is limited and there is no coverage at all in the desert.

Internet access

Most towns (even smaller ones) have internet cafés. The tariff usually is €1 per hour.

Emergency numbers

Police:	19
Fire brigade:	19
Ambulance:	15

Water

It is advisable not to drink tap water but to only use bottled water (or sterilize it yourself) before use. A 1.5l bottle of mineral water costs €0.40.

Climbing area Todra Gorge

Spring   Summer   Autumn   Winter

The High Atlas in central Morocco hides some of the most immensely impressive spectacles in the whole country. High limestone cliffs change colour in a magical effect as the day unfolds; weirdly shaped rock erosions and tall green palm trees form the setting of the much visited Todra Gorge. Even those who have been around and seen it all will gasp at the stunning rock architecture when they see it for the first time. Therefore the Todra Gorge is on the itinerary of many tours, especially on those from Marrakesh. Fortunately the majority of the day-trippers only visit the gorge for a couple of hours, have lunch at Hotel Les Roches or the Yasmina and leave again.

The Todra Gorge is the most developed sport climbing area in Morocco with over 400 routes. The variety of routes - all within walking distance of the accommodation - can't be surpassed. There are excellent easy slabs, incredible multi pitch routes following great lines and classic hard single pitches. Also the new-route potential is enormous.

The French bolted the first routes in the Todra Gorge in 1966. But it took almost two more decades before climbers truly discovered the area. Dutchman Ad van der Horst put up the first 8a in the 1980's and who named the first sectors (e.g. 'De Meuk'). Since then many more routes have been developed and the Todra Gorge is renowned for its special climbing across the world.

The Todra Gorge

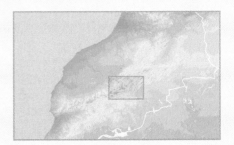

When to go

The best period for climbing is spring and autumn, late March to early May being the most favorable. As the gorge lies at an altitude of over 1.400 metres it cools down quite a bit in the evening - make sure you bring warm clothes. Winter can be very good too, especially during the middle of the day when the sun is shining. However, prepare yourself for very cold nights! In summer it is simply too hot to climb.

Crag

Ⓐ Todra Gorge

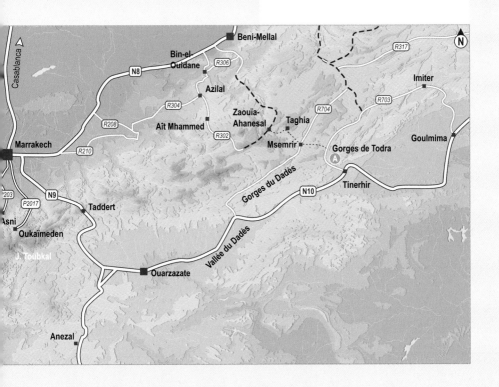

How to get to the area & how to move around

You don't need a car for the Todra Gorge - public transport is easily available. All climbing sectors are within walking distance from the hotels.

 By public transport from Marrakesh

To get to the Todra Gorge hop on one of the several buses to Tinerhir [7-8h, 110dh] which leave from the main terminal at Bab Doukkala in Marrakesh. It is best to take the 10am bus to enjoy the scenic ride during daytime. The service back to Marrakesh leaves Tinerhir at 6am. All buses stop in Ouarzazate.

Grand taxis operate between Tinerhir and the Todra Gorge. The fare is 6dh per person [20min] with a minimum of 6 persons.

If an 8hr-plus bus ride doesn't appeal to you sharing a grand taxi is a good idea, although this will only save about 2½ hours. The fare ranges between 800dh and 1000dh for a whole taxi, depending on your negotiating skills!

 By car

It is 360km from Marrakesh to Tinerhir via Ouarzazate. The most scenic part is between Marrakesh and Ouarzazate where the road winds its way up through the Atlas.

Hotel Les Roches and the Yasmina situated inside the gorge

A number of Bedouin still live inside the caves

Where to stay

There are many hotels to choose from in the gorge and the ones described here all provide hot water. (Always ask if there is hot water before checking in, especially in cheaper places.) Most hotels also have generators - electricity is usually only available in the morning and evening. Budget hotels are to be found just outside and at the start of the gorge. However, the price difference is very small – we advise making one of the mid range hotels, the Yasmina or Les Roches, your base. These two are situated right inside the most stunning and narrowest section of the gorge where the walls rise up several hundred metres. No joking, you could almost belay your partner from your room!

Hotel Les Roches

✉ Gorges du Todra, Tinerhir
☎ +212 24895134
@ h_les_roches@hotmail.com

📱 N 31°35'16,7 W 5°35'32,1

Price   Half pension costs 450dh per double room per night. A discount of 100dh is given for stays longer than 2 nights

Les Roches is situated in the prettiest and most dramatic part of the gorge. The hotel has clean rooms with private bathroom. The breakfast is basic but it will keep you going for a few hours. Dinner is served in a huge tent with good couscous and tajine on the menu.

Hotel Yasmina

✉ Gorges du Todra, Tinerhir
☎ +212 24895118
@ yasmina@todragorge.com

Price   Half pension costs 400dh
            per double room per night

*The Yasmina is located next to Hotel Les Roches
and is of a similar quality.*

Hotel El Mansour

✉ Gorges du Todra, Tinerhir
☎ +212 24895119

🖥 N 31°35'00,7 W 5°35'28,0

Price   Half pension costs 220dh
            per double room per night

*This hotel offers cheap basic rooms with shared
bathrooms and is situated in front of Sector
Aiguille Du Grabe.*

Hotel La Vallee

✉ Gorges du Todra, Tinerhir
☎ +212 24895126

🖥 N 31°35'00,9 W 5°35'29,6

Price   Half pension costs 340dh
            per double room per night

*Hotel La Vallee lies opposite El Mansour. It has
a restaurant and is very conveniently located to
the start of many routes.*

Wild camping is permitted. The best spots can be
found just next to the road at Sector Toxo de Lolla,
far away from the tourist hoards and where there is
some flat ground.

Vincent Massuger going for another nameless 6b+

The coloured limestone feels comfortable to climb on

Where to buy groceries?

As there is only one very small and expensive shop at the gorge, close to Hotel El Mansour, it is best to do your shopping in Tinerhir or Marrakesh. You will need some snacks to supplement the provided breakfast and dinners. There is only one international shop in Tinerhir, named Chez Michéle, owned by foreigners who sell, amongst other things, wine and beer. It is located on Av. Mohamed V. Most hotels sell water too.

Where to find the local climbing guidebook

There is one basic topo of the Todra Gorge, which is produced and drawn by hand by the author, Hassan Mouhajir. He sells it in French, English, Spanish, German, and Italian for 200dh to 250dh - he lets you decide on the price. The topo is rather expensive and most certainly not up to date - the author unfortunately seems to be spending more time drinking than climbing. However it is still useful. Hassan usually hangs around the Hotel El Mansour between August and May or can be contacted via his mobile: +212 10134294.

If you can't get in touch with Hassan either go to Hotel Les Roches or El Mansour. Both hotels can also provide route information and have a few photocopied articles from various climbing magazines.

Vincent Massuger looking for footholds

What else is there to see & do

Hiking
The area has some wonderful hikes and this is really the best thing to do on rest days. There is one highly recommended walk which will take about three hours: coming from Hotel Yasmina walk towards Sector Regression and turn left up the trail which starts between the craft stands. Follow the trail all the way up for about 1½ hours until you get to a flat plateau. Turn left and continue until you get to a Berber family living in a tent and cave. Continue left up the hill a bit more and then start descending from there, which takes 1 to 1½ hours. The trail finishes up at the last village of the gorge.

There are no ATM's in the Todra Gorge but there are in Tinerhir.

The Todra Gorge boasts over 400 single and multi pitch routes spread over 25 sectors that are all easy to reach. The quality and variety is immense for such a small area and the potential for further development is mind-boggling. A little more than half of the routes are single pitch although the very best climbs are multi pitch, which go up to 300 metres.

If you would like to get used to the rock and warm up before heading out to the multi pitch routes, head for Sector Dalle Hollandais or the enjoyable Le Petite Gorge. Both sectors are conveniently located next to the road, the latter a 3km walk from Hotel Les Roches. When climbing at Sector Dalle Hollandais you could collect royalties from all the tourists taking photos of you! At Le Petite Gorge you will find an excellent combination of fine rock, fine routes, fine views and relative solitude. A good selection of 5s and 6s occupy the north side whilst the south caters for 6s and 7s.

The easily accessible Sector Petite Gorge has many 6th and 7th grade routes

Sector Elephant also has some very attractive routes and a couple of multi pitch ones, most of them in the 6th and 7th grade. The route 'Pelier Du Guetteur' (6b) on Sector Aiguille Du Grabe' is a great route with fantastic views on each side of the gorge.

Past the Hotels Les Roches and Yasmina you will find Sector De Meuk, the first of the hard sectors. Unfortunately it suffers from dust from the passing jeeps so its walls are a bit dirty. But if you are into high 7th grade and 8th grade routes make sure to visit Sector Güllich. The latter is a good bet, is a brilliant venue with good views and amenable routes.

Be warned that hangers are occasionally removed by the locals (mostly by the children). This mostly occurs at the start of the route and on the belays. Bring some extra hangers as well as your usual rack. Also maillons could well be useful. Finally you will need some slings for those routes where the belays are completely missing. We advise using a 60m double rope, to deal with most eventualities.

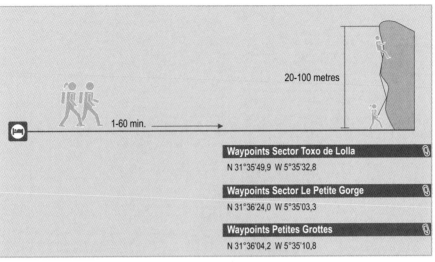

20-100 metres

1-60 min.

Waypoints Sector Toxo de Lolla
N 31°35'49,9 W 5°35'32,8

Waypoints Sector Le Petite Gorge
N 31°36'24,0 W 5°35'03,3

Waypoints Petites Grottes
N 31°36'04,2 W 5°35'10,8

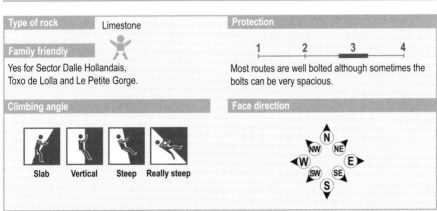

Type of rock
Limestone

Family friendly
Yes for Sector Dalle Hollandais,
Toxo de Lolla and Le Petite Gorge.

Climbing angle

Slab   Vertical   Steep   Really steep

Protection

1   2   3   4

Most routes are well bolted although sometimes the
bolts can be very spacious.

Face direction

N
NW NE
W   E
SW SE
S

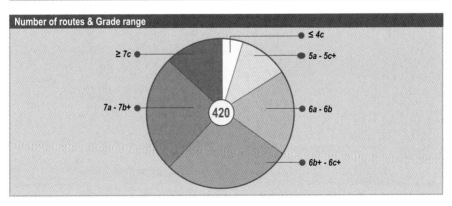

Number of routes & Grade range

≤ 4c

≥ 7c

5a - 5c+

7a - 7b+

420

6a - 6b

6b+ - 6c+

Wynand on the first of the 5 pitcher Pelier du Guetteur, Sector Aiguille du Grabe

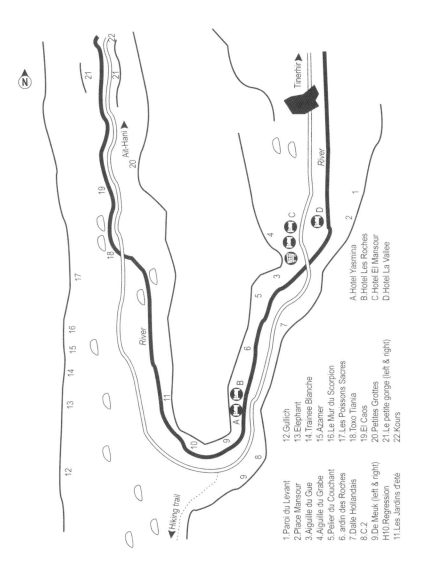

1. Paroi du Levant
2. Place Mansour
3. Aiguille du Gue
4. Aiguille du Grabe
5. Peiler du Couchant
6. ardin des Roches
7. Dalle Hollandais
8. C.2
9. De Meuk (left & right)
H10. Regression
11. Les Jardins d'été

12. Gullich
13. Elephant
14. Trainee Blanche
15. Azamer
16. Le Mur du Scorpion
17. Les Poissons Sacres
18. Toxo Tiania
19. El Caos
20. Petites Grottes
21. Le petite gorge (left & right)
22. Kours

A. Hotel Yasmina
B. Hotel Les Roches
C. Hotel El Mansour
D. Hotel La Vallee

Directions

► Once you have arrived inside the gorge it is fairly easy to find the sectors. There is only one road running through the gorge and the sectors are located on either side.

Climbing area Taghia Gorge

Spring   Summer   Autumn   Winter

For those who love long routes - up to 800 metres - on perfect limestone in a truly wonderful setting, Taghia is one of the most perfect climbing destinations in the world. Deep canyons, overhanging red walls, peaks reaching the 3000 metres, and verdant valleys create the breathtaking scenery of the gorge. Right in the middle lies the remote village of Taghia at 1900 metres. To get there you'll need to use a 4x4 to cover the 63 km from Aït Mhammed to Zaouia Ahanesal, from where you have to walk the last 8km with your equipment on the back of a donkey. Once in the friendly Berber village you'll find yourself in a completely different world where you'll loose all sense of time.

The area was first discovered by the mountaineer Manuel Punsola in 1974. The first routes were climbed in the following years by French climbers, and later in the 80's and 90's the area was visited by more French as well as Spanish climbers. However it was not until 2000 that there was a huge surge in new-routing activity. Petit, Piola, Larcher, Oviglia, Robert, and many more well known climbers have all contributed to the development of routes in the Taghia Gorge. The vast majority of climbers are still French and Spanish; other European climbers have only just discovered the beauty and potential of this area.

Taghia village

When to go

Climbing is possible from early April until the end of October. The weather in April can be a bit unpredictable but is generally good. July and August are fairly warm but climbing in the shade is possible, although this limits the number of feasible routes.

Crag

Ⓐ Taghia Gorge

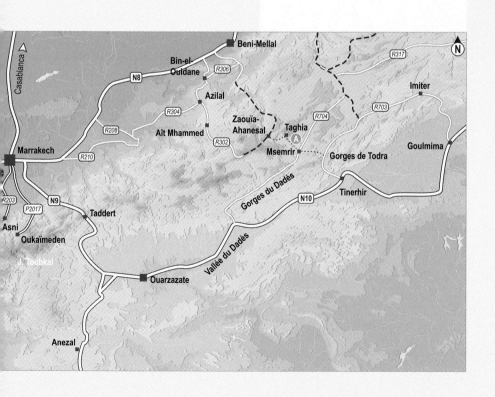

How to get to the area & how to move around

The closest and most convenient access to the area is from Marrakesh. Flying to Casablanca is also an option (you can sometimes find better flight deals there) but it will take you two days to get to the Taghia Gorge.

Arranging transport from Marrakesh airport is best done by contacting Youssef or Said, two gîte owners who live in Taghia, directly (see the where to stay section for contact details). They can arrange the whole trip from Marrakesh to Taghia for about 1700dh for groups of up to 6 people. This is simple and convenient.

However, you could also sort everything yourself and travel by public transport.

 By public transport

From Marrakesh take one of two daily buses from the Bab Doukala bus station to Azilal. Buses leave at 8.30am and 12.30pm [4h, 55dh]. From Casablanca buses leave the Ouled Ziane Gare Routière almost every half hour to Beni-Mellal [3½h, 50dh]. From Beni-Mellal there are 4 daily buses to Azilal [1½h, 25dh].

Once in Azilal take a shared taxi to Aît Mhammed [20min, 12dh] which leaves from the square where the bus stop is located. Then from Aît Mhammed you'll have to find a 4x4 that can take you to Zaouia Ahanesal [3h]. This could be the most difficult part of the journey! There are only a few 4x4 making the journey and they only leave when they are full (unless you are willing to pay the full fare of 400dh). The best day to travel from Aît Mhammed to Zaouia Ahanesal is Saturday - this is market day in Aît Mhammed and many people return to Zaouia Ahanesal at the end of the morning. If (and only if!) the road is completely dry you could also find a normal taxi to take you. The cost will be around 400dh-500dh per taxi. Upon arrival in Zaouia Ahanesal locals will approach you to offer you a donkey to carry your luggage to Taghia. This will typically cost you 100dh. The gentle walk takes 2½ hours.

The whole trip from Marrakesh to Taghia could be made in one long day if you take the early bus to Azilal. If you don't make it in one day you can spend the night in Azilal, Aît Mhammed, or even Zaouia Ahanesal.

The best choice in Azilal is the Hotel Assounfou, east of the town square on Hassan II. A double room is 200dh. Waypoints: N 31°57'39,3 W 6°34'01,1. Budget hotels include the friendly Hotel Dades with shared facilities, situated west of the town square on Hassan II. A double room costs 75dh. Waypoints: N31°57'34,5 W 6°34'25,9

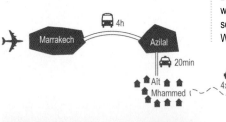

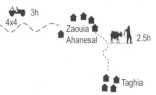

If you get stuck in Aît Mhammed ask for the Zouidi brothers (Mohammed and Hamid). They offer a room in their family house for 40dh per person including breakfast or 100dh including dinner as well. In Zaouia Ahanesal there are several gîtes available at 150dh per person, which include dinner and breakfast.

Girls in Taghia

By car

Azilal is 142km from Marrakesh and 280km from Casablanca. A standard car (i.e. non-4x4!) will be able to make the journey via Azilal-Aît Mhammed to Zaouia Ahanesal but only if the road is dry. Ask around about the road conditions in Aît Mhammed before setting off yourself. You can leave your car in Aît Mhammed if necessary, or also in Zaouia Ahanesal.

Where to stay

In Taghia there are basically two options: the gîtes belonging to either Youssef Rezki or Said Messaoudi. Both of them are equally popular and both serve breakfast (bread with cheese, jam, honey, coffee and tea) and dinner (alternating between couscous one night and tajine the next).

Gite of Youssef

Gite d'étape Said Messaoudi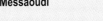

✉ Douar Taghia
🔔 Zaouia Ahanesal
@ 22000 Azilal
📞 +212 (0)68246536

📱 N 31°47'13,1 W 6°04'22,4

Price   150dh per person including breakfast and dinner

Said and his family have 8 rooms with shared squat toilets and a hot shower. They have mattresses and blankets but, again, best bring your own. Said speaks very little French and no English.

Directions
The gîte is close to the school on the east side of the village.

Gite d'étape Youssef Rezki

✉ Douar Taghia
Zaouia Ahanesal
22000 Azilal
📞 +212 (0)68909843
@ aoujdade@yahoo.fr

📱 N 31°47'20,4 W 6°04'25,6

Price   150dh per person including breakfast and dinner

Youssef is a certificated mountain guide and speaks good French, very little Spanish and no English. He has 8 rooms that can each accommodate 4 people. There are mattresses and blankets but you'd better bring your own bedding. There are shared squat toilets and a hot shower.

Directions
The gîte lies in the upper part of the village. Ask around, everyone knows Youssef!

Garden of Said

Marloes stepping through on the brilliant La Cascade

Where to buy groceries?

There is no shop in Taghia: bring snacks and fruit to supplement the meals. Also bring some toilet paper and bottled water or purification tablets. Shopping can be done in Marrakesh or Azilal.

Where to find the local climbing guidebook

The two websites to get climbing information from are *www.onaclimb.com* and *www.remi-thivel.com*. Both gîtes keep a route book and route information.

What else is there to see & do

Hiking
The Taghia Gorge offers some of the best scenery in Morocco and it is very popular with hikers. From Taghia there are a wide range of trails of varying lengths, including some multi-day hikes. Get information and advice from Youssef, who knows the area like the back of his hand. If you are planning on hiking it would be a good idea to pick up detailed area maps at home, as they are hard to obtain in Morocco. This applies to other areas in Morocco too.

The first pitch is a bit vegetated but Basesses et Tentations is a great route

A great way to combine climbing in the Taghia and Todra gorges is to walk between them! This trek is highly recommended and you'll experience some of the best scenery in the High Atlas. The best way to make all the necessary arrangements is to ask Youssef Rezki to sort everything out (email him in advance if you plan to do this). A donkey costs 100dh per day and the obligatory mountain guide 300dh per day. You then have two options to get to Todra. One is to hike from Taghia to Msemrir (two days) and continue by car via the beautiful Gorges du Dadès to the Todra Gorge (one day). Alternatively, you can hike all the way to the Todra Gorge from Msemrir (a further two days).

There are 115 equipped routes but it must immediately be said that the entrance ticket is a steady 6b climbing level. The vast majority of the routes (climbed free) are above 6c - if you don't climb this grade the route choice is limited. Although, having said that, it's probably fair to say that 90% of the climbers do only 10% of the routes. The following recommended routes are amongst the ones most often climbed:

- La rêve d'Aicha - on the Paroi des Sources, it is the easiest route in the Taghia Gorge: 255m (6a+, 5+ obligatory)
- Belle et Berbère - on the Paroi des Sources, it is an excellent first encounter with the Taghia Gorge: 330m (6b+, 6a+ obligatory)
- Au nom de la reforme - on the Taoujdad, it is a real classic: 340m (6c, 6b obligatory)
- Barraka (685m) - on the Oujdad, this is a beauty with just a few really hard moves: 685m (7b, 6b obligatory)
- Canyon Apache - on the Timrazine, a well protected technical climb: 355m (6c+, 6b obligatory)

The amount of fixed protection varies but the route descriptions give you good guidance to the necessary gear. Bring a full rack with you and also bring hangers for 8mm, 10mm and 12mm bolts - on some routes the local children have taken some of these!

Besides the long multi pitch routes there are also 39 bolted single pitch sport routes that are good for rest days or when there is unpredictable weather.

The Oujdad

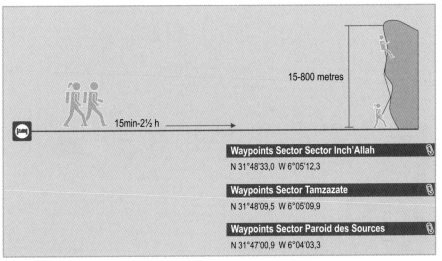

15-800 metres

15min-2½ h

Waypoints Sector Sector Inch'Allah
N 31°48'33,0 W 6°05'12,3

Waypoints Sector Tamzazate
N 31°48'09,5 W 6°05'09,9

Waypoints Sector Paroid des Sources
N 31°47'00,9 W 6°04'03,3

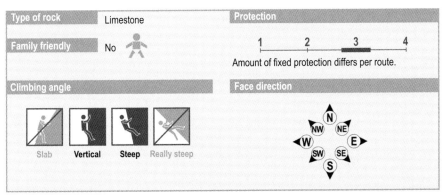

| Type of rock | Limestone |
| Family friendly | No |

Protection

1   2   3   4
Amount of fixed protection differs per route.

Climbing angle

Slab   **Vertical**   **Steep**   Really steep

Face direction

N NW NE W E SW SE S

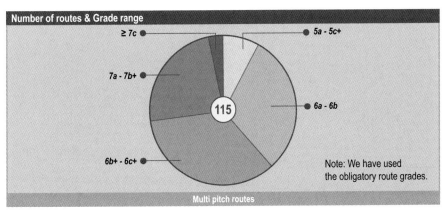

Number of routes & Grade range

≥ 7c

5a - 5c+

7a - 7b+

115

6a - 6b

6b+ - 6c+

Note: We have used the obligatory route grades.

Multi pitch routes

The scenic Taghia Gorge

Taghia Gorge

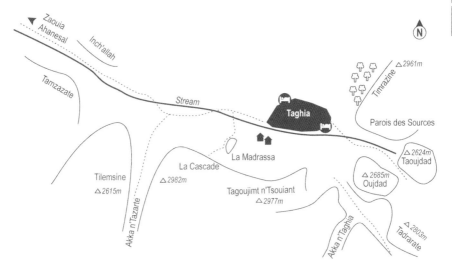

Directions

▶ See the detailed map. In both gîtes there is also plenty of access information available. You can always ask Youssef or Said if you're uncertain.

The red limestone of Taghia

Climbing area Tafraoute

Spring   Summer   Autumn   Winter

Tafraoute in the Anti-Atlas is a quiet but engaging town - The Rough Guide describes this as one of the most relaxed destinations in Morocco - some 143km southeast of Agadir. The majority of the locals spend most of their time either running small carpet shops or chilling out in the cafes. Tourists come here for the wonderful hikes in the Ameln Valley. The 26 small villages in this valley are set against the backdrop of the red quartzite rocks and they are absolutely stunning with their palm trees, springs, and brightly painted houses and mosques. Other famous sights in this region are the painted rocks and ancient rock carvings. Climbers come here either for adventurous bouldering or for traditional routes in the Jebel el Kest massif.

The whole area is scattered with granite boulders in the strangest forms ever seen. Wherever you look tasty looking boulders appear! The bouldering here is quite unexplored and there is no topo available, but this could make for a highly interesting trip for those after new problems. The traditional routes in the Jebel el Kest massif are described in a Cicerone guidebook. There are a wide variety of routes, all in a wonderful setting on extremely solid quartzite.

Tafraoute is an absolute winner for an adventurous climbing trip combined with fascinating culture and great weather during the winter months.

The Ameln Valley

When to go

February to the end of April, with October and November being the best months to visit this area. In summer the heat is excessive. The rainy period is from the end of November to early January and the landscape actually looks its best right after the winter rains.

Crag

Ⓐ Jebel el Kest massif
Ⓑ Tafraoute boulders

219

How to get to the area & how to move around

The best way here is to fly to Agadir and rent a car at the airport (a car really is a necessity). If you don't plan on climbing every day you could get away with travelling there by bus and using the taxi service run by Tafraoute-Aventure to get to the routes. They charge 150dh per car to drop you to the start of a route and pick you up later that day. They are located in the centre of Tafraoute, opposite the post office.

 By public transport

Take one of the six daily buses from Agadir or Inezgane to Tafraoute [5h, 70dh]. The bus station in Agadir is located on Rue Chair al Hamra Mohammed ben Brahim southeast of the centre and just beyond the souk. When en route from Agadir airport to Tafraoute it is easier to take a taxi to Inezgane and catch the bus to Tafraoute from there.

 By car

Several car rental agencies are located at the airport so shop around and bargain for the best deal. The most interesting route from Agadir to Tafraoute goes via Biougra and Aît-Baha. Along the way you'll see dramatic gorges and ancient villages perched in amazing positions. Take your time and enjoy the fantastic views!

Where to stay

Hotel Riad Tafraoute

✉ Centre Tafraoute 85450
📞 +212 (0)28800031
📠 +212 (0)28800032
@ info@riad-tafraout.com
🌐 www.riad-tafraout.com

📍 N 29°43'01,7 W 08°58'36,1

Price 350dh for a double room including breakfast

This is one of the best hotel options. It only opened in 2007 and has a beautifully decorated entrance and equally nice rooms with private bathrooms.

Directions
Follow the signs for "Hotel Les Amadiers" and you'll pass Hotel Riad Tafraoute just before the road climbs up to the Les Amadiers.

Bouldering in Tafraoute is always in extremely nice settings

Hotel Riad Tafraoute

Hotel Les Amadiers

Hotel Les Amadiers

✉ Centre Tafraoute 85450
📞 +212 (0) 28 800 008
@ reservation@hotel-lesamadiers.com
🏠 www.hotel-lesamadiers.com

📍 N 29°43'04,7 W 08°58'27,4

Price   400dh-500dh for a double room
including breakfast

This is the hotel where the first British climbers in the area stayed and they still keep a climbing log-book. However the only other advantage of this highly overrated and characterless hotel is its swimming pool.

Camping Les 3 palmiers

✉ Tafraoute
📞 +212 (0)66098403

📍 N 29°43'17,8 W 08°58'46,5

Price   45dh per night for 2 persons, a car
and a tent. A bungalow costs 45dh
for 2 persons

By Moroccan standards this is a very pleasant and clean campsite just outside the centre. The friendly Omar Sidki will make sure you enjoy your stay.

Directions
Follow the signs for "Les 3 palmiers".

Maison – Chambres d'hôte in Oemesnat

✉ Village Oemesnat – Tafraoute
📞 +212 (0)66917768 / +212 (0)66918145
@ maisondhote@gmail.com

📍 N 29°45'52,9 W 08°56'36,4

Price   150dh pp incl breakfast and dinner
for a room with shared bathroom
and 200dh pp for a room with
private bathroom

This nicely located small hotel is a very good choice if you want something special and quiet. It is very convenient for the climbing around Oemesnat (Sector O and P). There is also a family room.

Directions
Take the turn to Oemesnat and follow the signs for "La Maison Traditionelle" which shares the same owner and is next to the hotel.

Camping Les 3 Palmiers

Painted rocks of Tafraoute

One of the Ameln villages

Where to buy groceries?

In Tafraoute there are many small shops selling groceries.

Where to find the local climbing guidebook

The Cicerone guidebook "Climbing in the Moroccan Anti-Atlas - Tafraoute and Jebel el Kest" by Claude Davies is not on sale in Morocco so it is best to order it in advance (*www.cicerone.co.uk*). This guidebook describes all climbs and is a must-have, although it has only photo topos of climbs and no written descriptions. The author really has maintained the spirit of adventure!

There is no guidebook available for the bouldering.

What else is there to see & do

Hiking
You could spend days, if not weeks, wandering round the 26 villages of the Ameln Valley. Serious

Local climbers in the Souss valley, near Tafraoute

walkers could even go for the complete ascent of Jebel el Kest (2359m). Make sure you don't miss a walk to see the painted boulders in a sea of other boulders. The scenery is absolutely stunning.

4x4 tours
Tafraoute Aventure arranges several 4x4 tours. There are single day tours that include a drive to the Gorges Ait Mansour, including a 5 hour walk through the gorge [300dp per person including lunch]. A very nice 2-day tour takes you to the desert where you'll sleep [2000dh per person all-in].

Paragliding
This area is also famous for its great paragliding conditions. Book a course in advance with a paragliding school in your home country as it can't be arranged locally.

Surfing and kiting
There are loads of good surfing and kiting spots up the coast from Agadir. If you have the time head north - the coastal road is packed with camper vans full of kiters and surfers. Essaouira, north of Agadir, is a cool place to visit especially if you're chasing waves.

Bouldering around Tafraoute

There are no ATMs in Tafraoute so get money in Agadir or at the airport. If the ATM at the airport does not work and you've rented a car you'll pass a few ATMs on the way to Tafraoute.

The Jebel el Kest massif near Tafraoute is described by many as a trad-climbers dream. The first ascents were made by the pioneers Trevor Jones and Les Brown in 1991, when they first discovered the area. Soon Joe Brown and Claude Davies joined them and exploration continued over the following years. In 2004 a guidebook written by Claude Davies was published and, from that moment on, other trad climbers, mainly British, found their way to these remarkable rocks.

The main climbing is found in the two valleys either side of the area's highest peak, Jebel Um Kest. The most famous rock is called "The Lion's Face". No prizes for guessing what it looks like! There are many kilometres worth of clean, solid orange quartzite, generally with good protection. Routes range from single pitch wall climbs to huge, rambling, alpine-like ridges. The majority of the climbing is only an hour or so from the road, making it an even more pleasing area!

The Cicerone guidebook has good descriptions of how to find the crags with realistic times for the walk-ins but it doesn't give exact route descriptions, so finding the starts can be tricky. But this just adds to the adventure, so enjoy it!

Quartzite

Noreen Brown on the Great Ridge of the Lion's Face

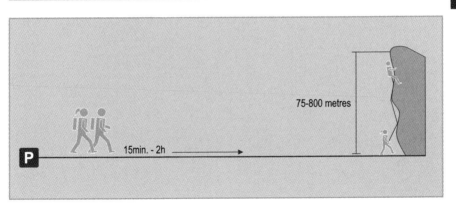

75-800 metres

P

15min. - 2h

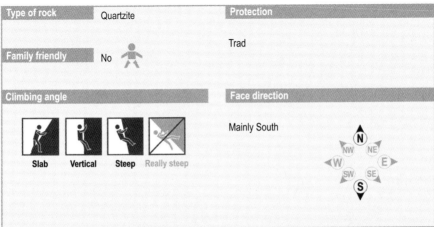

Type of rock	Quartzite	Protection	Trad
Family friendly	No		

Climbing angle

Slab Vertical Steep Really steep

Face direction

Mainly South

Number of routes & Grade range

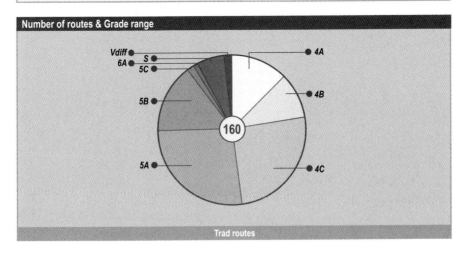

Vdiff
S
6A
5C
5B
4A
4B
160
5A
4C

Trad routes

Oumsnat village in the Ameln Valley

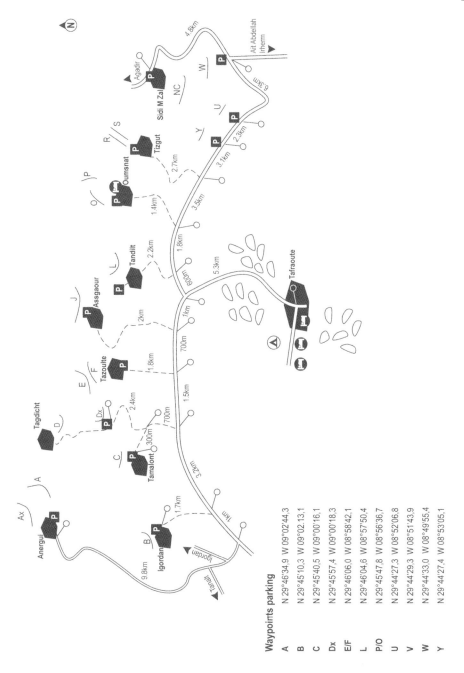

Waypoints parking

A	N 29°46'34.9 W 09°02'44,3
B	N 29°45'10,3 W 09°02.13,1
C	N 29°45'40,5 W 09°00'16,1
Dx	N 29°45'57,4 W 09°00'18,3
E/F	N 29°46'06.0 W 08°58'42,1
L	N 29°46'04,6 W 08°57'50,4
P/O	N 29°45'47,8 W 08°56'36,7
U	N 29°44'27,3 W 08°52'06,8
V	N 29°44'29,3 W 08°51'43,9
W	N 29°44'33,0 W 08°49'55,4
Y	N 29°44'27,4 W 08°53'05,1

The Tafraoute granite boulders are probably the most famous boulders in the world among non-climbers - they are touted in so many tourist guidebooks! In 1984 the Belgian artist Jean Veran found his way here - not for climbing but for art's sake. Together with a team of Moroccan firemen he hosed some 18 tons of paint over many different boulders. Even though their sharpness has faded over the years, a weird landscape of blue and red boulders remains. Today a visit to the painted rocks is on every tourist's agenda.

For a climber, the sight of those blue and red boulders, and the thousands of other ones of every shape and size, will get you itching to climb! There are not many recorded problems but boulderers have certainly been here.

Apart from the painted rocks area, there are boulders all around Tafraoute. The best advice we could give you is to drive and walk around and pick your sport. However, bear in mind that while the granite has great friction it is not so solid and can be rather crumbly, meaning that you quite easily loose your footholds. For this reason it will never become an enormously popular area. However it is an absolutely wonderful playground.

Directions

▶ Leave Tafraoute in the direction of Tiznit. After 2.4km you will reach the village of Agard Oudad. Turn right here and follow the road all the way through the village. Continue on this road. You will pass a small gate and on your right a huge rock will come into view, called Le Chapeau de Napoléon (Napoleon's hat). Continue along the road and don't take any side roads, until you see the first painted boulders. Parking is possible anywhere along the track.

Bouldering around Tafraoute, photo by Klemen Demsar

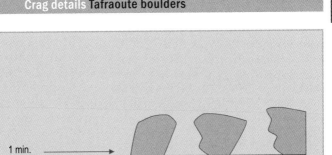

Waypoints painted boulders

N 29°40'40,0 W 08°58'37,3

Type of rock	Granite
Family friendly	Yes

Climbing angle

Slab Vertical Steep Really steep

Face direction

N NE E SE S SW W NW

Last sun of this winter day in Tafraoute, photo by Klemen Demsar

...Europe's sunniest destination...

Portugal

Ricardo Belchior flashing his first 7c+ at Rocha da Pena

Alright, we'd better say it now, Portugal is not particularly famous for any one crag and it might not be your first choice as a climbing destination. However, it's certainly a great place to climb when on holiday as it does have a good selection of high-quality smaller crags. Oh, and don't forget to take your surfboard!

Portugal is one of the most popular holiday destinations in Europe. This also applies to its capital Lisbon. It is without doubt one of Europe's most wonderful cities with outstanding monuments, castles, churches, and the delights of fantastic beaches and untouched countryside within striking distance.

If a bit of sun worship is your thing and you're trying to buff up your tan, try the beautiful and long beaches on the Algarve, which are surrounded by amazing cliffs and crystal clear waters. It has the best weather in Europe throughout the whole year - in winter it feels like spring and summers are kept relatively fresh by the Atlantic breeze.

Portugal also is the place on the Atlantic for surfers of all kinds, whether plain vanilla, wind, or kite. It has a huge variety of waves and swells, and is a popular destination with surfers of all abilities. It is also a good place to learn to surf - there are lots of places offering surf lessons and packages. In other words, Portugal is your ideal destination for that combined climb and surf trip!

Climbing information

Although Portugal doesn't really have any single crag that is world famous, there are around 25 crags and bouldering areas, some of which have really great climbing and are most certainly worth visiting. There are crags near Lisbon, in the north of Portugal, and in the sunny Algarve. We'll only describe the most worthwhile areas, in terms of size, variety of routes, beauty, and ease of access and accommodation.

Climbing area Lisbon

Around Lisbon there is a good collection of small crags that have both sport climbing and bouldering. In the hills of beautiful Sintra, just outside Lisbon, there is climbing on a nice granite slab. The coastline to the west of Lisbon offers a variety of sport climbing and bouldering next to the sea.

Climbing area Algarve

In the far south of the Algarve, the crags are just far enough away from the busy holiday resorts to find some peace. Here you'll find Rocha da Pena, a very worthwhile crag inland from Faro. Further west there are the sea cliffs near Sagres with a combination of DWS, sport and trad climbing.

Farol Da Guia is where the locals come to learn to climb

Portugal | Introduction

233

Marc Xavier on Kamet (6c) at Rocha da Pena

Climate

Portugal has a very mild Mediterranean climate which is heavily moderated by the Atlantic. Droughts are common in the south and the north is far greener due to slightly cooler winter temperatures.

Spring and autumn are definitely the best times of year to visit mainland Portugal. Winter starts in November or December and lasts till February or March. It can be rainy in the winter, especially in the north and central regions, including Lisbon. The weather usually stays very warm from May to September.

The Algarve is moderate year-round, with extremely hot summers but with a sea breeze that makes things bearable even in the winter.

Month	Average temperature (°C)	Average rainfall (mm)
Jan	11	111
Feb	12	76
March	14	109
April	16	54
May	17	44
June	20	16
July	22	3
Aug	23	4
Sept	22	33
Oct	18	62
Nov	14	93
Dec	12	103

Climate table Lisbon. Winter rainfall in the Algarve is about 35% less and up to 75% less in summer. Minimum temperatures in the Algarve are consistently a few degrees higher than Lisbon.

Getting there

 By plane

There is no shortage of budget flights to Portugal. There are several airports to choose from but the best options are to fly to Faro (in the Algarve) or Lisbon. Ryanair and Easyjet have flights to these cities, amongst others.

 By train

It is possible to travel by train from Paris to Lisbon in 19 hours. There is a daily high-speed TGV from Paris to Irun on the Spanish frontier at 3:50pm, which arrives in Irun at 09:23pm. The famous overnight Sud Express takes you from here to Lisbon, leaving Irun at 10pm and arriving in Lisbon (Oriente Station) at 10:42am. Sleeping-car and couchettes places are available. It is also possible to travel via Madrid and spend some days there. For prices and up to date timetables check *www.spanish-rail.co.uk, www.renfe.es* and *www.cp.pt.* From London you can get easily to Paris by taking the Eurostar.

Moving around

A car is very convenient for getting you to the crags in Portugal. You can easily rent a car upon arrival in the airport or rent one for a few days at your end destination. If you'd rather not spend money on a car the best crags to visit are along the coastline to

Small harbour at Sagres

Torre de Belem in Lisbon

the west of Lisbon since these can be reached by bus from the campsite.

 Lisbon airport information

Lisbon airport is 10km northeast of the city centre.

There are several buses to and from the airport. Bus 44 provides the link between the train station Gare do Oriente - Parque das Nações (North/South) and the airport. Bus 91 makes the run between Lisbon Airport and the city centre. Services begin at 07:45am and end at 08:15pm, running every 20 minutes.

A taxi to the city centre should cost around €20. Pre-paid taxis are available from the tourist desk in arrivals.

Faro airport information

Faro airport is only a few kilometers out of Faro and close to Quarteira. The bus stop is just outside of the main terminal building and buses leaving at regular intervals take you to the centre of Faro. From the bus terminal in the centre there are a wide range of travel options. For further information go to the main Algarve bus company's website at *www.eva-bus.net*.

A taxi to Quarteira should cost about €36.

 By public transport

The "Lisboa card" allows you to use all public transport facilities in the city and trains between Lisbon and Sintra or Cascais, and it also offers you free entrance and discounts for monuments, museums, or other tourist attractions. It costs €14.85 for 24 hours, €25.5 for 48 hours and €31 for 36 hours.

There is a vast network of regional, inter-regional, and suburban trains covering the whole of the country. Caminhos de Ferro Portugueses (CP) is the national railway company. The top-of-the-range "Alfa pendular" trains are the fastest and most comfortable rail link between Lisbon and the Algarve. The cheaper "Intercidades" (Intercity) service also covers the Lisbon-Algarve routes. *Check www.cp.pt* for timetables. Tourist tickets are the ideal choice for those traveling a lot by train. They are personal, non-transferable tickets that are valid for an unlimited number of journeys for 7, 14 or 21 consecutive days, at any time of year and for any category and class of train.

Buses are also commonly used and these tend to drop you right in the town centre. There are 2 bus companies: Rede Expressos and Eva Bus. The latter also runs the local buses in the Algarve. Check out their websites for a complete overview of routes, times, and prices: *www.rede-expressos.pt* and *www.eva-bus.net*.

Typical Portuguese ceramics

Marloes on Factor Solar (5c) at Baia Do Mexilhoeiro

Taxis are usually cream in colour, although there are still some painted black with a green roof in traditional Portuguese style. The fare is always shown on the taximeter.

 By car

All motorways are marked with internationally recognized signs and motorists have to pay tolls on most of them.

Car rental in Portugal is relatively cheap and it's best to surf the internet for the best deals. Rates for a small car start at €130 per week. Check out *www.portugal-auto-rentals.com* for an initial price comparison.

Pasteis

Accommodation

Portugal has plenty of choice in accommodation - hotels ranging from luxury to basic, boarding houses, inns, and hostels. Many tour operators offer package deals, mostly to the Algarve, and these are often the most cost efficient options if you're after a comfortable stay in the Algarve. There are also many relaxed campsites throughout the country that make for an inexpensive holiday. The usual price in low season for 2 people, with a car and a tent is €11, going up to €22 in high season (July and August).The wind in Portugal can blow real strong, so chose your pitch wisely and bring that 4-season tent!

Portugal has some of the best surfing in Europe

Typical menu at a Portuguese bar

best to order this guidebook in advance as it is not available in Portugal. Try *www.cordee.co.uk*.

Another great resource is the website *www.socurtir.com*, however, it is only in Portuguese. The Faro climbing club (AMEA) also gives some information on its website: *www.amea.pt*. The website *www.gmesintra.com* provides good information too including a full freely downloadable topo of Sintra and Farol da Guia.

Route information for Sagres is currently only available from the Dromedario Bar in Sagres.

Food & drinks

Portuguese cuisine is characterised by rich, filling, and flavourful dishes. It is a seafaring nation at heart, and this is reflected in the amount of fish and seafood eaten. Fish is served grilled, poached (in which case it is always flavoured with olive oil), fried, or even roasted. Tuna, swordfish, red mullet, bacalhau and sea bream are just a few of the varieties you'll find. The most popular meat dish is Bife à Portuguesa: sirloin steak topped with smoked ham, cooked in a clay dish and served with French fries.

It is easily possible to eat out in a nice restaurant for €10 per person for a fish or meat menu. A large beer would normally go for €2 and a coffee will cost between €1 and €2. Supermarket prices are the same as other Western European countries although some fruit and vegetables may be cheaper.

Climbing guidebook

There is one guidebook covering most areas in Portugal, the Portugal Sport Onsight & Bouldering by Jingo Wobbly Topo Guides. This nicely made full color guidebook provides topos of 16 different climbing areas. Except for Sagres, it includes all the areas described in this Rock Climbing Atlas. It is

Zé Maria on Ovamaltine (6a+) at Farol da Guia

Facts about Portugal

Facts & figures

Population:	11 million
Religion:	Roman Catholic (84%)
Capital:	Lisbon
Time zone:	GMT
Telephone code:	+351

Language

The official language of Portugal is Portuguese.

Goodmorning	*Bom dia*
Thank you	*Obrigado*
Goodbye	*Adeus*
Yes / No	*Sim / Não*
Right / Left / Straight	*Direito / Esquerda / Em frente*
Rock climbing	*Escalada*

Money

Currency:	Euro
ATM machines:	widely available

Visas & formalities

EU	Other European nationalities	USA / Canada	All other nationalities
No visa required for a period of up to 90 days.			Most other nationalities do not require a visa for a period of up to 90 days.

Safety

Portugal has a relatively low rate of violent crime. However, petty crime is, as everywhere, something to be aware of. Take the normal precautions and don't leave any valuables inside your car.

Use of mobile phone

Several mobile operators cover the whole country.

Internet access

Available in most towns for around €3 per hour.

Emergency numbers

General:	112

Water

It is not advisable to drink tap water in Portugal - it is better to use bottled water. The price for six 1.5l bottles of water is around €2.

Climbing area Lisbon

Spring

Summer

Autumn

Winter

A trip to Lisbon purely for the climbing is probably not so worthwhile but climbing while in the area for other reasons does make sense. Lisbon is the most visited city in Portugal and a very attractive tourist destination: it has a charming historic downtown, fabulous food, lively nightlife, museums, and lovely beaches that are within easy reach. Around Lisbon there are some ten different climbing and bouldering areas - all very small, but all good for a one-day visit. The three most interesting venues are described in this chapter. One of them is Sintra, some 30km west of Lisbon, and it is one of the most delightful places to be found in Portugal. The area is very popular with tourists because of its picturesquely situated royal castles and its beautiful forest gardens where European kings spent their weekends. The granite slab climbing here is not very special yet it is in a nice quiet setting below a castle. Plus it is easy to reach by public transport from Lisbon.

The coastline to the west of Lisbon, known as the Costa do Estoril, is popular for its huge waves, pleasant beaches, and great sunbathing weather! Here you'll also find two very nice climbing spots next to the Atlantic Ocean. One is great for bouldering and the other is perfect for bolt clipping. The south-facing orientation, protection from the dominant wind, high quality limestone, and easy accessibility turns this area into an attractive year-round climbing destination both for beginners and advanced climbers.

Palacio da Pena

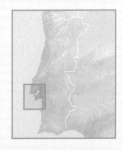

When to go

Lisbon is the mildest European capital. Spring is cool to warm (between 10°C and 27°C) with plenty of sunshine but also some showers once in a while. Summer months are mostly sunny, dry, and hot with temperatures between 16°C to 36°C. Autumn is mild and unsettled with temperatures between 8°C and 23°C and winters are typically rainy, windy, and cool with some sunny days (temperatures between 2°C and 18°C), usually hovering around an average of 10°C.

Crag

- Ⓐ Sintra
- Ⓑ Farol Da Guia
- Ⓒ Baía Do Mexilhoeiro

Portugal | Lisbon

241

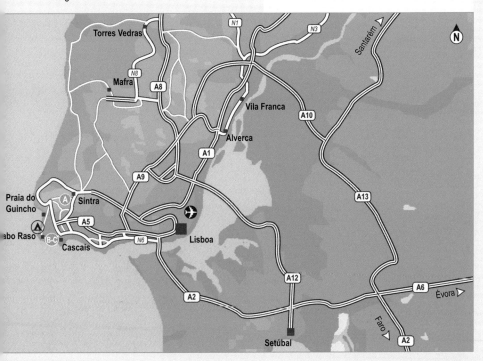

There are quite a few easier routes at Farol da Guia

How to get to the area & how to move around

It's easiest to use a car but all the crags described here can be reached by public transport too.

 By public transport

If you are not able to hire a car, catch a train from the Cais do Sodré terminal station in Lisbon (reached by the subway on the green line) to Cascais [40min, €3] and from there a local bus, number 405 or 415, to Guincho. This bus passes Farol da Guia and Baía do Mexilhoeiro on its way to Guincho. There is a bus stop just before Camping Guincho. It is also possible to take a direct hourly bus from Lisbon airport to Cascais. Get off at Areia, close to the campsite [45min, €7].

Bus 403 runs between Cascais and Sintra.

 By car

From Northern Europe it is quite a drive to Portugal so most people would opt for a fly and drive. However, you may like to combine a road trip to Spain with a visit to Portugal. The distance from Madrid to Lisbon is 630km, for reference.

Where to stay

Lisbon is full of nice hotels in all price ranges and it is not difficult to find something suitable. There is also a campsite just outside of Lisbon (*www.lisboacamping.com*). If your trip is more rock or wave focused, the campsite in Guincho is a better.bet. This gives good access to the beaches and picturesque villages of the enchanting Costa Azul region.

Camping Guincho

View from the granite of Sintra

Camping Guincho

✉ Lugar de Areia/EN 247-6
2750-053 Cascais/Guincho
☎ +351 214870450
@ info@orbitur.pt
🖰 www.orbitur.pt

📍 N 38°43'21.3 W 09°28'05.6

Open   Year round

Grade

1	2	3	4

Price   €11.30/€18.40 (low/high season)
for 2 persons, a tent and a car

This large campsite is most conveniently located to reach all crags in this area. It has a lot of shady pitches under pine trees and it is only 1km from the beach. It has a tennis court, restaurant and a small supermarket. It also rents small bungalows.

Directions:
From Lisbon take the A5 in the direction of Cascais. At the end of the motorway follow the signs to Guincho. The campsite is well signed.

Where to buy groceries?

There are supermarkets in Malveira, Sintra, and a big supermarket in Cascais. Camping Guincho has a small supermarket too.

Where to find the local climbing guidebook

There are no shops in Portugal selling the Jingo Wobbly guidebook. Buy it in advance or get your information from the internet. The best source is *www.gmesintra.com* which has free topos for Sintra and Farol da Guia.

Wynand on Bikini (6b) at Baia Do Mexilhoeiro

What else is there to see & do

Surfing

Near Guincho there are excellent conditions for surfing, windsurfing and kitesurfing. The Moana Surf School rents equipment (€15 for a board and a wetsuit for 2 hours) and offers courses. A 4 day course (1½ hour per day) costs €75. Check out *www.moanasurfschool.com*.

Relaxing at the beach

Beaches continue to be one of the greatest attractions of this region, and you have a choice of those that are situated in Cascais' sheltered bay or near Guincho.

Sintra

Sintra is beautiful and it really has retained its essentially medieval layout, with narrow and labyrinthine lovely streets, steps, and arcades. Every corner in town is different! The main architectural feature in Sintra is the Palacio Nacional. Besides the historic centre there are many picturesque royal castles with beautiful forest gardens - it's great for hiking. On the

Historic centre of Sintra

outskirts of the town is one of the most beautiful and important creations of the Romantic movement, the nineteenth-century Palacio da Pena. You should not miss this!

Cascais

Situated close to the sea and traditionally a fishing village, Cascais is now a stylish summer resort. The town itself is good for shopping or to enjoy a few moments' rest at one of the many outdoor cafés and restaurants scattered around the place.

Castelo dos Mouros above the granite slabs of Sintra

Farol Da Guia

Sintra

The climbing sectors in Sintra are right under the Moorish Castle just above the historic centre. The climbing is purely on granite slabs in an atmospheric and quiet setting but you don't get many holds on the routes here! There is a good selection of hard climbs but there is also perfect slab climbing in the lower grades. Most are single pitch but there are a couple of multi pitch climbs too. Views from the top are pretty. All sectors are north and west facing and can be cool and damp in autumn but very warm in summer. Generally, if Sintra is chilly go to Guia da Farol - if Guia is baking go to Sintra.

Marloes using the friction at Sintra

Directions

▶ *Directions by car from Camping Guincho*
Take a left turn when leaving the campsite and turn right at the next junction towards Malveira. In Malveira turn right to Alcabdeche but then immediately left, following the signs for Palacio da Pena through the beautiful forest. At a certain point the road to Palacio da Pena veers left and Sintra will be signposted straight on. Continue straight towards Sintra and after 1.3km you will find a green gate just before a sharp bend to the left: park here. Go through the gate and after 100m turn right following the steps that will lead you to the crags.

▶ *Directions by train from Lisbon*
Take one of the frequent trains to Sintra from the Rossio train station in Lisbon [1/2h, €4]. Sintra is at the end of the line. From the train station in Sintra walk towards the historic centre. Follow the signs for Palacio da Pena. The walk takes about 40 minutes in total. Access to the crags is through the green gate - see detailed drawing and route description above.

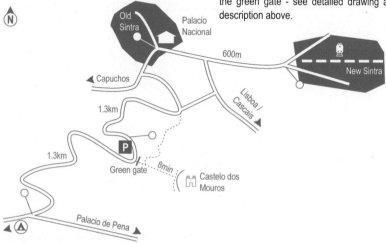

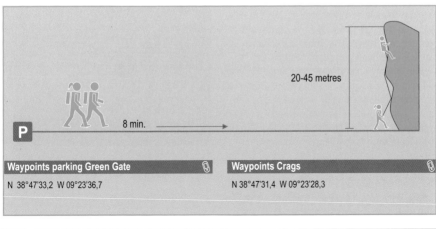

Waypoints parking Green Gate

N 38°47'33,2 W 09°23'36,7

Waypoints Crags

N 38°47'31,4 W 09°23'28,3

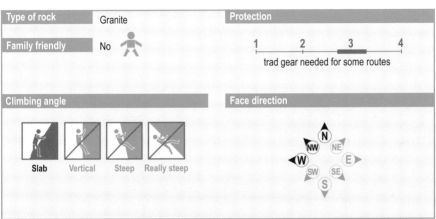

Type of rock	Granite
Family friendly	No

Protection

1 2 3 4

trad gear needed for some routes

Climbing angle

Slab Vertical Steep Really steep

Face direction

N NE E SE S SW W NW

Number of routes & Grade range

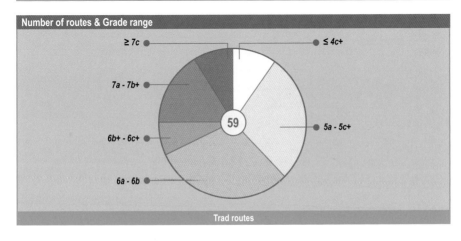

≥ 7c
7a - 7b+
6b+ - 6c+
6a - 6b
≤ 4c+
5a - 5c+

59

Trad routes

Farol Da Guia

This crag is used by a local climbing school in Guia - the sectors have a lot of easier routes and all are very well bolted. The yellow limestone is very textured and has many easy to find pockets. The setting is simply superb, right next to the sea but without any tide issues. All sectors face south and are both exposed to the sun and protected from the prevailing NW wind. It is an ideal winter crag but in summer it can be unbearably hot, with climbing between 10am and 6pm simply not possible.

The easier routes are slowly getting polished but most are still very much ok. There are some boulder problems too but for bouldering Baía Do Mexilhoeiro offers a greater choice.

Easy route finding at Farol Da Guia

Directions

▶ *Directions by car from Camping Guincho*
From the Guincho campsite head towards Guia. Park opposite the Repsol gas station with the giant artificial pine tree. There is a sign above the entrance to the crag, "Escola de Escalada da Guia".

▶ *Directions by bus from Camping Guincho*
Take the bus from Camping Guincho to Cascais. Ask the driver to drop you off just before Boca del Inferno.

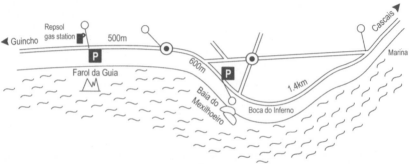

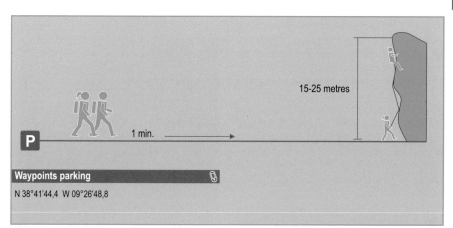

Waypoints parking

N 38°41'44,4 W 09°26'48,8

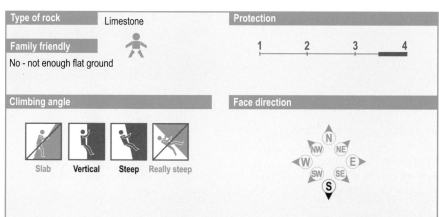

Type of rock

Limestone

Family friendly

No - not enough flat ground

Protection

1   2   3   4

Climbing angle

Slab   **Vertical**   **Steep**   Really steep

Face direction

N NE E SE S SW W NW

Number of routes & Grade range

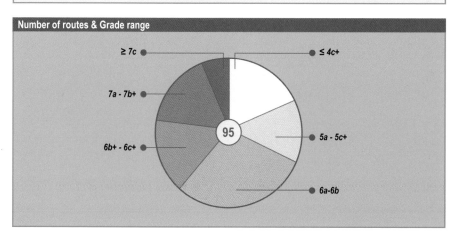

≥ 7c   ≤ 4c+

7a - 7b+   5a - 5c+

6b+ - 6c+   6a-6b

95

Baía Do Mexilhoeiro

If you're in the area, you really shouldn't miss the bouldering here. The whole area is covered with great limestone blocks, of which some touch the Atlantic. Tidal bouldering is a key skill to master here! The ground is flat and wide and this makes for an ideal playground for children too, although you have to be careful as the sea gets deep immediately. There is a huge variety of problems, from easy to difficult and facing all directions. In summer the best time to visit is in the morning when the rock is still cool or in the evening when the rocks turn yellow from the sunset and there is a refreshing breeze.

We recommend bringing a bouldering mat. Besides the bouldering there are also around 40 bolted sport routes, but it must be said that Farol da Guia is the better venue for sport climbing.

Baia Do Mexilhoeiro

Directions

▶ *Directions by car from Camping Guincho*

From the Guincho campsite head towards Guia and follow the signs for Boca do Inferno. When the road splits turn right and park the car after 300m. Steep steps lead down to the rock platforms.

▶ *Directions by bus from Camping Guincho*

Take the bus from Camping Guincho to Cascais. Ask the driver to let you out as close as possible to Boca del Inferno.

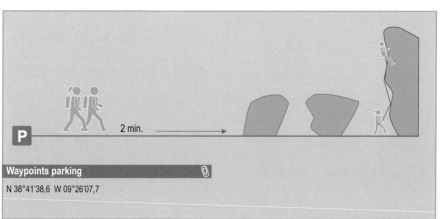

Waypoints parking

N 38°41'38,6 W 09°26'07,7

Type of rock

Limestone

Protection

1   2   3   4

Family friendly

Yes, but steep stairs go down
so small children must be carried.
Also watch your kids don't fall into the sea!

Climbing angle

Slab   Vertical   Steep   Really steep

Face direction

N   NE   E   SE   S   SW   W   NW

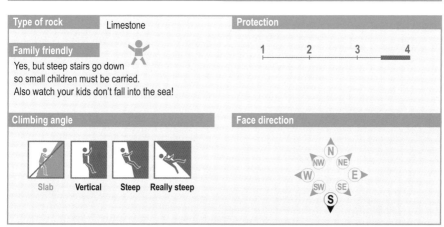

Number of routes & Grade range

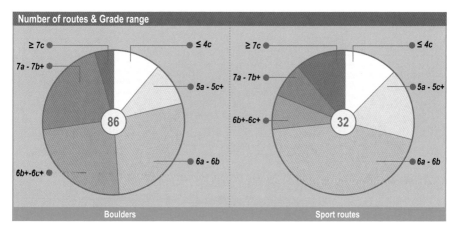

≥ 7c
7a - 7b+
6b+-6c+
≤ 4c
5a - 5c+
6a - 6b

86

Boulders

≥ 7c
7a - 7b+
6b+-6c+
≤ 4c
5a - 5c+
6a - 6b

32

Sport routes

Climbing area Algarve

Spring

Summer

Autumn

Winter

The Algarve is the southernmost region of Portugal and it is one of Europe's favourite holiday destinations, well known for its year round sunshine, fantastic scenery, and excellent sandy beaches. It has no shortage of cheap package holidays and for those after a (family) beach holiday or surfing destination combined with a bit of climbing the Algarve is a good choice.

There are two areas of interest. The climbing venue Rocha da Pena is near the fully fledged tourist resorts of Quarteira and Albufeira, and the coastline near Sagres and Cape St Vincent contains a wealth of big limestone sea cliffs. Rocha da Pena could be considered one of the most interesting sport climbing venues in the whole of Portugal. It is nicely situated, just far enough away from the busy tourist resorts yet still quick to reach, and with a short approach from the car to the crags. There is a good variety of rock structures and routes span the entire grade range.

Around Sagres there are a couple of bolted venues as well as some very good deep water soloing. The majority of the sea cliffs however are for trad climbing. Opinions on this area vary: some say that the rock is rather bad and suitable only for Mick Fowler and his ilk; others find it a wonderful place with top class adventure climbing. Well, we'd personally probably not rate it as the best spot in Europe. However, if you're there on holiday it is definitely worth checking out. You never know, you might find yourself in heaven!

Ricardo Belchior on Ghost Shit at Rocha da Pena

When to go

With over 3,000 hours of sun a year, the climate in the Algarve makes it a favourite destination. Summers are hot and dry and winters are mild with hardly any rain (50 days with rain and 500 mm on average each year), combined with very inviting springs and autumns. Be aware that during summer the Algarve gets very hot (it can go over 40°C/100°F exceptionally) and the sun is out for long periods in the day. If it's like this then DWS is your only option.

Crag

Ⓐ Rocha da Pena

Ⓑ Sagres

Portugal | Algarve

253

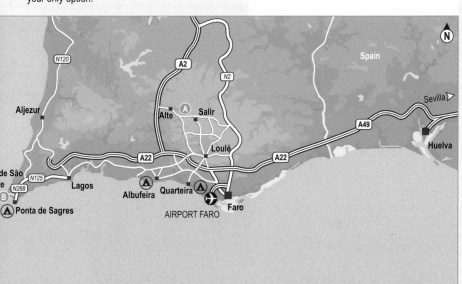

Ricardo Belchior on Pujanca (7a+)

How to get to the area & how to move around

You are better off with a car here so consider renting one, at least for a few days, to get you to the crags and back.

 By public transport

If you book a package deal then your airport transfer (most likely Faro) to your hotel or apartment will have been arranged, and you don't have to worry any further. If you're coming from Lisbon you can either take a train or a bus to the Algarve.

Bar das Grutas at Rocha da Pena

A train from Lisbon to Faro costs between €19.5 and €26 on an Alfa Pendular train and from €18 to €23.5 on an InterCity. Check the timetables (*www. cp.pt*). Coming from Lisbon on the bus is more straightforward. The bus company Rede Expressos runs about 12 buses daily to Quarteira [3½ h, €17.50] and 6 daily to Albufeira [2¾h, 17.50]. For timetables see *www.rede-expressos.pt*. Eva Buses run services too (*www.eva-bus.net*).

For Sagres from Lisbon you're best taking one of the frequent buses to Lagos [3¾h, €17.50] and then another bus from Lagos to Sagres [1h].

 By car

From Lisbon it is 277km to Quarteira, 261km to Albufeira, and 283km to Sagres. From Faro to Quarteira it is 20km, to Albufeira 45km, and to Sagres 118km. Clearly you can also combine the Algarve with Southern Spain. The distance from Malaga to Faro is 410km, for example.

Car rental is best arranged at Faro or Lisbon airports.

Where to stay

Quarteira, originally a quiet little fishing village, has metamorphosed into a fully-fledged tourist resort and has thus lost all of its charm. The same goes for Albufeira. Nevertheless those with families and interests other than pure climbing will have a wonderful time here. For Rocha da Pena one of these two places will be your best base. If you are not on a package deal there are several campsites along the coast.

It is also possible to camp wild near the Rocha da Pena. Ask the owner of the "Bar das Grutas" down in the valley below the crags for permission, as he owns the land. He will let you camp for free with the expectation that you'll provide him some business in his bar.

Down towards Sagres there is a good campsite close to two of the best beach breaks in Europe, Tonel and Beliche and close to the many sea cliffs suitable for climbing.

Guincho beach

Camping Orbitur Quarteira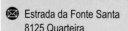

✉ Estrada da Fonte Santa
  8125 Quarteira
☎ +351 289302826
@ info@orbitur.pt
🖱 www.orbitur.pt

📱 N 37°04'02,0 W 08°05'13,2

Open   Year round

Grade   1 ——— 2 ——— 3 ■■■ 4

Price   €11.70/€21.50 (low/high season)
       for 2 persons, a tent and a car

This huge campsite has a restaurant, bar, disco, playground, tennis courts, and a small supermarket. The beach is only 600m away. There are also bungalows for rent.

Directions:
Head to Quarteira and then take the main road (with the sea on your right) towards Faro. The campsite is about 2km from the centre of Quarteira.

Camping Albufeira

✉ Estrada das Ferreiras
  8200-555 Albufeira
☎ + 351 289587629
@ campingalbufeira@mail.telepac.pt

📱 N 37°10'63,9 W 08°25'36,1

Open   Year round

Grade   1 ——— 2 ——— 3 ■■■ 4

Price   €14.50/€26.50 (low/high season)
       for 2 persons, a tent and a car

This is quite a large and luxurious campsite with all facilities you would need - it even has a swimming pool. It is a bit further from Rocha da Pena than the Quarteira campsite.

Directions:
The campsite is 1.5km away from Albufeira and 5km from Oura. On the N125 turn towards Ferreiras. From here head towards Albufeira. The campsite is 3km further on the left.

Old canon at the Fortaleza de Sagres

Bar Dromedario in Sagres

Campsite Sagres

⊠ E.N.268 Cerro das Moitas
Sagres 8650

☎ +351 282624371

Open Year round

Grade 1   2   3   4

Price €9.80/€17.60 (low/high season)
for 2 persons, a tent and a car

This is a basic but pleasant campsite that also rents bikes. Bring a solid tent - the wind blows hard here!

Directions:
From Sagres drive in the direction of Cabo de São Vicente. The campsite is well signposted.

Where to buy groceries?

Each town has a good range of supermarkets and groceries. All campsites have small supermarkets too.

Where to find the local climbing guidebook

For Rocha da Pena the best guide is the Jingo Wobbly one or get information from internet before arrival. The pleasant Dromedário Bar in the centre of Sagres (Avenida Comandante Matoso) keeps a book with detailed information on the sport, trad and DWS routes.

What else is there to see & do

Explore the traditional Algarve
Loulé is the Algarve's largest inland town and most interesting to visit on a Saturday morning when the market is in full swing. In the back streets you will come across dimly-lit workshops with traditional craftsmen working with copper and brass, leather, and wood. Alte, quite near Rocha da Pena, is a picturesque traditional village with a fine church and nice spots for a picnic. The surrounding area is also good walking country with panoramic views from the surrounding hills.

Rocha da Pena itself is also a famous hiking area and is well known for its indigenous plants and wildlife. There's a good trail of approximately 4.7km (which should take you 2½ hours) that enables you to see some interesting aspects of the flora, fauna and geology as well as to enjoy the magnificent landscape.

Water sports
Water sports are naturally big in this region. Sailing, jet skiing, paragliding, scuba-diving, snorkelling, water-skiing, and windsurfing are on offer all along the coast. Near Sagres you'll find two of the best beach breaks in Europe: Tonel and Beliche.

The beautiful coastline of the Algarve

Rocha da Pena

Rocha da Pena is a long ridge of some 2km in length 19km north of Loulé, close to Salir. It has many different sectors. The rock structure is really varied and every sector offers something completely different - from highly pocketed red limestone to tiny sharp holds on compact grey limestone. All sectors face south so climbing in summer during the day is not possible, though early morning and late afternoon can be bearable. In the morning, head to the sectors at the left end to catch the shade. In the early evening you may be lucky and catch some refreshing wind.

There's not much flat ground at the base of the crag, so it's not really a place to bring young children.

View from Rocha da Pena

Directions

▶ Rocha da Pena is 37km from the campsite in Quarteira. First go to Loulé and from there follow the signs to Salir. In Salir follow the signs for Alte until you see the signs for Rocha da Pena.

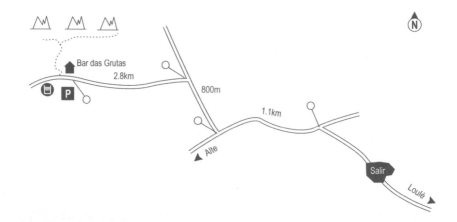

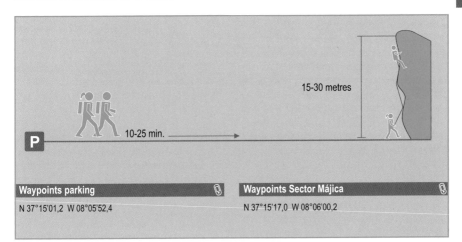

Waypoints parking	Waypoints Sector Májica
N 37°15'01,2 W 08°05'52,4	N 37°15'17,0 W 08°06'00,2

15-30 metres

10-25 min.

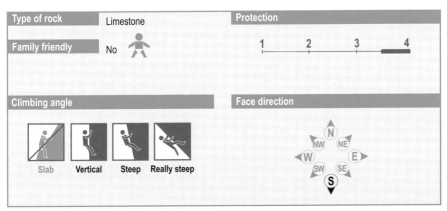

Type of rock — Limestone

Family friendly — No

Protection — 1 2 3 4

Climbing angle — Slab · Vertical · Steep · Really steep

Face direction — N NW NE W E SW SE S

Number of routes & Grade range

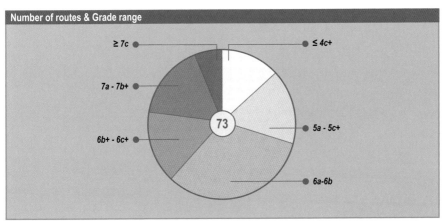

≥ 7c

7a - 7b+

6b+ - 6c+

73

≤ 4c+

5a - 5c+

6a-6b

DWS

This is the place for those who like adventure! The area around Sagres and Cape St Vincent contains a wealth of big limestone cliffs towering above the Atlantic. The setting is great, the limestone is pretty ok, and the weather is always sunny, however the big downside of this area is the fishermen. They don't like you climbing anywhere near them and they (but also other people) don't believe in taking rubbish (including broken glass bottles) home. Even so, to avoid problems, please remember that the fishermen were here first.

There is a comprehensive logbook located in the Dromedario Bar in Sagres with route descriptions (Avenida Comandante Matoso, waypoints N 37°00' 30,0 W 08°56'17,8). It cannot be taken from the bar so bring a pen and paper.

The vast majority of the routes are trad - over 600 routes - but more and more bolted routes are now being developed too. Additionally there is also some fantastic deep water soloing at the Fossil Cave and Covo del Garcia. Most routes finish at an acceptable height above the sea. A water proof bag is needed to gain access to some of the routes. Climbing is possible at low and high tide. There are 37 sport routes described in the topo that is available at the Dromedario Bar. The easiest are 6a/6b but there are only three at this grade. The rest are 6b+ and higher with 23 routes at 7a or higher.

Most trad routes are at the Fortaleza of Sagres. This old fort is nothing fancy and after entering you will only find the remnants of the walls and an old church. Entrance to the fort costs €1.50 per person which you do have to pay every time you go climbing. A standard rack suffices for the trad routes. You have to abseil to get to the start of the routes.

The best sport climbing is found at Armação Nova, with 37 routes of which 8 are in the 6a/6b range, 9 are around 6c, and the rest are 7a or harder. Some routes can be reached by abseiling down and can be belayed from the ground though most routes have the open sea beneath them.

Armação Nova

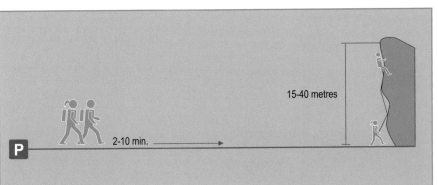

15-40 metres

2-10 min.

Type of rock

Limestone

Family friendly

No, the area is family friendly but you'd better not take your kids climbing with you!

Protection

1 2 3 4

This ony applies to the sport routes.
The fixed protection on the trad routes varies.
Always take a full rack.

Climbing angle

Slab **Vertical** **Steep** Really steep

Face direction

N
NW NE
W E
SW SE
S

Number of routes & Grade range

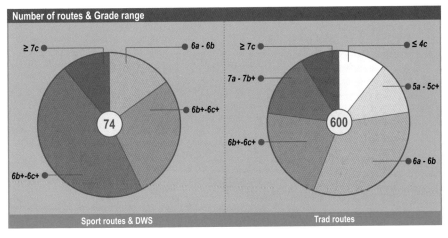

≥ 7c   ● 6a - 6b

● 6b+-6c+

74

6b+-6c+ ●

Sport routes & DWS

≥ 7c ●   ● ≤ 4c

7a - 7b+ ●

● 5a - 5c+

600

6b+-6c+ ●

● 6a - 6b

Trad routes

Sea cliffs at Sagres

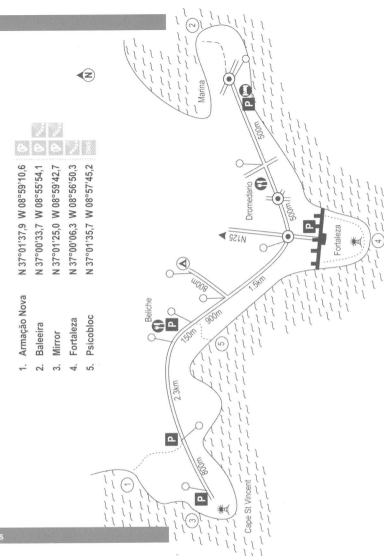

1.	Armação Nova	N 37°01'37,9 W 08°59'10,6
2.	Baleeira	N 37°00'33,7 W 08°55'54,1
3.	Mirror	N 37°01'25,0 W 08°59'42,7
4.	Fortaleza	N 37°00'06,3 W 08°56'50,3
5.	Psicobloc	N 37°01'35,7 W 08°57'45,2

Directions

▶ *Directions Armação Nova*
There's car parking about 800 metres before the lighthouse at Cape St Vincent.

▶ *Directions Baleeira*
Head towards the small harbour and park either at Aparthotel Orguidem or continue on the dirt track by car to the end.

▶ *Directions Mirror*
Park your car at the lighthouse at Cape St Vincent.

▶ *Directions Fortaleza*
Park at the big car park for the fort and walk from there.

▶ *Directions Psicobloc (Fossil Cave and Covo del Garcia)*
Park 150m at a lay-by before restaurant Beliche. A dirt track leads to a gulley with a descent ramp. Facing out to sea the Fossil Cave is on your right and Covo del Garcia on your left.

...where climbing is a true passion...

Spain

Youri van Vliet on the spectacular Dosis (8b+) at Sella, photo by Paul Lahaye

It is easy to get to with plenty of cheap flights and accommodation, it has great weather in winter, fantastic scenery with a stunning rural countryside, and a great coastline, but above all it is the ultimate playground for climbers. Spain has so much rock you'll need a few lifetimes to see it all - no matter where you choose to go, the experience will be unforgettable!

This is the country of passionate Flamenco, bullfights, tapas, Las Ramblas, Picasso, and Gaudí. Spain has an incredible history which is reflected in its many palaces, ruins, and cathedrals. Spain's cultural uniqueness is rooted in its history - the Spanish nation was made up of a conglomeration of separate kingdoms, each bringing their own flavour to the pot. Over the past few decades Spain has become well loved by foreigners whom come to admire its great cities, gorgeous coast line, and beautiful landscape. And, of course, to appreciate the Jamón and the culture!

Its rugged landscape is packed with top quality climbing areas. The climbing is extremely diverse and you'll be hard pressed to find a climbing style that isn't represented here - granite slabs, long multi pitches, tufa-and-stalactite fests, trad climbs, long cracks, huge roofs, fingery vertical walls... we could go on and on! The crags are beautifully situated and the ambience is always super relaxed. A trip to Spain in winter is ideal for those who long to get away from the inhospitable winters of Northern Europe, which hinders climbing activity so much. But also there are venues that are suitable in summer. Whatever your choice, flights are cheap year round and the accommodation options are endless and, outside the high tourist season, very reasonably priced. Many areas even have a typically relaxed climbers campsite with bungalows, which really adds to the holiday feeling. Yes, Spain is definitely one of those countries that make you want to come back to over and over again.

Climbing information

Climbing is possible almost everywhere in Spain - from the Pyrenees to the Canary Islands and from the Mediterranean to the North Atlantic coastline. Actually it sometimes feels as if the whole country is made out of rock and despite there being hundreds of developed crags there seems to be unlimited rock waiting to be climbed. The Spanish themselves are, unsurprisingly, very able and strong climbers - have a look at the world sport climbing ranking list of the UIAA!

Most of the rock is good quality limestone but there is also granite and conglomerate to be found. In general the routes are always very well bolted and have good lower-offs, which makes it a perfect place to try harder stuff and push your limits with confidence.

Since Spain has so many climbing areas it is an almost impossible task to choose the best. Nevertheless we have tried to give an overview of, in our opinion, the most interesting and unique areas.

Climbing area Pre-Pyrenees

In the north the foothills of the Pyrenees host a number of impressive crags. Not far away from the French border, Riglos and Rodellar, both have some fantastic climbing. Riglos is exceptional for its huge red-coloured conglomerate pillars. Rodellar is without doubt one of the best sport climbing destinations in Europe.

Climbing area Madrid

The best crags around Madrid, La Pedriza and Patones, are situated north of the capital. Each offers a completely different style of climbing - from pure slab climbing to technical moves on steep and overhanging rock! It is a great opportunity to combine good climbing with a visit to Madrid.

Climbing area Malaga

Malaga is home to the world famous El Chorro. This fantastic place offers all a climber could dream for! The setting in a deep gorge is simply stunning and the climbing is tremendous. Another fabulous nearby crag, Desplomilandia, makes your whole trip complete.

Climbing area Costa Blanca

The Costa Blanca is mainly known for its beautiful coast line with the most stable winter weather in Spain. It also has some very nice crags, such as Sella, Sierra de Toix, and Gandia.

Climbing area València

Hidden away about a two hour drive inland from València is the best bouldering destination in Spain. Some even say that Albarracin is only second in Europe after Fontainebleau for bouldering. Closer to València you'll find Montanejos, with a large number of sport and traditional routes where one can happily spend a few months.

Climbing area Costa Daurada

South west of Barcelona are two supreme crags - Siurana and Montsant. This is one of the cheapest and easiest to reach destinations in Spain, favoured by many. Siurana is already widely known for its fantastic limestone and incredibly chilled atmosphere. Nearby Montsant is still a secret to some but is also on its way to becoming one of Spain's top venues.

Climbing area Mallorca

The island of Mallorca situated in the Mediterranean Sea provides truly excellent rock climbing in beautiful surroundings. It is a good choice for both families and hard rock climbers, and for those who enjoy good nightlife. It also has fantastic deep water solo possibilities.

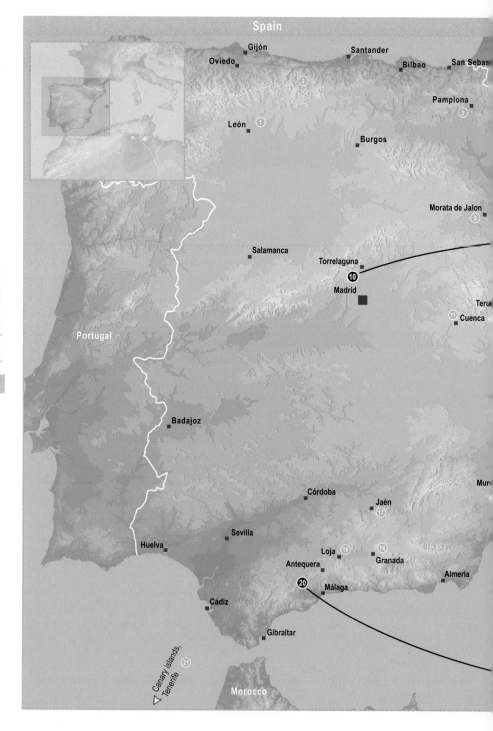

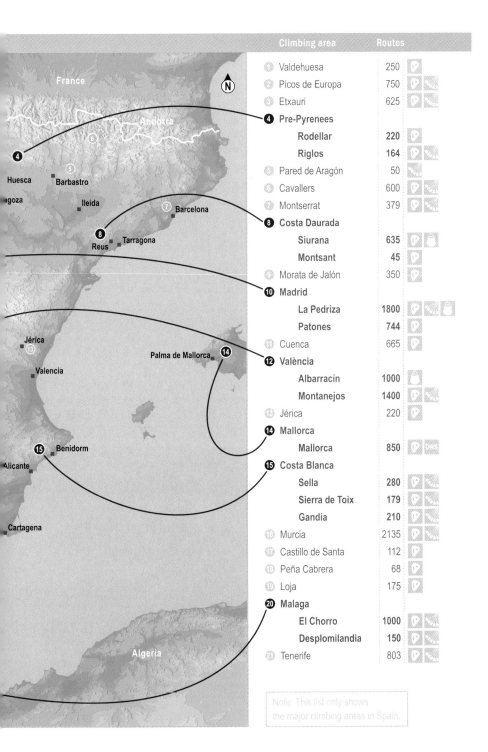

Climbing area	Routes	
① Valdehuesa	250	
② Picos de Europa	750	
③ Etxauri	625	
❹ Pre-Pyrenees		
Rodellar	220	
Riglos	164	
⑤ Pared de Aragón	50	
⑥ Cavallers	600	
⑦ Montserrat	379	
❽ Costa Daurada		
Siurana	635	
Montsant	45	
⑨ Morata de Jalón	350	
❿ Madrid		
La Pedriza	1800	
Patones	744	
⑪ Cuenca	665	
⓬ València		
Albarracín	1000	
Montanejos	1400	
⑬ Jérica	220	
⓮ Mallorca		
Mallorca	850	
⓯ Costa Blanca		
Sella	280	
Sierra de Toix	179	
Gandia	210	
⑯ Murcia	2135	
⑰ Castillo de Santa	112	
⑱ Peña Cabrera	68	
⑲ Loja	175	
⓴ Malaga		
El Chorro	1000	
Desplomilandia	150	
㉑ Tenerife	803	

Note: This list only shows the major climbing areas in Spain.

Climate

Spain can be unbearable hot in high summer. During the months of July and August most visitors either stay up high, in any of its mountain ranges, or along the coast, where the water provides some refreshment. Roughly speaking the north is quite a bit cooler than the south for the rest of the year. The higher regions, such as the Pyrenees and Madrid, can get very cold during winter.

The best time to go climbing is during spring and autumn. However climbing along the south and the east coasts in winter can be really pleasant - Spain is, not without reason, a highly favoured winter climbing destination for Northern Europeans. The worst time for climbing generally is July and August but there are still crags that are suitable.

Month	Average temperature (°C)	Average rainfall (mm)
Jan	6	35
Feb	7	37
March	10	39
April	12	44
May	15	43
June	21	31
July	24	11
Aug	25	11
Sept	21	34
Oct	14	47
Nov	9	52
Dec	6	44

Climate table Madrid

The average temperatures along the Mediterranean coast are a few degrees higher from October to May.

Getting there

 By plane

A large number of budget airlines operate flights between numerous European cities and several different Spanish destinations. Amongst them are Ryanair, Easyjet, Thomsonfly, BmiBaby, Air Berlin, TUIfly, Transavia and Vueling.

For the Pre-Pyrenees area the quickest way there is to fly to Zaragoza but the best deals are often found to Barcelona. For the crags around Madrid it is naturally best to fly to Madrid. For El Chorro fly to Malaga. Alicante is the cheapest and quickest for any of the crags on the Costa Blanca. For the bouldering at Albarracin or the sport climbing at Montanejos fly to València. Book a flight to Barcelona if you are heading for the Costa Daurada and when going to Mallorca, Palma de Mallorca is your place.

If you're coming from the USA or Canada it often is cheaper to fly to some European cities outside Spain, such as London, Dusseldorf, or Amsterdam. From any of these cities hop on one of the low cost airlines operating flights to a number of Spanish cities. If you choose to fly directly either Iberia or British Airways is a good starting point for your search. Iberia now offers round trips from $512 between Madrid and several cities in the USA.

 By train

Spain is well connected by train from many other European countries. An excellent website to start your search is: www.reiseauskunft.bahn.de. Check the prices carefully as plane tickets often are a cheaper and quicker alternative of getting there. The

Spain offers some fantastic sea cliff climbing - here at the Costa Blanca, Sierra de Toix

Spanish national railways website *www.renfe.es* gives information on train schedules within Spain and some international destinations. If you're travelling a lot by rail, a rail pass might work out cheaper, especially if you are a student - *www.inter-railnet.com* provides all information.

 By bus

Travelling to Spain by bus is still popular although mostly only with younger people. Madrid, and the cities along the coast - Barcelona, Alicante, and València - are all popular destinations. Start searching at *www.eurolines.com*.

 By car

Spain is a long drive from most other European countries but if time is on your side then it is a very worthwhile drive. The drive from France into Spain through the Pyrenees is very pleasant indeed, especially if you take any of the smaller roads like the D929 / A138 via the Bielsa tunnel.

Moving around

For most areas mentioned in this chapter you'll really need to have a car to move around with the exception of La Pedriza, Montanejos, Siurana and El Chorro.

 Airport information

All Spanish airports are modern and well organized, and it goes without saying that all national and international car rental agencies are always located in the arrivals hall. Transport from the airport to the city centre is generally by bus.

 By public transport

Spain has an extensive bus and train network and it is usually possible to take a train or bus to the nearest city. However your own wheels still

Paddy Clarke enjoys evening sunshine on Yellow Arrete (6b), El Chorro, photo by Eoin Lawless

come in handy to get from the bus station to your accommodation or campsite. A lot of climbers also choose to hitch a ride for this last bit. The national railway company in Spain is called Renfe and their website *www.renfe.es* gives train information.

 By car

The road conditions in Spain are generally good with clear road signs. Most roads are toll free except for several highways along the coast.

Cars can be rented easily at the airports. The best deals are found on Mallorca where daily rates can go rock bottom at €20 for the smallest class and unlimited mileage. On the mainland rates usually start at €30 per day and €175 per week. Make sure you book ahead on the internet as this is almost always cheaper than arranging a car on the spot.

Soak up the tranquil atmosphere of the Costa Blanca, photo by Paul Lahaye

Accommodation

Spain has a wide range of accommodation. There are plenty of campsites, mountain huts, farm houses (called fincas), hotels, and apartments. Camping prices range from €10 to €20 per night for 2 persons, a car and a tent. Budget hotels usually start at €35 for a double room. The months of July and August are high season in Spain and prices easily go up 25% compared to low season.

Food & drinks

The Spanish cuisine is deeply influenced by the different cultures that have passed through the Iberian Peninsula - from the Romans to Moors. One of the best ways to sample Spanish food is to try tapas which are served at any time of day in local bars. A tapa literally translates as a lid or a cap - traditionally, a tapa was a free snack (hot or cold) served on a small plate on top of your glass when ordering a drink in a bar. Nowadays, tapas are generally ordered separately and most bars have a wide range available, so it's possible to eat a full meal this way. Many Spanish people make an evening of going from bar to bar drinking Spanish wine or beer (cerveza) and trying different tapas. Certain bars specialise in, and have reputations among the locals for particularly good, say, seafood or cured

A typical old Spanish village

meat tapas – have a look around and order what the locals are eating, and you'll have a great time!

Many of the specialties of Spanish cuisine are based on seafood, although regional specialties are easier to find inland than along the coast. Also the Spanish paella has a well-deserved reputation. It can be prepared in many ways, based on meat or seafood. Eating out in Spain is still relatively cheap, however prices along Las Ramblas in Barcelona are outrageous compared to what you would pay in those small charming cities which you'll pass through on your way to the rocks. Here a good meal with a beer would cost you something like €15. A cappuccino shouldn't cost more than €2 and the same goes for a good glass of beer. For lunch, a Bocadillo is the way to go, which is a large filled sandwich - virtually all bars and bakeries will prepare you one fresh in the morning and wrap it up to take away (para llevar) for €2-€3.

Spain has convenient large shopping centres. These clusters of shops are often located along the highway and signposted as 'zona commercial'. These have huge supermarkets such as 'Carrefour'

One of Mallorca's beautiful coves

where you can get all you need in one place. Prices are comparable to Western Europe though fruits and vegetables will mostly be cheaper.

Climbing guidebook

Guidebooks exist of all the areas described in this chapter. See the 'Where to find the local climbing guidebook' section for each area for more details.

A beautiful lake not far away from El Chorro

The old part of Albarracín

Facts about Spain

Facts & figures

Population:	45 million
Religion:	Roman Catholicism
Capital:	Madrid
Time zone:	GMT +1
Telephone code:	+34

Money

Currency:	Euro (€)
ATM machines:	widespread

Language

Goodmorning	*Hola / Buenos Dias*
Thank you	*Gracias*
Goodbye	*Hasta luego / Adios*
Yes / No	*Si / No*
Right / Left / Straight	*Derrecha / Izquirda / Todo recto*
Rock climbing	*Escalar*

Visas & formalities

EU	*Other European nationalities*	*USA / Canada*	*All other nationalities*
No visa required.	No visa required for a period of up to 90 days.		Most other nationalities do not require a visa for a period of up to 90 days.

Safety

Spain is a safe country to spend a holiday. Take the normal precautions when parking your car and don't leave any valuables inside.

Use of mobile phone

There is wide GSM coverage although some of the crags which are located in National Parks have limited or no network availability.

Internet access

Internet cafés are spread throughout the country. Prices range from €1 to €4 per hour.

Emergency numbers

General:	112

Water

Always check if you can drink the local water from the tap. It usually is ok although it often tastes bad. A 1½ litre bottle of mineral water costs around €0.50.

Climbing area Pre-Pyrenees

Spring   Summer   Autumn   Winter

The Pyrenees form a natural border between France and Spain and, whether it is for hiking, mountain biking, climbing, skiing, canyoning, or simply the desire for adventure, it is a very popular destination for those who love the outdoors. As well as a huge range of outdoor activities, this beautiful mountain range also features many picturesque mountain villages that form a great base for a holiday.

It shouldn't surprise you then that the Pyrenees are host to a wide variety of crags but two of them, Rodellar and Riglos, are certainly the pick of the bunch. Both are situated in the foothills of the Pyrenees in Aragón, one of the seventeen Spain provinces. They are not too far from the French border and this makes them easily accessible by car from much of North western Europe.

The limestone paradise of Rodellar lies deep in the Sierra de Guara and it is an absolute heaven for strong climbers. It boasts incredible rock features with a multitude of huge overhanging caves, arches, roofs, tufas, and pinnacles. All the routes require a good dose of power and you will enjoy it most if you lead 6b at the very least. The very small village of Rodellar is located at the end of a 30km road and lies in one of the least inhabited areas of Spain. Only two of the houses are occupied throughout the whole year and most visitors here are either climbers or hikers, or come for the canyoning.

Riglos is a totally different place. At first sight, Riglos is pretty overwhelming as the huge red coloured pillars behind the picturesque village dominate the whole scene. The place offers both sport

Riglos

and traditional climbing but we've got to say that climbing here requires a special style since the rock is conglomerate.

There are almost 500 routes at both venues combined which is more than enough to spend weeks in this fantastic area.

Crag

Ⓐ Rodellar

Ⓑ Riglos

When to go

The best months for climbing are March, April, May, September and October. The summers are boiling hot and winter it is too cold.

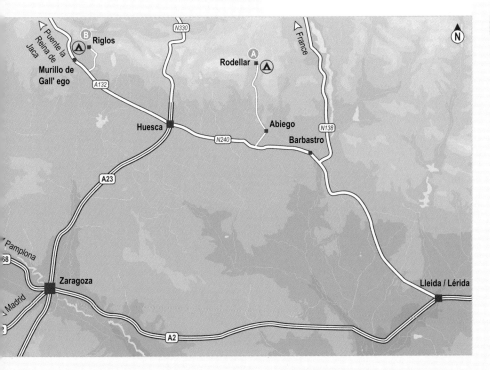

How to get to the area & how to move around

You will need your own wheels. Although Riglos can be reached directly by public transport from Madrid and Barcelona, you still need a car to get to the campsite and from there to the crags. You definitely need a car to get to Rodellar - there are no buses - but once at the campsite you can walk to the crags.

Rodellar and Riglos lie 105km away from each other.

 By public transport

Even though the closest airport is Zaragoza, it is better to fly to Barcelona or Madrid as this is much cheaper. Car rental is possible at these airports.

If you plan to hitchhike to Rodellar you should start by taking the daily bus between Barcelona and Huesca [4h20, €15.20] and hitch from there. Services in Barcelona leave from the main bus station, named Estació del Nord (Carrer d'Ali-Bei 80).

 By car from Toulouse in France

Coming from Toulouse in France take exit 16 on the E80 / A64 to Spain via the Tunnel de Bielsa. Continue towards Huesca.

 By car from Barcelona

From Barcelona take the A2 to Lleida. Take exit 458 at Lleida which is the N240 to Huesca.

Be aware that there is no petrol station in Rodellar. Make sure you fill up your car before leaving the N240.

Where to stay

There are two campsites in Rodellar which both offer bungalows for rent too. Riglos doesn't have any campsites in the village itself but there are two located relatively close although these are still too far away to walk to the crags.

The campsites in Rodellar are the most family friendly.

View from Riglos

Sector Delfin at Rodellar

Rodellar

Camping Mascún

- 22144 Rodellar
- +34 974 318367
- camping@guara-mascun.com
- www.campingmascun.com

N 42°16'54,5 W 00°04'29,8

Open	April - end October

Grade 1 — 2 — **3** — 4

Price €18 for 2 people, a tent and a car; bungalows (4 to 6 people) are €65 - €85 per night

Many climbers stay at this campsite. It has a restaurant, bar and a small shop. There is also internet access. The owners rent bungalows for up to 6 people. The bathrooms are reasonably clean.

Directions:
The campsite lies on the right side of the road just before you enter Rodellar. It is very conveniently located for the Mascún Valley.

Camping El Puente

- 22144 Rodellar
- +34 974 318312
- Info@campingelpuente.com
- www.campingelpuente.com

N 42°16'14,6 W 00°04'48,3

Open	April - end October

Grade 1 — 2 — **3** — 4

Price €18 for 2 people, a tent and a car; bungalows for up to 6 people are €61 - €78

The campsite has the same facilities as Camping Mascún but the bungalows are of better quality for a lower price.

Directions:
The campsite lies 2km before Rodellar and is well signed.

Rodellar is pleasantly quiet in the low season

Riglos

Camping Armalygal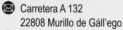

✉ Carretera A 132
  22808 Murillo de Gáll'ego
☎ +34 974 383005
@ welcome@armalygal.com
🌐 www.armalygal.com

🧭 N 42°20'05,9 W 00°44'41,1

Open End March - October

Grade 1 — 2 — **3** — 4

Price €16.40 for 2 people, a tent and a car

A pretty campsite with a beautiful view of the Riglos pillars from its swimming pool. It has a restaurant but dinners are only served on request. Clean bathrooms.

Directions:
You'll find signs for the campsite in Murillo de Gáll'ego - it is 11km away from Riglos. It is the closest campsite to the climbing of the ones around.

Casa Escaleretas

✉ C/ La Iglesia 3
☎ 22808 Riglos
@ +34 974 383096
🌐 isabel_ubiergo@hotmail.com

🧭 N 42°20'54,3 W 00°43'34,2

Open March - December

Price Double room without breakfast €45

The pension is situated right in the middle of Riglos and it is a nice place to stay for those wanting a bit more comfort.

Directions:
The pension is signposted within the village.

Camping Armalygal at Riglos

Camping La Banera

✉ 22800 Ayerbe
☎ +34 974 380242
@ labanera@wanadoo.es
🌐 http://labanera.turincon.com

🧭 N 42°16'52,6 W 00°40'30,5

Open Year round

Grade 1 — 2 — **3** — 4

Price €11.30 for 2 people, a tent and a car

A quiet campsite outside La Banera. It has a restaurant and clean bathrooms.

Directions:
Drive towards Ayerbe which lies along the A132. In the village take the turn to Loarre. The campsite lies on the right side of the road after 1km.

Small village in the Pre-Pyrenees

Where to buy groceries?

There are no shops in Rodellar although the campsites there have small shops. There is nothing in the village itself. In Riglos there is a small shop that only offers the very basics. Therefore make sure you do your shopping on your way in Huesca or any of the larger villages around.

Where to find the local climbing guidebook

The topo for Rodellar is sold at both campsites there (€17). It gives a good overview of the whole climbing scene. It's only drawback is the quality of the drawings, which are not always very clear and can make it difficult to find the right route.

The topo for Riglos is sold at the very first shop, named La Francesa, on the left side of the street when you get to the village (€20).

What else is there to see & do

Canyoning
Rodellar was originally unearthed for canyoning reasons and the valleys are now known worldwide among canyoning enthusiasts. Both campsites in Rodellar can provide information on canyoning and they sell guidebooks.

Hiking
The National Park La Sierra y de los Cañones de Guarra at Rodellar has many marked hiking trails. Another more popular destination for hikers is the National Park of Ordesa, north of Rodellar and Riglos, close to the French border. It is a 2 hour drive from Riglos and 1 hour more from Rodellar. A one day trip wouldn't really do the place justice but a couple of days hiking are certainly worthwhile, and is easily combined with a few days of climbing. Head to Torla on the N260 where many trails start.

The Mascún valley in Rodellar

Right behind Rodellar one descends into the Mascún valley, which is the central and most developed of the three valleys around. The valley mainly has bolted single pitch routes although there are also a few longer ones up to 260 metres in length. However most of the multi pitch routes can't be climbed from December 1st to June 1st due to the birds breeding restrictions.

The typical style of climbing is on overhanging rock where strong arms and stamina are your best friends. Many routes are very hard and demanding, and the majority are in the 7th and 8th grade. Most of the sectors in the Mascún valley are situated either on the west or on the east side which makes climbing possible all day long. The dominating Sector 'Gran Bóveda' is a real must if you feel really strong and like tufas. It has 7th and 8th grade challenges up to 40 metres. Come here in the afternoon as it faces east. If you like slopers head for Sector 'El Camino' which faces west

Sector El Camino

and has shorter 6th and 7th grade routes. Roof climbing takes centre stage at Sector Ventanas Del Mascún. Some of the sectors, such as 'El Camino', are unfortunately starting to get polished as the number of climbers visiting Rodellar keeps on growing. Despite this we are confident that Rodellar will keep on being one of the jewels of Spain for a very long time!

Sector Gran Boveda

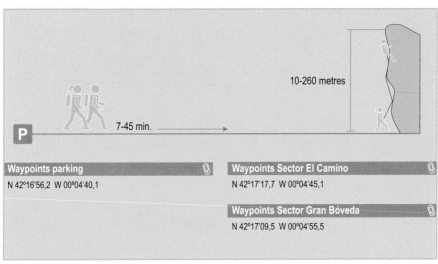

10-260 metres

7-45 min.

P

Waypoints parking

N 42°16'56,2 W 00°04'40,1

Waypoints Sector El Camino

N 42°17'17,7 W 00°04'45,1

Waypoints Sector Gran Bóveda

N 42°17'09,5 W 00°04'55,5

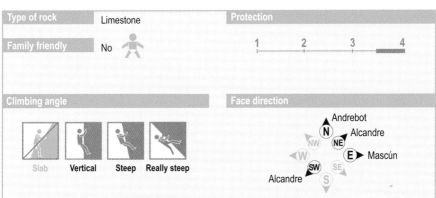

Type of rock	Limestone

Protection

1 2 3 4

Family friendly	No

Climbing angle

Slab **Vertical** **Steep** **Really steep**

Face direction

Andrebot
N Alcandre
NW NE
W E ▶ Mascún
SW SE
Alcandre S

Number of routes & Grade range

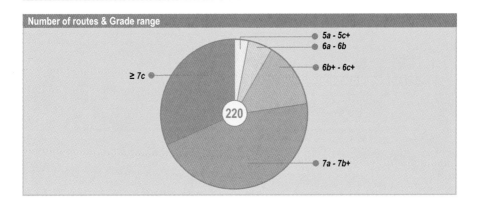

- 5a - 5c+
- 6a - 6b
- 6b+ - 6c+
- ≥ 7c
- 220
- 7a - 7b+

Cranking through the slopers at Sector El Camino

A.Camping Mascun
B.Camping El Puente

1.Andrebot Valley
2.Mascun Valley
3.Alcanadre Valley

Directions

Signpost in the Parque de la Sierra y de los Canones de Guara

► Coming from Huesca follow the N240 towards Barbastro. Leave the N240 after Angüés towards Abiego and continue all the way to the end and Rodellar. From Huesca it is 63km to Rodellar. If you're coming from Barbastro leave the N240 for Abiego after Lascellas.

Water is available from a fountain on the main square in the village. There is also a pay phone as there is no GSM coverage.

The beauty of the setting in which the climbing of Riglos takes place is indisputable. The group of pillars, of which 'El Pisón' dominates the lot, are simply enormous - a sight which is hard to find anywhere else in Europe. However whether you will like the style of climbing here is questionable. The conglomerate type of rock means that most parts of the walls are anything but smooth: there are numerous smaller pebbles and larger stones, known locally as patatas, sticking out. This type of rock surely has to suit you well to really enjoy the climbing here. Most of the work is done on vertical and slightly overhanging rock.

The routes on the pillars go up to 300 metres in length and both sport and traditional climbing is found here. Even though the sport routes are well bolted, always bring trad gear as some sections can be really exposed. Two 60m ropes are sufficient and always wear a helmet as parts of the rock can come off. Also take plenty of water - these extra kilograms will not be redundant as the routes are south facing (think of it as a training aid!). Don't miss out of the four star classics Carnavalada (7a/b) and Alberto Rabadá o Murciana (6c) on El Pisón!

Riglos's conglomerate rocks

Climbing on El Pison

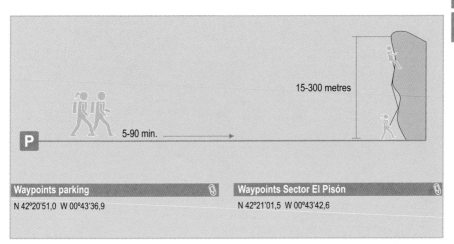

15-300 metres

5-90 min.

P

Waypoints parking

N 42°20'51,0 W 00°43'36,9

Waypoints Sector El Pisón

N 42°21'01,5 W 00°43'42,6

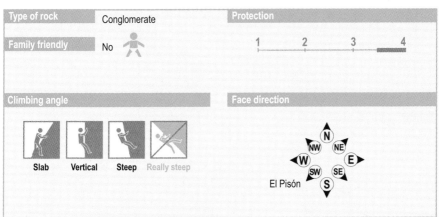

Type of rock Conglomerate

Family friendly No

Protection

1   2   3   4

Climbing angle

Slab   Vertical   Steep   Really steep

Face direction

N
NW NE
W   E
SW SE
El Pisón   S

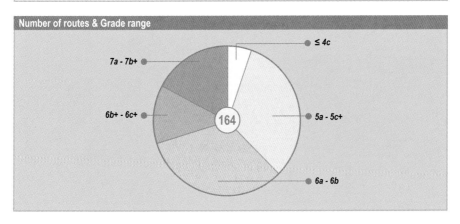

Number of routes & Grade range

164

≤ 4c
7a - 7b+
6b+ - 6c+
5a - 5c+
6a - 6b

Riglos village

Riglos

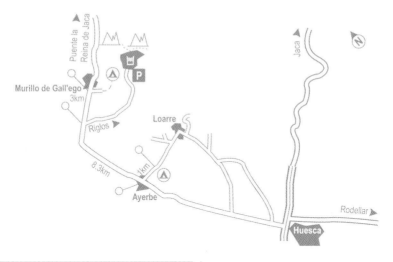

El Pison

▶ *By car*
From Huesca follow the A132 towards Ayerbe. Continue on the same road. Riglos is well signposted. It is 42km from Huesca to Riglos.

▶ *By bus*
There are bus services between the central bus station of Huesca (Calle Cavia 8) and Riglos.

Water is available from the fountain in the village.

Climbing area Madrid

In the heart of Spain lies the lively capital of Madrid characterized by intense cultural and artistic activity. Madrid has become one of the most important cities of Europe and each year a large flow of tourists find their way here to explore its historical buildings, famous museums, and vibrant night life.

Spring   Summer   **Autumn**   Winter

Not far away from bustling Madrid to the north, you'll find two excellent climbing venues, La Pedriza and Patones. Both are beautifully situated and very unique. La Pedriza is located in the 'Parque Regional de la Cuenca Alta del Manzanares', close to the village of Manzanares El Real, and offers a huge amount of granite climbing in an area of thirty square kilometres. Mind you, almost all of it is slab climbing! The other crag, Patones, lies east of La Pedriza. The different sectors are located around the village of Torrelaguña and are mainly bolted single pitch affairs on limestone, mostly in the 6th grade.

Altogether both venues offer over an incredible 2000 routes to choose from and, due to its proximity to Madrid, are easy to reach. You can even get to La Pedriza without a car making it perfectly combinable with a visit to Madrid!

When to go

Early spring and late autumn are the best periods to go. Winter is definitely too cold and summer way too hot.

Parque Regional de la Cuenca Alta del Manzanares

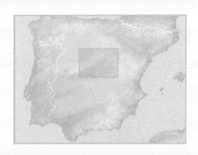

Crag

Ⓐ La Pedriza
Ⓑ Patones

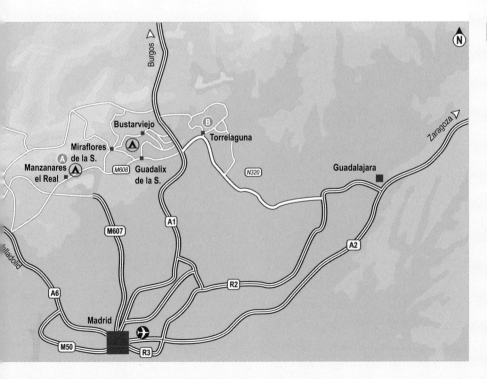

How to get to the area & how to move around

Madrid Barajas Airport is the most convenient one to fly to. You can get to La Pedriza by public transport from Madrid. Once at La Pedriza the campsite is near enough not to need a car. However you'll need a car to reach the different sectors of Patones. La Pedriza and Patones are a 45 minutes drive from each other.

🚌 By public to La Pedriza

Line 724 operates between Madrid and Manzanares El Real [50 min, €3]. The bus leaves the Plaza de Castilla bus station in Madrid and runs twice per hour from 7am onwards.

🚗 By car from Madrid

Coming from Madrid take the E5 in the direction of Burgos. Leave the motorway at exit number 50 either in the direction of Torrelaguña (for Patones) or Guadalix de la Sierra (for La Pedriza).

One of the very fingery and steep 8a's at Patones

Where to stay

There is one recommended campsite, El Ortigal, located close to La Pedriza. From here it is a few kilometres to the entrance of the park and a car is not a necessity. A few other campsites are dotted around between La Pedriza and Patones. From any of these it takes between 15 and 25 minutes to reach either crag. For families with children or for those after a slightly better campsite, Camping Piscis is recommended. It is also closer to Patones than El Ortigal.

There should also be a refugio (Refugio Giner de los Ríos) in the park at 1220m over the way from Prado Peluca and near Canto del Tolmo. It supposes to have food, water, light and 50 bunk beds and should be open at weekends including Fridays. At the time of research it was closed and we couldn't get in touch with the guardian to check this information.

Camping El Ortigal

✉ C/ Montañeros, 19
   28410 Manzanares el Real
📞 +34 91 8530120

📍 N 40°44'30,1 W 03°52'27,3

Open	Year round

Grade

1	2	3	4

Price   €23 for 2 people, a tent and a car

This campsite is in a convenient location for La Pedriza. It feels like a small village - most people rent their own small place here for a whole year. On the weekend you'll need to reserve a pitch because it gets very popular with the Madrileños.

Directions:
There are signs to the campsite in Manzanares el Real and it lies on the road that leads to the park entrance.

Camping D'Oremor

⊠ Cabanillas de la Sierra
  28721 Madrid
📞 +34 91 8439034
@ doremor@doremor.com
🌐 www.doremor.com

📍 N 40°49'15,7 W 03°38'14,4

Open   Year round

Grade   1 —— 2 —— 3 ▬▬ 4

Price   €18.80 for 2 people, a tent and a car;
          mobile home for €320 - €360 per week

A campsite with a small supermarket and a swimming pool. They also rent mobile homes for up to 6 people. This is one of the noisier campsites around and only recommended if the others are full.

Directions:
Coming from Madrid leave the E5 at exit 50 in the direction of Guadalix de la Sierra. Almost immediately, turn off the M608 in the direction of Cabanillas de la Sierra. The campsite is located on the left hand side.

Camping Valle

⊠ Bustarviejo
  28720 Madrid
📞 +34 91 8443587

📍 N 40°50'34,9 W 3°45'01,8

Open   Year round

Grade   1 —— 2 —— 3 ▬▬ 4

Price   €20 for 2 people, a tent and a car

This is an expensive campsite for the quality on offer. There are only a few spaces for tents.

Directions:
Coming from Madrid leave the E5 at exit 50 in the direction of Guadalix de la Sierra. Almost immediately, turn off the M608 in the direction of Cabanillas de la Sierra and continue on to Bustarviejo. The campsite lies between Bustarviejo and Miraflores de la Sierra.

Patones, Sector Ponton de Oliva East Side

Camping Piscis

✉ Navalafuente
28729 Madrid
📞 +34 91 8439034
@ campiscis@campiscis.com
🕐 www.campiscis.com

📱 N 40°48'30,1 W 03°41'28,0

Open	Year round

Grade 1 2 3 4

Price €21.40 for 2 people, a tent and a car;
€65 per night for a bungalow which
sleeps 2

*A very large campsite with tennis courts, swimming
pool, shop, and a restaurant. Bungalows and
mobile homes are also for rent. The best choice
for families.*

Directions:
Coming from Madrid leave the E5 at exit 50 in
the direction of Guadalix de la Sierra. Turn right
at Guadalix de la Sierra towards Navalafuente.
The campsite is located on the left hand side.

Lots of slaby granite in La Pedriza

The castle of Manzanares El Real

Hotel Parque Real

✉ Padre Damián 4
28410 Manzanares el Real
📞 +34 91 8539912
@ info@hotelparquereal.com
🕐 www.hotelparquereal.com

📱 N 40°43'37,1 W 03°51'51,2

Open	Year round
Price	Double room without breakfast €61

*A nice two star hotel with everything you could
desire at this price.*

Directions
The hotel is just off the main square in Manzanares
el Real towards the castle.

Where to buy groceries?

There are several large supermarkets in Manzanares
el Real and in Torrelaguña.

Where to find the local climbing guidebook

There are two guidebooks for La Pedriza. There
is a comprehensive one published by Barrabes,
Guía De Escalada La Pedriza (€29.50), the Bible

for the place! Another is published by Desnivel, Pedriza, vías conocidas y desconocidas (€15). Both have crag photos but the Desnivel ones are much clearer. Both guides also have a basic map of the National Park.

We also strongly recommend you buy a detailed map of the park called 'Mapa Deportivo Excursionista de La Pedriza del Manzanares'. You will definitely need it if any of the sectors deeper into the park are on your hit-list. The guidebooks and the map are sold at 'El Refugio', Piazza de Postiguillo 3 in Manzanares el Real. The street is just off the main square. Also 'La Papeleria', located north east of the main square, at Calle Morales 7, sells the Barrabes guidebook.

The Patones topo is published by Desnivel and is for sale at 'El Refugio' too (€15.30). The guidebook has photos of the sectors.

What else is there to see & do

Hiking
You can spend weeks hiking in the 'Parque Regional de la Cuenca Alta del Manzanares', however the number of boulders will most probably

Plaza Mayor in Madrid

distract enough to limit your ability to complete long walks! If you plan on hiking make sure you pick up the map as mentioned before.

Castle Tripping
The region is famous for its castles and many come here to spend their holiday going from one to the other.

Patones de Arriba
This small village is a lovely place to spend a free afternoon and enjoy a Spanish meal. The village is located near Sector Patones Pueblo.

Madrid
The capital of Spain is the largest city in Europe after London and Paris. The best known attraction in Madrid is the Palacio Real (Royal Palace of Madrid). Other must-see places are the Museo del Prado, one of the most important art museum in the world, and 'El Parque de Retiro', the most beautiful park in Madrid. The San Isidro bullfighting festival takes place during May and June, in case you want to experience an event Spain is well known for.

Patones de Ariba

La Pedriza

If slab climbing is your thing, then this is your newly found heaven. If it isn't, go somewhere else! La Pedriza is one big maze of boulders and much larger granite rock formations. It is hard to find any other location in Europe where there is so much slab climbing in one concentrated area. There is no need for strength here but don't forget to bring your feet and your balance!

La Pedriza has a mix of sport and traditional routes. Some very good sectors are El Pajero and El Yelmo. Sector El Pajaro has the mega-classic route of the area, 'Sur clásica', a beautiful 5 pitch pleasure. If you want to get used to this type of climbing head for Sector La Tortuga, which isn't far away from parking P1. The sector has some nice single pitch routes to start with, which allow you to get acquainted with the style of climbing.

Both guidebooks for La Pedriza have a small map of the whole place but buying the more detailed map 'La Pedriza Del Manzanares' is a very worthwhile luxury, which will more than pay itself back. Besides the outdoor shop in Manzanares el Real, as mentioned before, the small hut on the track between P1 and P2 sells it as well. Here you can also get other general information about the park.

Juan Pablo Trigo enjoying his weekend at Sector La Tortuga

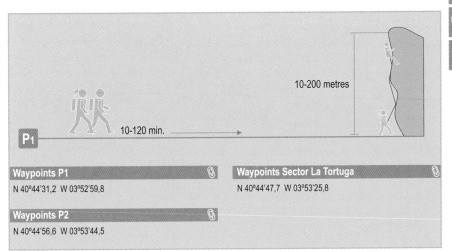

10-200 metres

10-120 min.

P1

Waypoints P1
N 40°44'31,2 W 03°52'59,8

Waypoints Sector La Tortuga
N 40°44'47,7 W 03°53'25,8

Waypoints P2
N 40°44'56,6 W 03°53'44,5

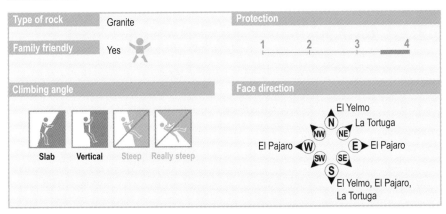

Type of rock Granite

Family friendly Yes

Protection
1   2   3   4

Climbing angle

Slab   Vertical   Steep   Really steep

Face direction

El Yelmo
N — La Tortuga
NW NE
El Pajaro ◄ W   E ► El Pajaro
SW SE
S
El Yelmo, El Pajaro,
La Tortuga

Number of routes & Grade range

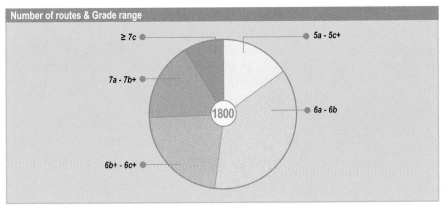

≥ 7c
5a - 5c+
7a - 7b+
6a - 6b
1800
6b+ - 6c+

Fantastic slab climbing at Sector La Tortuga

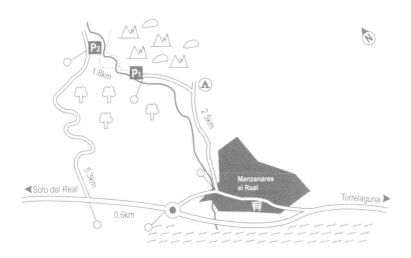

Directions

Plenty of bouldering at La Pedriza too

▶ Coming from Madrid take the E5 towards Burgos. Leave the motorway at exit number 50 towards Guadalix de la Sierra. Continue on the M608 to Manzanares el Real. Once in Manzanares el Real follow the signs for the campsite, after which it is another 2.5km to the entrance of the park.

Patones

Those with allergies to slabs, who've scuttled away from La Pedriza, should spend their time at Patones, which has everything but slabs! The venue actually consists of 5 different sectors that are separate from each other and can only be reached by car. The variety of routes here is simply huge - from pocketed vertical walls to overhanging jug fests. It goes without saying that this place is well visited, especially at the weekends when Madrid ejects climbers.

Patones's prime attraction is the big dark wall of Sector Pontón de la Oliva with mainly 6th and 7th grade routes. It is a real pleasure to climb here and the long single pitch routes on mainly vertical rock have excellent views! If you want to pump yourself up, head for Sector Los Alcores by the water. It has short and overhanging routes.

Have a beer at the end of the day at the lively village of Torrelaguña.

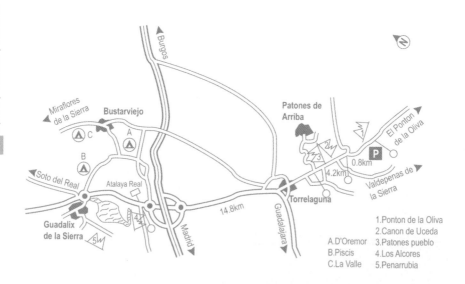

1. Ponton de la Oliva
2. Canon de Uceda
3. Patones pueblo
4. Los Alcores
5. Penarrubia

A. D'Oremor
B. Piscis
C. La Valle

Directions

▶ Coming from Madrid leave the E5 at exit 50 and head for Torrelaguña. For Sector Pontón de la Oliva continue towards El Atazar. You'll see a sign to the right for 'El Pontón de la Oliva' just before you come to a left hand bend. This is some 6km after Torrelaguña. If you're heading for Sector Los Alcores turn left on the M608 in the direction of Guadalix de la Sierra. Cross the roundabout and turn left again soon into a small road signposted 'Atalaya Real'. From here it is 1km to the car park on the right hand side of the road.

Sector Ponton de Oliva, West Side

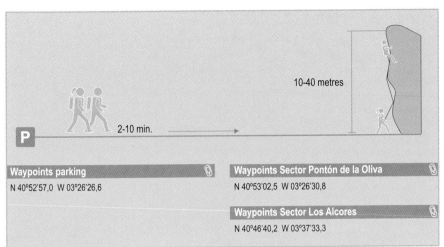

Waypoints parking

N 40°52'57,0 W 03°26'26,6

Waypoints Sector Pontón de la Oliva

N 40°53'02,5 W 03°26'30,8

Waypoints Sector Los Alcores

N 40°46'40,2 W 03°37'33,3

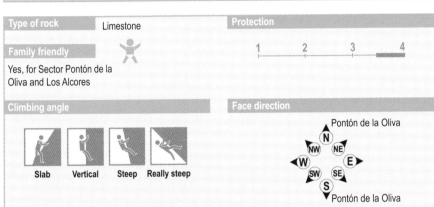

Type of rock Limestone

Family friendly

Yes, for Sector Pontón de la Oliva and Los Alcores

Protection

1   2   3   4

Climbing angle

Slab   Vertical   Steep   Really steep

Face direction

Pontón de la Oliva

N   NE   E   SE   S   SW   W   NW

Pontón de la Oliva

Number of routes & Grade range

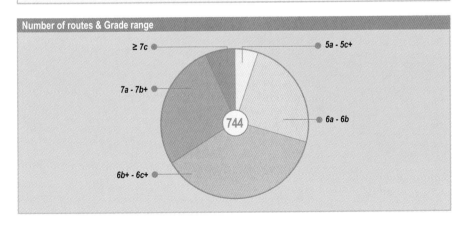

≥ 7c

7a - 7b+

6b+ - 6c+

5a - 5c+

6a - 6b

744

Climbing area Malaga

Situated in the south of Spain, Andalucía is one of its most visited areas. Apart from the world famous city of Seville, people particularly come here to see the Alhambra, the Moorish fortress and the palace in Granada, the Mesquita, a Roman Catholic cathedral build inside a mosque in Cordoba, and to hike in the Sierra Nevada mountain range. The coast has further attractions: the Costa de la Luz, east of Cádiz, is one of Europe's best windsurfing hotspots; the Costa del Sol has the dubious distinction of being Spain's most visited beach holiday destination, with all that brings with it!

Andalucía also has a large number of crags, both big and small. The very best crags can be found near Málaga. These world class crags, El Chorro and Desplomilandia, are situated one hours drive inland from Málaga around the tiny village El Chorro. Honestly, if there is one place in Spain you should climb at in your life, it's El Chorro! The village is surrounded by a spectacular landscape marked by a 200 metres deep gorge 'El Garganta del Chorro'. The gorge itself leads to some stunning turquoise lakes, a few kilometres away from El Chorro.

A trip to El Chorro will surely be unforgettable and it attracts climbers from all over the world. So if it rains and it is cold during the winter months at home, you know where to come!

When to go

El Chorro and Desplomilandia are excellent winter destinations. As it gets unbearably hot in summer, the climbing season starts in October and lasts until April. Even though the rainy season runs from November to May, it usually doesn't rain more than a few days in a row, although the showers can be heavy. Bring warm clothes - it can get cold in the gorge.

 Spring Summer Autumn Winter

Bridge crossing the El Chorro Gorge

Crag

A El Chorro
B Desplomilandia

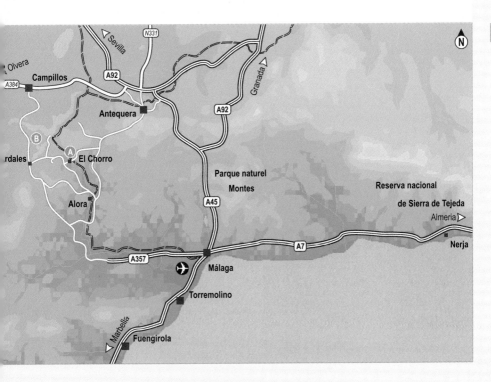

How to get to the area & how to move around

El Chorro is accessible by public transport. Once there, the sectors can be reached on foot from the campsites. However, you will need a car to get to Desplomilandia.

 By public transport

Flying directly to Málaga is your best option, it's the closest airport to El Chorro. There are a number of European low cost airlines operating flights. Flybmi, Veuling, Ryanair, Transavia and Air Berlin all have flights to the south of Spain, as well as some others.

There are direct trains from the airport to the main train station, Málaga Renfe. From here there is only one direct train to El Chorro at 7.15 pm [41 min, €4.15]. If you miss this one take any train to Álora which leaves every hour. From Álora take a taxi [€20] to El Chorro. The direct service returning from El Chorro to Málaga leaves at 3.11 pm.

 By car

From Málaga airport follow the signs to Granada for a short while. Then take the A357 to Cártama and continue on to Ardales where you'll see signs for El Chorro. It takes a bit more than one hour. A somewhat shorter alternative is to drive via Álora but the road is a bit twisty.

Be aware that there is no petrol station in El Chorro so fill up in Álora.

Camping Finca La Campana at El Chorro

Where to stay

The best option is to stay in El Chorro itself: you can walk to the sectors and Desplomilandia is no too far away by car. There are several accommodation options.

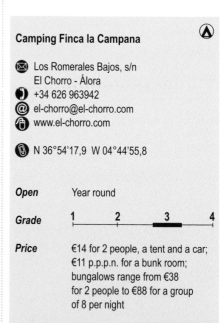

Camping Finca la Campana

✉ Los Romerales Bajos, s/n
   El Chorro - Álora
☎ +34 626 963942
@ el-chorro@el-chorro.com
🌐 www.el-chorro.com

📍 N 36°54'17,9 W 04°44'55,8

Open	Year round
Grade	1 2 3 4
Price	€14 for 2 people, a tent and a car; €11 p.p.p.n. for a bunk room; bungalows range from €38 for 2 people to €88 for a group of 8 per night

This typical climbers' campsite lies just outside the village and is run by Juan and Christina, a very friendly Swiss couple. They can organize just about everything - from caving trips to kayaking on the lakes. They rent nice bungalows and campers can make use of the kitchen and the large communal room, which feels like a living room. You could quite easily come here on your own and hook up with climbing partners. There is also internet access.

Directions
Once in El Chorro go past the train station and take the first road on your right. From here it is just a bit over 1km to the campsite which is signposted.

Camping El Chorro

Estación del Chorro, s/n
29500 El Chorro - Álora

+34 952 495244

info@alberguecampingelchorro.com

www.alberguecampingelchorro.com

N 36°54'40,0 W 04°45'40,0

Open	Year round
Grade	1 2 **3** 4
Price	€16 for 2 people, a tent and a car; cabins range from €42 to €70 per night

This campsite is a lot bigger than Finca la Campana. It has a hostel and cabins which sleep up to 6 persons. There is also a swimming pool and the trees provide shelter from the sun.

Directions
When arriving in El Chorro take the first road on the left after the dam. The campsite is on the right after 200 metres, overlooking the lake.

Paul Lahaye on the fingery Arzapua (7b), photo by Hans Snijders

Sector El Recodo at El Chorro

La Almona Chica

✉ P.O. Box 161
Las Casillas del Choro
El Chorro – Álora
29552 Málaga
📞 +34 952 119872
@ sumitch@mercuryin.es
🏠 www.holiday-rentals.co.uk property 2678

📍 N 36°54'14,2 W 04°45'23,7

La Almona Chica

Open   Year round

Price   €270 to €300 per cottage
(2-6 people) per week

This lovely old farmhouse is run by two friendly Brits, Susan and Dell. They have four cottages for 2 to 6 people to rent. The authentic cottages have a very relaxed atmosphere and, in case you overheat, the swimming pool is just outside.

Directions
When arriving in El Chorro go past the train station. Continue for another few hundred metres. La Almona Chica is located on the left hand side of the road.

Apartments La Garganta

✉ El Chorro s/n
29552 Álora
📞 +34 952 495119
@ informacion@lagarganta.com
🏠 www.lagarganta.com

📍 N 36°54'24,2 W 04°45'33,4

Open   Year round

Price   €45 for a 2 person apartment

You can't fail to spot this apartment complex when arriving in El Chorro. The apartments have a great view over the lake. There is also a restaurant but it might be better to cook for yourself. Be your own judge! From La Garganta you can walk to the sectors.

Directions
The complex is opposite the train station.

El Chorro, Sector 'Los tres techos'

The train station in El Chorro

Where to buy groceries?

As El Chorro only has two very small shops, make sure you do your shopping either in Málaga or Álora. There is a Mercadona supermarket in Álora, for which you'll see signs when you enter the town.

Where to find the local climbing guidebook

Both Camping Finca La Campana and the climbing shop in El Chorro sell the topo 'Escalada en Malaga – El Chorro'. It is written by Javier Romero Rubiols and Desplomilandia is included as well.

The topo has two maps with overview of the sectors and the author has used colour photos. It is written in both Spanish and English. The climbing shop is located between Camping El Chorro and the train station.

VERSANTE SUD
climbing and mountaineering guidebooks
VERSANTE SUD
www.versantesud.it

Flo Babolat working her way up on Sheik tu Dinero (7a), photo by Paul Lahaye

What else is there to see & do

Caving
There are some very special caves in the area. A guided trip costs between €40 and €60 per day.

Mountain biking
Around El Chorro there are numerous biking trails. Rental rates per day are €12 to €18.

Kayaking & Ardales lakes
The beautiful turquoise lakes of Ardales attract many locals from Málaga. One of the best ways to see it is from the water itself, in a kayak.

The equipment required for caving, mountain biking and kayaking can all be rented at Camping Finca la Campana.

Hiking & Via-Ferrata
The El Chorro gorge is great to hike around, especially if you don't plan on climbing at any of the sectors inside the gorge itself. Without a doubt, the highlight will be the awesome via-ferrata on the King's Path. The path, named 'El Camino del Rey', 100 metres up the gorge was originally built for King Alfonso XII who wanted to be able to see the dam and the gorge at the same time. The government has formally closed the path as it has almost completely fallen apart. Even though a lot of climbers still use it for access to the surrounding sectors, it's use is fully at your own risk!

El Chorro

The outstanding limestone, the quality of the routes, and the exceptional setting are the reasons for El Chorro's world-class status. The climbing takes place at the sectors north of the village and in the gorge itself. There is a mixture of both sport and traditional climbing.

The vast majority of the sectors face south so forget about climbing here during summer. In winter it can get very busy but this normally is not a problem as the place is fairly spread out. The majority of the sectors can only be approached on foot. Even though it is strictly forbidden and not recommended, most climbers use the train tunnels to get to the routes as this is by far the quickest way. If you choose to do this then take good care - trains can enter from both ends of the tunnels. Be aware that at the weekend the train company places guards at the tunnel entrances and, if you are caught, the fine can be enormous!

Some of the best routes are found at Sector Makinodromo, Frontales Medias, and right inside the gorge near the bridge. A lot of routes start from the King's path within the gorge. As the path is no longer trustworthy and is in a serious state of disrepair it is wise to always clip into the via-ferrata when walking or belaying.

These days El Chorro has 44 sectors and more than 1000 bolted routes.

The awesome Sector Makinodromo, photo by Jean-Bernard Hofer

El Chorro Lake

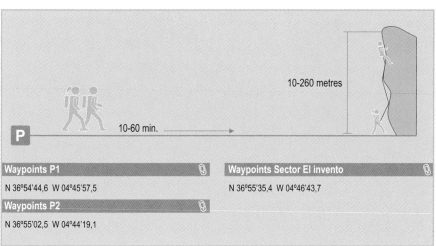

10-260 metres

10-60 min.

P

Waypoints P1	Waypoints Sector El invento
N 36°54'44,6 W 04°45'57,5	N 36°55'35,4 W 04°46'43,7

Waypoints P2

N 36°55'02,5 W 04°44'19,1

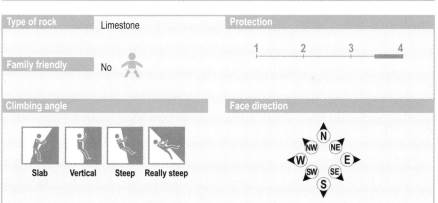

Type of rock	Limestone
Family friendly	No

Protection

1   2   3   4

Climbing angle

Slab   Vertical   Steep   Really steep

Face direction

N   NW   NE   W   E   SW   SE   S

Number of routes & Grade range

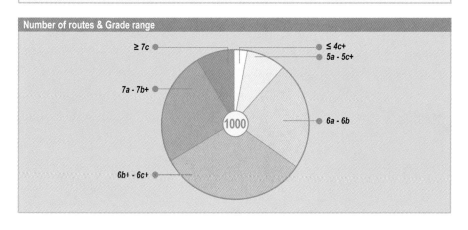

≥ 7c

7a - 7b+

6b+ - 6c+

≤ 4c+

5a - 5c+

1000

6a - 6b

Sector Makinodromo

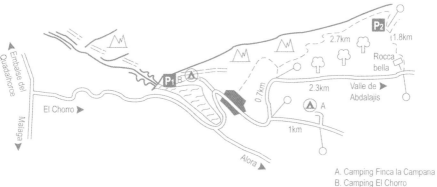

A. Camping Finca la Campana
B. Camping El Chorro

Directions

Carole McGloughlin enjoying the perfect structure
of Sector Los Ibercones, photo by Eoin Lawless

▶ *Directions from MA444*

After crossing the dam take the first road to the left
which leads to Camping El Chorro. Either park there
or 600 metres further up the unpaved road, from
where the routes at the gorge can be approached.
For any of the sectors north of the village either park
at Sector Las Encantadas and walk from there or
continue on the MA226 until the sign 'Roca bella'.
Turn onto this unpaved road and continue until the
parking spot, which is 1.8km up the way.

Desplomilandia

It is not as famous as El Chorro but Desplomilandia is a top spot too. The pocketed red limestone complete with tufas guarantees good climbing. The crag is also popular because the sectors face north and are thus a very nice place to escape to on warm days. As a bonus the crags are very close to the parking. Most of the routes are vertical and overhanging, with a good mixture of technical climbs and pumpy 'no-brainers'.

One of the first sectors you come to approaching from the parking at the bottom is Buena Sombra. It has some good warm ups on the right before continuing onto some more serious routes, like the powerful 'Lirón careto' (7c) on the left hand side of the sector. If you are keen to climb more overhanging rock, head towards Sector Como La Vida Misma, a bit further to the left. Don't miss 'Al Andalus', 6c+. Even though it is getting a bit polished it remains a first class route!

The views from Desplomilandia are simply fantastic...

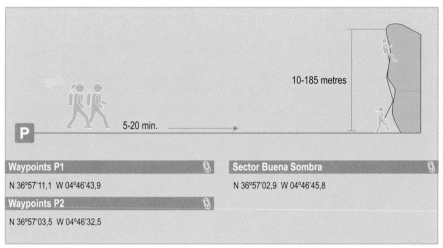

10-185 metres

5-20 min.

P

Waypoints P1

N 36°57'11,1 W 04°46'43,9

Sector Buena Sombra

N 36°57'02,9 W 04°46'45,8

Waypoints P2

N 36°57'03,5 W 04°46'32,5

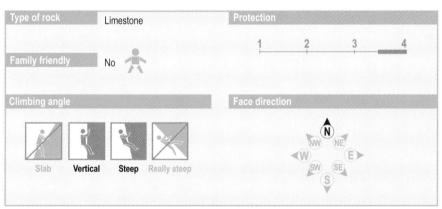

Type of rock Limestone

Protection

1   2   3   4

Family friendly No

Climbing angle

Slab **Vertical** **Steep** Really steep

Face direction

N
NW NE
W E
SW SE
S

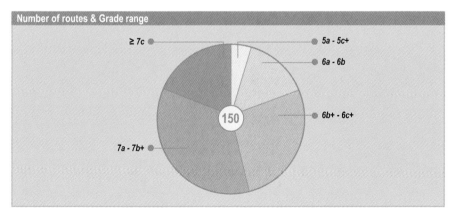

Number of routes & Grade range

≥ 7c   5a - 5c+

6a - 6b

150   6b+ - 6c+

7a - 7b+

Martin Heywood making big moves on The Great Liron Careto (7c),
Sector Buena sombra at Desplomilandia

Desplomilandia

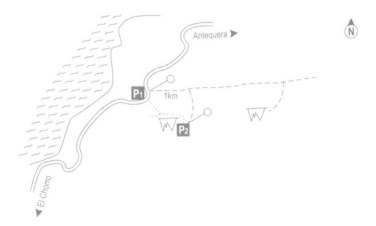

Directions

▶ Coming from El Chorro drive towards Embalse del Guadalhorce and follow the signs for Antequera. It is almost 12km from El Chorro to the parking. The obvious crag on the right hand side of the road cannot be missed.

Desplomiliandia

Climbing area Costa Blanca

For many the Costa Blanca stands for cheap flights and accommodation, 24 hour night and beach life, and lots of sun. Well, all of this is true. The authentic coastal villages of this part of Spain have morphed over time into large tourist resorts and business is booming. Places like Benidorm attract bus loads of mainly youngsters who come to drink the night away. Luckily, if you drive only a few kilometres inland it is a whole different world. And this is where the climbing starts!

The Costa Blanca has numerous good limestone crags. Most climbers visit this area mostly during the winter. Many crags face south and even in winter it can still be pleasantly warm. Of all crags in this region there are three that really stand out - Sierra de Toix, Gandia, and Sella, the latter sticking out with head and shoulders over the other two. The whole area has both multi pitch and single pitch climbs and a good blend of bolted and traditional routes.

Spring   Summer   Autumn   Winter

When to go

The best time for climbing runs from November to the end of January. It rains in October and February. If you choose to go in March and April you will most likely be confined to north facing sectors. Summer climbing? Forget about it!

The Costa Blanca: a great place to enjoy the winter

Crag

Ⓐ Sella

Ⓑ Sierra de Toix

Ⓒ Gandia

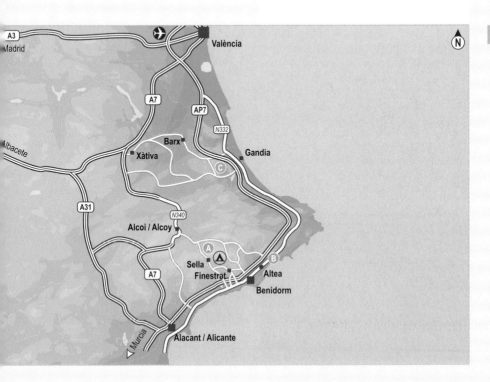

How to get to the area & how to move around

A car is required to get to all crags in this region.

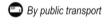 *By public transport*

The best thing to do is to fly to Alicante, one of the coastal cities on the Costa Blanca. Amongst others, the low-cost airlines Jet2, Bmibaby and Ryanair operate routes to Alicante.

 By car

Alicante is most easily approached by the A7 motorway and lies north east of Murcia and south of València.

Where to stay

The Costa Blanca has a huge range of accommodation. Be it a self catering apartment, a big villa, a room in a hotel or pension, or just a place to pitch your tent, the Costa Blanca has it all. Package deals with flights and accommodation are also very popular. These can work out very cheap and the accommodation will be somewhere on the coast, but, in general, accommodation prices reduce as you head inland and you can find good deals if you look.

We have chosen to list the accommodation around Sella as this is the best crag here and not too far away from the others. The campsites at the coast tend be overly expensive and there is some uncertainty as to their operation. At the time of research all the campsites we visited were closed - and this was in the tourist season - and it was unknown whether they would open again in the future. Therefore these campsites are not included here.

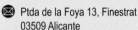

The Orange House

✉ Ptda de la Foya 13, Finestrat
   03509 Alicante
☏ +34 965 878251
@ sam@theorangehouse.net
🏠 www.theorangehouse.net

📍 N 38°33'44,7 W 00°12'46,6

Open   Year round

Price   €18 for 2 people, a tent and a car;
             €9 p.p.p.n. for a bunk room;
             €16 to €25 p.p.p.n. for a double room

Over the years The Orange House has become widely known within the climbing community. This relaxed place is run by the adventurous and very welcoming Sam and Rich, a couple from the UK. The house can be rented as a villa or you can take a room. They also allow limited camping. There is a communal kitchen, a pool, TV room, bar, and internet. There are also a few dogs and cats who seem to live in harmony with each other... Don't forget to make a reservation.

Directions

Coming from Alicante on the A7 take exit 65A to Finestrat. Just before Finestrat you'll see signs for The Orange House.

The beautiful Sector Pared de Rosalia in Sella

The Orange House

Jemma Powell working her way up A Golpe de Pecho (7a+), Sector Wild Side

Casaroc

 C/Sant Xotxim 25
03579 Sella

📞 +34 965 879281

@ casaroc@sella-alicante.com

🏠 www.casaroc.com

📍 N 38°36'32,9 W 00°16'19,0

Open	Year round
Price	4 person apartment costs €370 per week

Casaroc offers one apartment high up in Sella. It sleeps up to 4 people and has a nice terrace.

Directions

Sella lies north west of Benidorm. Leave the A7 either at junction 66 or 65A depending on which direction you come from. Follow the signs for Sella and head towards the houses high up when in the village. The place itself is a bit of a maze but the locals are very friendly and will help you find your way round.

Youri van Vliet on the beautiful Black is Black (7b) at Sector Wild Side in Sella, photo by Paul Lahaye

Villa Pico

✉ Calle Cirineo 21
03579 Sella
☎ +34 965 879238
@ info@villapico.com
🏠 www.villapico.com

📍 N 38°36'33,7 W 00°16'17,9

Open   Year round

Price   Rooms start at €23 to €36
for the apartment p.p.p.n.

The owners of Villa Pico have transformed the house in a picturesque place with a great atmosphere. There are several rooms, including one done in a Moorish style, plus an apartment, which is the highest one in the village. There is a small pool, internet, and a big terrace.

Directions
For information how to reach Sella see 'Directions' to the Casaroc accommodation. Calle Cirineo lies all the way at the top of the village.

View from the terrace of Villa Pico in Sella

El Refugio Font de L'arc

✉ Sella

📍 N 38°37'11,8 W 00°14'03,9

Open   Should be open year round

Price   €6 p.p.p.n.

Basic hut from where you can walk to the climbing in Sella. Guests can use the kitchen facilities and they sell drinks and beer. The hut has a shower but hot water is rare. A tent can be pitched around the hut.

Directions
See 'Directions' to Sella how to get to the crag. The refugio is next to the parking.

Finestrat, photo by Paul Lahaye

El Refugio in Sella

Where to buy groceries?

Alicante and Gandia have several large supermarkets. There is a Carrefour at the exit to Finestrat on the N332. Smaller shops can be found in Sella and Finestrat.

Where to find the local climbing guidebook

Rockfax has a guide for the Costa Blanca (€30). It is pretty extensive and covers a large number of crags in this part of Spain. It is named 'Costa Blanca' and is written by Chris Craggs and Alan James. It is for sale at The Orange House in Finestrat. The climbing shop 'El Refugio' in Alicante (c/ Capitán Segarra, 29) sells a number of local guide books as well.

There is one topo for Sella produced by the locals called 'Aitana Sur' (€7). It should be for sale at the Refugio Font de L'arc at Sella. However at the time

of our research it had been sold out for a few months.

What else is there to see & do

Excursions
You should be able to arrange excursions through your accommodation. There are a wide variety of trips on offer, such as a visit to the castle of Guadalest, Safaripark Aitana, Wildpark Terra Natura, the island of Tabarca, or to Aqualandia, a huge water park.

Penón de Ifach
This more than 300 metre high tower is the most remarkable landmark of the Costa Blanca. Even if you don't plan on climbing here it is nice to visit. It is located at Calpe and really can't be missed. Bring your gear in case you change your mind!

Hiking
There are a number of great walks. For example head out to the 'Embalse de Guadalest' where people hike next to the lake. Also you can walk for days in a row around Sella without getting bored.

Magnficent view over Penón de Ifach

Sella

Sella is one of the best venues in the Costa Blanca region, maybe even the best. This is down to the large number and wide variety of routes - from fingery technical moves on slabs to some wild dancing on steep tufas! It definitely makes you want to come back, over and over again. Every now and then the bolting may feel a bit spaced but, generally, it is nothing to complain about. The majority of the routes are single pitch but Sella also has some outstanding multi pitch challenges, such as those at the north facing Sector Pared de Rosalia.

It is good to warm up at any of the sectors near the Refugio, like at Culo de Rino or Techo del Rino, before heading to one of the best and hardest sector, Wild Side. Here the easiest route is at 7a. Be aware that Sector Wild Side is located on private land. Climbing there is allowed as long as you keep the place clean and don't make too much noise.

The majority of the sectors of Sella face south. This is very nice during winter but on hot days in spring and autumn you'll have to avoid climbing during midday.

Gaby Kostermans focusing on Valor y Coraje (6a+), Sector Techo del Rino

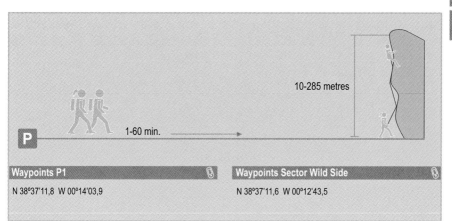

Waypoints P1

N 38°37'11,8 W 00°14'03,9

Waypoints Sector Wild Side

N 38°37'11,6 W 00°12'43,5

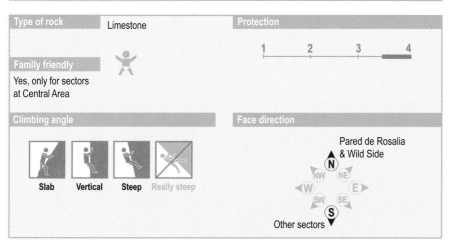

Type of rock

Limestone

Family friendly

Yes, only for sectors
at Central Area

Climbing angle

Slab   Vertical   Steep   Really steep

Protection

1   2   3   4

Face direction

Pared de Rosalia
& Wild Side

NW NE
W   E
SW SE

Other sectors

Number of routes & Grade range

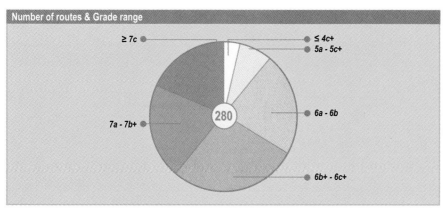

280

≥ 7c
≤ 4c+
5a - 5c+
6a - 6b
6b+ - 6c+
7a - 7b+

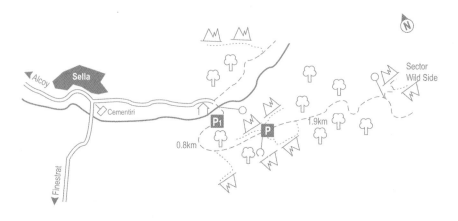

Directions

Youri van Vliet on Blanco nato (6b) at Sector Techno del Rino, photo by Paul Lahaye

▶ Coming from Benidorm or Alicante leave the A7 at either junction 66 or 65A. Follow the signs to Sella. Just when you enter the village take a right turn marked 'Cementiri' (cemetery). Follow this road for 4km until the Refugio appears on your right. Either park there or continue for 800 metres on a gravel road to the other parking.

Gandia

Gandia is a town mid-way between Benidorm and València. West of this town is an imposing crag, characterized by its rock structure that has many holes and tufas. Unfortunately many routes have become slippery due to the popularity of the place. Nevertheless it is a good crag to hone your skills for overhanging routes. Even though it faces south the overhanging routes are in the shade from the early afternoon on. The crag is well bolted and has proper belays. Make sure you do some routes at Sector Potent. It has some excellent 7th grade routes, such as Muluk el targui and Enya!

Even though there is nothing to do for young children apart from watching their parents climb, it is a family friendly place as the walk-in is short and the ground beneath the routes is fairly flat.

The immaculate Sector Vici

Enjoying the late afternoon shade at Gandia

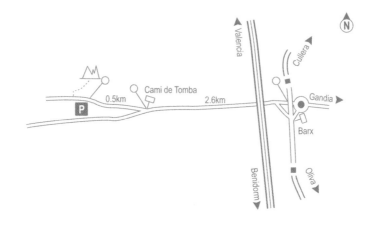

Directions

*Ralf Brunckhorst on the power sapping
Quien Molonda (7a), Gandia*

▶ Take the A7 in the direction of València and exit at junction 61 for Olivia. Continue on the N332 towards Gandia. Leave the N332 at the exit for 'Barx'. Turn left under the N332 and the A7 and continue for 2.6km until a sign 'Camí de Tomba' points to a road to the right. Follow this road and park after 500 metres. The crag is easy to spot on your right hand side.

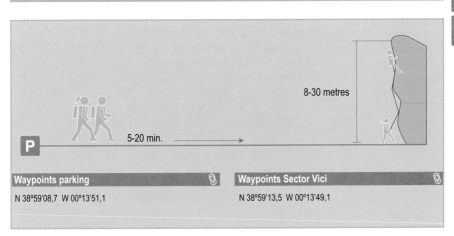

Waypoints parking

N 38°59'08,7 W 00°13'51,1

Waypoints Sector Vici

N 38°59'13,5 W 00°13'49,1

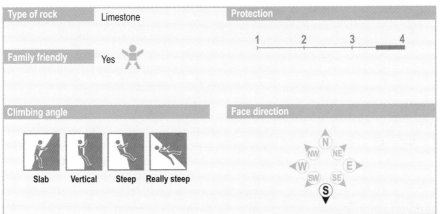

Type of rock	Limestone

Protection

1   2   3   4

Family friendly Yes

Climbing angle

Slab   Vertical   Steep   Really steep

Face direction

N NW NE W E SW SE S

Number of routes & Grade range

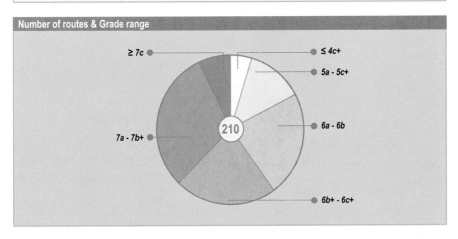

210

≥ 7c

7a - 7b+

≤ 4c+

5a - 5c+

6a - 6b

6b+ - 6c+

Sierra de Toix is a crag along the coast just south of Calpe. It has eight sectors and some of them offer great views over the coastline and the striking Penón de Ifach. In general this is a very good place for beginners and intermediate climbers as there are many lower and mid grade routes.

Sector Toix Este is one of the sectors with clear views over the Penón. The sector lies directly next to the road which doesn't get any traffic. The routes here are sharp with many positive holds and the only polish is on the start of the routes. The appearance of the bolts, as well as some of the belays, might put you off a bit as they have turned rusty in this harsh salty environment, but the fixed gear appears safe. As ever, exercise a bit of judgement.

One of the best sectors is Toix TV which has long, powerful, mainly single pitch routes with some small tufas. Don't miss Monkey Wall (6c) and Painted Wall (6b+)! The Amphitheatre section of Sector Toix TV is a real sun-trap which makes it an ideal venue in the winter. If you enjoy climbing directly above the water head for Sector Raco del Corv or, even better, Sector Candelabra del Sol.

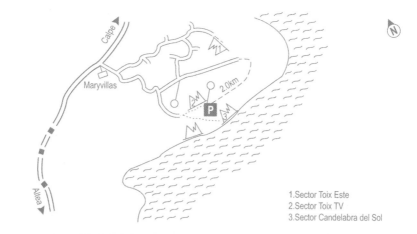

1.Sector Toix Este
2.Sector Toix TV
3.Sector Candelabra del Sol

Directions

Monkey Wall (6c), a favourite route at Sector Toix TV

▶ Coming from Benidorm follow the N332 to Calpe. Just past the tunnels turn right at a sign for 'Maryvillas' (Maryvillas is a holiday resort where many older foreigners reside). Follow the signs for 'Toix Mirador' to get to Sector Toix TV. For Sector Este head east towards the sea. It is best to chill and take your time when finding the sectors for the first time - Maryvillas is one giant maze of small streets...

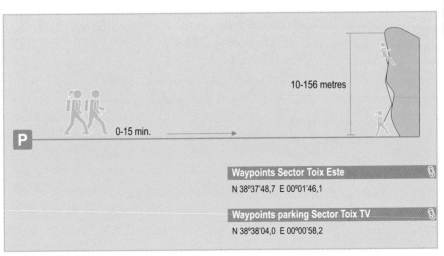

10-156 metres

0-15 min.

Waypoints Sector Toix Este
N 38°37'48,7 E 00°01'46,1

Waypoints parking Sector Toix TV
N 38°38'04,0 E 00°00'58,2

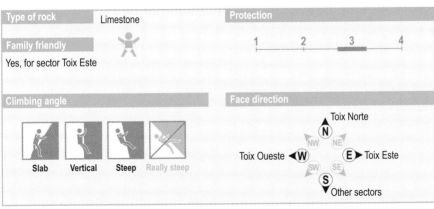

Type of rock	Limestone

Protection

1   2   3   4

Family friendly

Yes, for sector Toix Este

Climbing angle

Slab   Vertical   Steep   Really steep

Face direction

Toix Norte
N
NW   NE
Toix Oueste ◄W   E► Toix Este
SW   SE
S
Other sectors

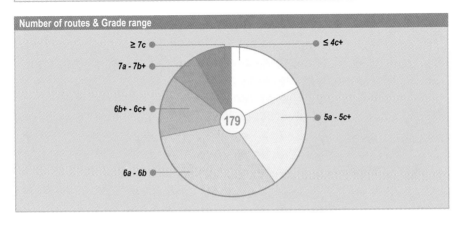

Number of routes & Grade range

≥ 7c   ≤ 4c+

7a - 7b+

6b+ - 6c+

179   5a - 5c+

6a - 6b

Climbing area València

València is the third largest city in Spain and is situated on the Mediterranean Sea. Like Alicante it receives a very large number of tourists each year who mainly come to enjoy the pretty beaches. Inland, the countryside changes rapidly and the rough interior is home to some splendid crags and a fantastic bouldering area.

Spring   Summer   Autumn   Winter

One of the best kept secrets of Spain lies close to a little medieval village named Albarracín. It's Spain's bouldering paradise and the sandstone boulders are located just outside the village. Fontainebleau's little brother would be a good description, although it certainly doesn't receive the same number of climbers as its French counterpart. The friendly environment is also great for families with children. Albarracín is 180km from València.

Montanejos is the other pearl of the València area. The climbing here is mainly on pocketed limestone and there is a combination of bolted routes and traditional climbing. There is a choice of more than 1400 routes spread out over 80 sectors. And there is a potential for thousands of more routes! The green environment is simply beautiful with a big lake called Embalse de Arenoso and plenty of spots to take a dip in thermal pool! This crag is located 90km from València and 115km from Albarracin.

So if you are after great bouldering or you simply want to do some challenging sport routes, head for València, rent a car, and explore the region!

Albarracín is one of the prettiest villages in Spain

When to go

The optimal times of year for climbing are spring and autumn. Albarracín lies at an altitude of 1200 metres, which makes it cold during the winter when it can also snow. Although the pine trees provide some relief from the sun, the summers are still way too hot. The same also applies to Montanejos. Early autumn is still a little hot for Montanejos, so the best time is from the end of September until November.

Crag

Ⓐ Albarracín
Ⓑ Montanejos

Spain | València

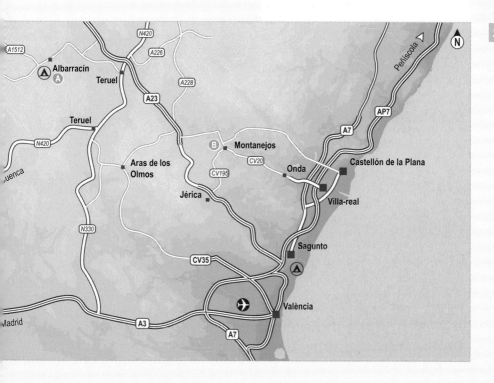

How to get to the area & how to move around

A car is required for Albarracín but not for Montanejos. From any of the hotels in Montanejos you can walk to the crags.

 *By public transport*

There are several airlines flying between València and other European cities: Transavia, Vueling, German Wings, Air Berlin, Jet2 and Ryanair. An alternative for Albarracín only is to fly to Zaragoza.

The bus company 'Autocares Herca' has twice daily services on work days between València's bus station at Menéndez Pidal 11, and Montanejos. It leaves València at 10am and 4.30pm during the week and 8pm on Sunday's. It returns at 6.30am and 1pm on weekdays and 4.45pm on Sunday.

 By car

València is situated between Alicante and Castellón. The city lies close to the A7 motorway.

Where to stay

Both Albarracín and Montanejos have a wide range of accommodation. Albarracín has a campsite which Montanejos lacks, although the Refugio in Montanejos has a few spaces reserved for tents.

The beautiful surroundings of Albarracín

Albarracín

Camping Ciudad de Albarracín

✉ Camino de Gea, s/n
   44100 Albarracín
☎ +34 978 710197
🌐 www.campingalbarracin.com

📱 N 40°24'43,8 W 01°25'44,1

Open   Year round

Price   €12.60 for 2 people, a tent and
              a car; bungalow €60 - €85 per day
              up to 6 people

This is a very quiet campsite with clean bathrooms. It has a bar and is a favourite place to stay with climbers.

Directions
When arriving in Albarracín follow the road to Bezas. The campsite is signposted.

Casa de Oria

✉ C/Garita 5
   44100 Albarracín
☎ +34 978 700351

📱 N 40°24'29,7 W 01°26'12,3

Open   Year round

Price   €38 for a double room
              without breakfast

This hostal is the cheapest place to stay in Albarracín after the campsite. Surprisingly rooms are very tasteful decorated by the friendly owners. Try to get a room on the top floor!

Directions
When arriving in Albarracín take the turn for Bezas. The hostal is found on a narrow street a few hundred metres after the turn on your right.

The pine forest provides good shelter from the sun at the boulders of Albarracín

Hotel Prado Del Navazo

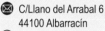

✉ C/Llano del Arrabal 6
  44100 Albarracín
☎ +34 978 700350

📱 N 40°24'29,2 W 01°26'18,9

Open   Year round

Price   €58 for a double room without
            breakfast and €68 for a suite

A two star hotel with clean rooms not far away from the old part of Albarracín.

Directions
When arriving in Albarracín take the left turn for Bezas and go past the café El Molino del Gato. The hotel is next to the road after a few hundred metres.

The narrow streets of Albarracín

The stunning Sector Los Miradores, Estrecho del Mijares of Montanejos

Habitaciones Los Palacios

✉ C/Los Palacios 21
  44100 Albarracín
☎ +34 978 700327
🌐 www.montepalacios.com

📱 N 40°24'31,6 W 01°26'44,3

Open   Year round

Price   €40 for a double room
            without breakfast

This hostal has simple but fine rooms with a great view over Albarracín.

Directions
The hostal is situated in the old part of Albarracín, a few minutes on foot from the Plaza Mayor.

Impressions of the bouldering in Albarracín

Albarracín is great for families

An authentic sundial

Hotel Arabia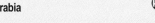

✉ Bernardo Zapater 2
44100 Albarracín
☎ +34 978 710212
@ reserves@montesuniversales.com
🖥 www.montesuniversales.com

📱 N 40°24'28,8 W 01°26'28,4

Open	Year round
Price	€65 for a double room; €80 - €120 for a 2 to 8 person apartment

This huge place has many rooms and apartments that can sleep up to 8 people. The size of the hotel does no favours for the atmosphere.

Directions
When arriving in Albarracín don't take the turn for Bezas but continue on the same road for a few more metres. Take the first turn on your right which is the street Bernardo Zapater.

Montanejos

Albergue El Refugio

✉ Carretera de Tales 27
Montanejos
☎ +34 964 131317

📱 N 40°04'18,1 W 00°31'36,1

Open	Year round
Price	€15 p.p.p.n.in the bunk room including breakfast and diner; €32 - €45 per night for the hut

The friendly refugio is a great place to meet other climbers and is conveniently located for the climbing. It has a bunk room and two separate huts which sleep 4 to 6 people.

Directions
Coming from the direction of Caudiel continue through Montanejos. The refugio is on the left after the bridge and just before the turn to Zucaine.

Hotel Arabia

Refugio of Montanejos

Hotel Gil

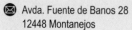

- ✉ Avda. Fuente de Banos 28
  12448 Montanejos
- ☎ +34 964 131380
- @ info@hotelgil.com
- 🌐 www.hotelgil.com

- 📍 N 40°04'09,8 W 00°31'29,2

Open   February - December 15th

Price   €60 for a double room
             including breakfast

One of the cheaper hotels in Montanejos. It has clean rooms that lack ambiance.

Directions

Coming from Caudiel follow the main road through Montanejos. The hotel is on this road on the right.

Hostal Casa Ovidio

- ✉ C/Elvira Peiró 41
  12448 Montanejos
- ☎ +34 964 131309
- 🌐 www.casaovidio.com

- 📍 N 40°03'59,8 W 00°31'32,1

Open   Year round

Price   €50 for a double room with breakfast

The hostal has basic rooms, a bar and a restaurant.

Directions

Coming from Caudiel the hostal is situated directly on the right side of the road as you enter Montanejos.

Where to buy groceries?

Albarracín has some small supermarkets. There is a supermarket situated a few hundred metres after the turn for Bezas on the road to the campsite and the boulders. The bakery is opposite the supermarket. Nevertheless it is better to do your shopping in Teruel which has a Mercadona supermarket. To get to this, follow the signs to the centre coming from A23. The supermarket is signposted and lies close to the main road leading through town.

There are also shops in Montanejos but Sagunto and València have a much wider selection.

Where to find the local climbing guidebook

There's a very small topo for Albarracín. It is mainly a promotional leaflet for a manufacturer making climbing holds but some of the areas are described on the back. It can be picked up for free in Albarracín at the café 'El Molino del Gato' which is situated at the turn for Bezas.

Montanejos has two guides. One is called 'Montanejos' (€25) and is both in Spanish and English, and a more extensive (and expensive) one is called 'Escalada en Montanejos' (€38). Both books are sold at Albergue El Refugio in Montanejos.

What else is there to see & do

Albarracín

Albarracín village
A tour around this National Monument is a must! Around every corner in town you'll find narrow cobbled streets and ever more delightful picturesque houses. If you look up to the walls of the castle it still feels like the village is protected by it. Once inside, this highly photogenic place breaths out an atmosphere of peace and quietness.

Hiking & Mountain biking
There are endless opportunities for hiking and mountain biking in the woods of Albarracín! The surroundings are simply beautiful. The forest also hides several ancient rock paintings. The tourist office, which is situated just of Plaza Mayor, can provide information.

Fantastic ambiance at Estrecho del Mijares in Montanejos

Montanejos

Kayaking & Mountain biking & Caving
There are many adventures to be had around Montanejos. The tourist office on C/Carretera de Tales can provide information on prices and how to make arrangements.

Thermal baths
'Montanejos, Villa Termal' it tells you on driving into town. The village is famous for its thermal baths and many come to enjoy the water, which is at a constant temperature of 25°C. It is very relaxing and good for the muscles after a hard day's climbing!

Albarracín

Albarracín is not as big as Fontainebleau but is equally beautiful. There are a large number of magnificent boulders hidden in a pine forest waiting to be developed. This is obvious from the 'clean' nature of the majority of the boulders, which are, as yet, unsullied by chalk. The sandstone has perfect friction, which comes in handy as a number of the boulders are as high as 4 to 6 metres. This place will keep a boulderer busy for a very long time!

Generally the problems are hard and only a small number are graded below 6a. There are many roofs to add to the challenge, and the top outs are mostly on slabs with not much to go on... Don't let this put you off, Albarracín really is a dream destination if you can climb 6a and higher. The place is packed with 6th and 7th grade problems, as well as some harder ones. But it is a huge place and problems can always be found for the less experienced climber. Some of the 4th and 5th grade problems are documented in the free topo guide.

The topo gives an overview of the sectors where climbing is allowed and tells you about prohibited areas. Between P1 and P2 (see detailed drawing) there are some very good vertical boulders that are easily accessible. This is a good place for the first day or two, so you can get used to the sandstone. The majority of the other sectors lie on the east side of the road. As it is easy to get lost in the forest it is best to follow the S1 & S2 signs that mark a path. This leads automatically to a good number of boulders.

Albarracín has a petrol station and an ATM.

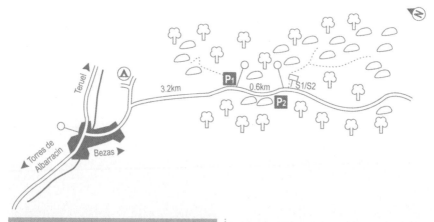

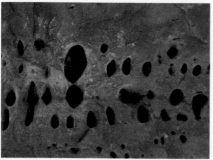

One of the typical sandstone structures

► From València take the A7 towards Sagunto. Continue on the A23 to Teruel. Coming from Zaragoza take the A23 directly to Teruel. From Teruel follow the A1512, which takes you the 33km to Albarracín.

Once in Albarracín follow the road to Bezas through the village until you come to a Y junction. Take the right hand branch and continue for 3.2km until the first parking (P1) on the left or another 600 metres till the second parking (P2) on the right.

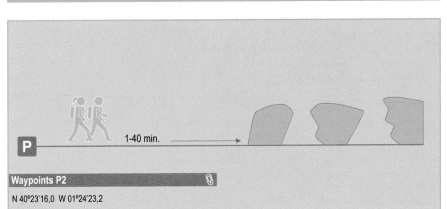

1-40 min.

Waypoints P2

N 40°23'16,0 W 01°24'23,2

Type of rock   Sandstone

Family friendly   Yes

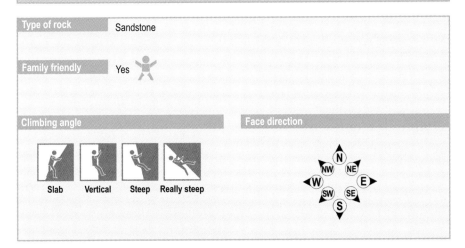

Climbing angle

Slab   Vertical   Steep   Really steep

Face direction

N
NW   NE
◄ W   E ►
SW   SE
S

Number of routes & Grade range

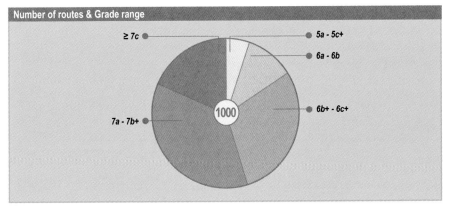

≥ 7c

7a - 7b+

1000

5a - 5c+

6a - 6b

6b+ - 6c+

Montanejos

Montanejos offers a choice of more than 1400 routes spread out over 80 sectors with routes up to 260 metres in a stunning environment.

The two most important and popular zones are the 'Maimona Gully' (Barranco de la Maimona) and the 'Mijares Gorge' (Estrecho del Mijares). Maimona has lots of overhanging routes while climbing at the Mijares is all about mainly vertical rock. At these two zones the climbing takes place on both sides of the river on good quality rock. The routes at Estrecho del Mijares are more concentrated and easily accessible compared to those at Barranco de la Maimona. But this has the longest routes in the area and is definitely the most impressive, as well as being in a lovely setting.

The cover photo of the Montanejos guidebook is taken in Sector Centro del Estrecho at Estrecho del Mijares. The climber is on the classic 'Pericondrio tragal' which has a very interesting traverse with a spectacular view. Even though the first pitch of the four is polished, it is a highly recommended route. The friendly couple living in the Albergue El Refugio can give a lot of good tips for routes to do and those not to waste your time on.

The sectors on the east side of the river, Estrecho del Mijares zone

Sector Entrada a Miradores

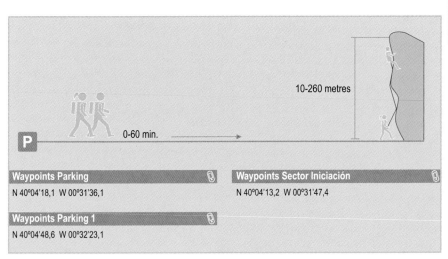

Waypoints Parking

N 40°04'18,1 W 00°31'36,1

Waypoints Parking 1

N 40°04'48,6 W 00°32'23,1

Waypoints Sector Iniciación

N 40°04'13,2 W 00°31'47,4

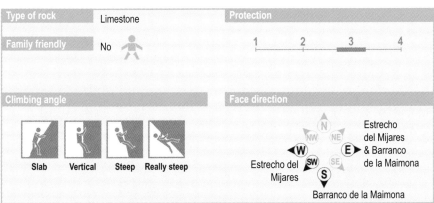

Type of rock	Limestone
Family friendly	No

Protection: 1 2 3 4

Climbing angle: Slab · Vertical · Steep · Really steep

Face direction:
Estrecho del Mijares & Barranco de la Maimona (E)
Estrecho del Mijares (SW)
Barranco de la Maimona (S)

Number of routes & Grade range

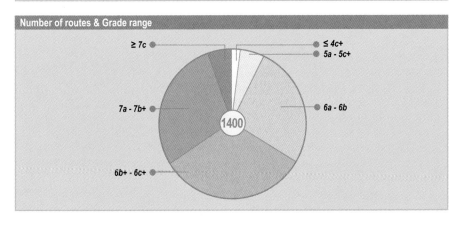

1400

≥ 7c
7a - 7b+
6b+ - 6c+
≤ 4c+
5a - 5c+
6a - 6b

Guy Maddox getting his footwork sorted on one of the brilliant 6c routes at Sector La Polaca in Montanejos, photo by Jon Bibby

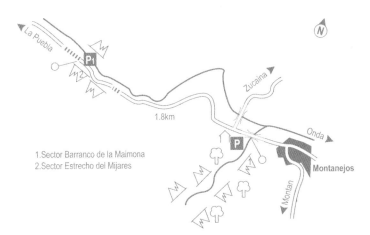

1. Sector Barranco de la Maimona
2. Sector Estrecho del Mijares

Directions

Welcome to Montanejos

▶ From València take the A7 towards Sagunto. Continue on the A23 in the direction of Teruel. Take the exit for Caudiel, on the CV195, and continue to Montanejos.

Climbing area Costa Daurada

Spring   Summer   Autumn   Winter

The Costa Daurada or Golden Coast stretches for more than 200km along the north east coast of Spain. Nearby Barcelona is the best known and most popular destination in the area. Its Art Nouveau architecture is world famous and its fantastic nightlife attracts many visitors from all over the world.

South West of Barcelona, near the city of Reus, lies one of the top crags of Spain, Siurana. Some even say Siurana is the best place for climbing in Spain, but that's for you to decide! The variety of routes is enormously - cracks, tufas, slabs, roofs, crimpy pockets, big jugs, and so on. And a good job has been done of the bolting, thanks to the Spanish and a number of international climbers. This is a place to push your limits though it is not really for beginners! It's also worth mentioning that Siurana is one of those places where you can come alone; the welcoming campsite at Siurana is a great place to meet other climbers.

Montsant, in contrast, is far less spoken of and written about, but the climbing is still great. It is situated west of Siurana, not too far away. This crag is a bit of a hidden gem, with mostly hard routes too. It is on its way to becoming a very important venue on the Costa Daurada.

In short, if you are looking for a prime sport climbing destination for those long and dark days in the winter put the Costa Daurada on your tick list!

When to go

The best time to visit the Costa Daurada is from October to May, the months October, November, March and April being the best. In the winter it can rain and can get cold although there is still a very good chance of fine weather. The summer months are too hot.

Neeltje Tops warming up on one of the few 6a's of Siurana at Sector Can Marges

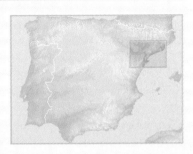

Crag

A Siurana

B Montsant

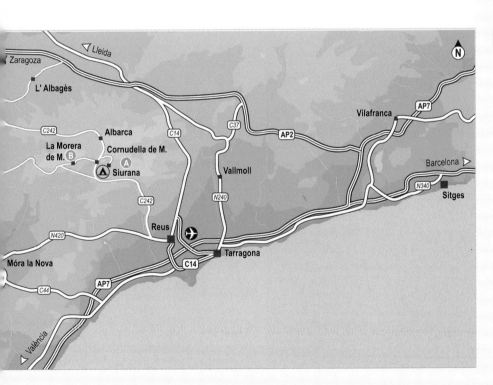

How to get to the area & how to move around

A car will come in very handy, although you can get very close to both Siurana and Montsant by public transport. From the campsite in Siurana you can walk to the sectors. Montsant lacks nearby accommodation so a car is required to get there if you're staying at Siurana.

 By public transport

The usual low cost airlines fly to Barcelona. There's also a new airline on the scene, Clickair *(www. clickair.com)*, which has cheap flights between Barcelona and other European cities. Also check out the option of flying to Reus - Ryanair operates direct flights from the UK, and there are charter flights serving the coastal resorts.

From Barcelona airport take one of the Renfe trains to Barcelona-Sants station. From here, trains to Reus leave daily on a frequent basis [1h20]. From Reus take the bus to Morera de Montsant ,which leaves at 7pm from the central bus station. Get out at Cornudella de Montsant from where you need to hitchhike the last 7.7km to Siurana. The bus returns to Reus at 9.45am from Morera de Montsant.

Hans van Uden cranking through the steepness on No Dan Bolsa (6c+), Sector Can Marges, Siurana

Early morning at Siurana, photo by Eoin Lawless

By car

From Barcelona take the AP7 to Tarragona and continue on to Reus. In Reus take the N420 for a short while until you see the directions for Les Borges del Camp. Continue on the C242 to Cornudella de Montsant. From here either take the TV7021 to La Morera de Montsant (7km) or head through Cornudella de Montsant in the direction of Albarca for Siurana. The turn-off for Siurana is past the village on your right after less than 1km.

Where to stay

There is not particularly a wide choice of accommodation around Siurana and La Morera de Montsant. No worries - nearly all climbers stay in Siurana itself and make day trips to Montsant.

Camping Siurana

✉ Siurana
📞 +34 629 480602
📧 aarbones@ati.es

📍 N 41°15'41,4 E 00°56'30,3

Open	Year round

Grade 1 — 2 — **3** — 4

Price	€12 for 2 people, a tent and a car; €25 for a double room; €35 to €60 per day for a bungalow up to 4 people

This campsite is where the majority of climbers stay. It has a bar and a simple inexpensive restaurant. The owners or their son Tony, the author of the topo, are always willing to help out with any questions you might have. They also rent bungalows.

Directions
Coming from Cornudella de Montsant, the campsite is on the right hand side of the (only) road a few hundred metres before the village.

The popular zone Barranc de Fontscaldes of Siurana

coronn.com

rock climbing TOPOS

Refuge Siurana

✉ Siurana
📞 +34 977 821337

📍 N 41°15'31,5 E 00°55'57,4

Open	Year round
Price	€11 p.p.p.n. in a bunk room (a special price for climbers only)

The friendly refuge can sleep 18 persons. It has hot showers and they do dinners as well. Inside you can practice your bouldering and it has a supremely pleasant terrace with a fantastic view!

Directions
When arriving in Siurana the refuge is on your right and can't be missed.

The interior of the Refuge

Many great walls in Siurana

Hotel La Siuranella 🛏

✉ C/Rentadors, Siurana
☎ +34 977 821144
@ siuranella@siuranella.com
🏠 www.siuranella.com

📱 N 41°15'28,6 E 00°55'54,9

Open   Feb 16th - Jan 14th

Price   €90 - €120 for a double room
               with breakfast

Climbers looking for a very comfortable holiday can stay at this pretty two star hotel situated in the village.

Directions
The hotel is located inside the village. As the village only has a few small streets, you'd be doing well to miss it!a few minutes on foot from the Plaza Mayor.

Siurana

Where to buy groceries

There are no shops in Siurana selling food. Do your shopping at any of the small shops in Cornudella de Montsant or, even better, in Reus.

Where to find the local climbing guidebook

The local guide book 'Guia d'escalades Siurana' is sold at the campsite and at the refuge (€20). Unfortunately the writers have used very simple drawings instead of pictures to show the lines. This makes it hard to get your bearings right. There is no separate topo of Montsant (yet).

There is another guidebook called 'Costa Daurada', published by Rockfax (€24). Even though it is very outdated - it was published in 2002 - it gives a good overview of all the Costa Daurada has to offer. Montsant is included but is given very limited coverage.

What else is there to see & do

Hiking
The countryside around Siurana is great walking country. Either start or finish in the village itself which is extremely quiet and has fantastic views.

Wine Tasting
The wines from Montsant and nearby Priorat rank among the best in Spain but the area has not received much international attention so prices aren't that silly yet. Take the opportunity to sample the local vintages! For a list of local producers and cellars, visit *www.domontsant.com* or *www.doqpriorat.org* - there are a cluster based in Cornudella de Monsant that you can easily visit.

Barcelona
It is not often that you encounter a city with great nightlife, a gorgeous beach, a rich culture, numerous small tapas bars, and some of the best climbing not too far away! If your fingers beg you for a day of rest take the great opportunity to explore this magnificent city.

There is lots of hiking around Siurana if the weather is not that good

Morera de Montsant

On the windy road up from Cornudella de Montsant to Siurana the crag soon comes into view and you will quickly understand why this is a world class climbing destination! Excellent limestone rises on both sides of the road and there is an enormous range of different sectors. In total there are 40 sectors and over 600 routes. The majority of the routes, and also the best ones, are in the 7th and 8th grades. Sector Can Piqui Pugui and L'Olla have, without question, the most testing and demanding routes of 8a and above. These overhanging sectors are also good when it rains. If you are looking for some good easier routes (5 and up) head to Sector Can Marges. Sector Esperó Primavera has a few excellent 7th grade routes.

Siurana can get very busy at the weekend. But even though it is a popular destination, it still feels very relaxed, especially during the week.

John Mehegan enjoying the routes at the village crags of Siurana in late winter, photo by Eoin Lawless

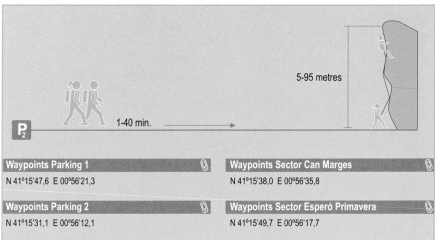

Waypoints Parking 1	
N 41°15'47,6 E 00°56'21,3	

Waypoints Sector Can Marges	
N 41°15'38,0 E 00°56'35,8	

Waypoints Parking 2	
N 41°15'31,1 E 00°56'12,1	

Waypoints Sector Esperó Primavera	
N 41°15'49,7 E 00°56'17,7	

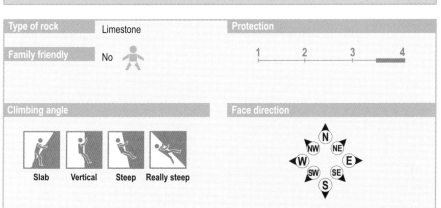

Type of rock — Limestone

Family friendly — No

Protection — 1   2   3   4

Climbing angle — Slab, Vertical, Steep, Really steep

Face direction — N NE E SE S SW W NW

Number of routes & Grade range

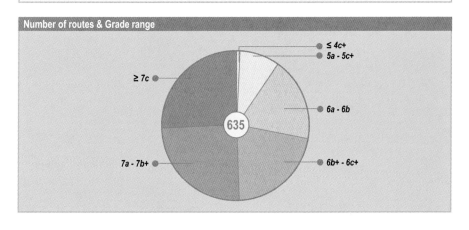

635

- ≤ 4c+
- 5a - 5c+
- 6a - 6b
- 6b+ - 6c+
- 7a - 7b+
- ≥ 7c

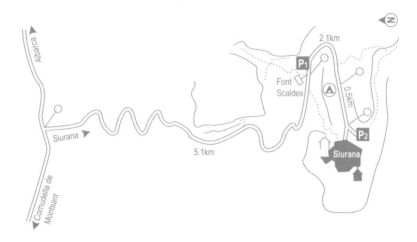

Directions

*Remco den Dulk enjoying one of the many
7a's in Siurana, Sector Corral Nou*

▶ From Barcelona take the AP7 to Tarragona and continue to Reus. In Reus take the N420 for a short distance until you see the directions for Les Borges del Camp. Continue on the C242 to Cornudella de Montsant. Go through the village in the direction of Albarca and turn right towards Siurana some 800 metres further. It is a nice 7.7km drive from Cornudella de Montsant to Siurana. Park either at the campsite or the big car park just before the village.

Montsant

As Siurana is enormous and still has so much potential, nearby Montsant has never really been in the spotlight. A shame, because this has nothing to do with the quality of the rock, which consists of excellent pocketed limestone, coated with conglomerate. The routes at Montsant are sustained and steep. Those climbing less than 6b will literally find nothing to do here!

Sector Barrots is one of the best at Montsant. It is a real treat climbing here and the views are simply magnificent. Climbing here makes a great change from Siurana!

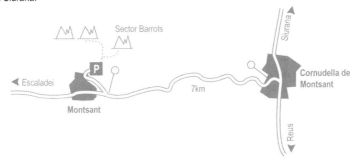

Directions

▶ From Barcelona take the AP7 to Tarragona and continue to Reus. In Reus take the N420 for a short distance until you see the directions for Les Borges del Camp. Continue on the C242 to Cornudella de Montsant. In the village take the TV7021 to La Morera de Montsant (7km). On entering the village, take the first road on your right up the hill and park after 300 metres at the 'big' car park.

Montsant

Montsant offers fantastic rock, photo by Adrian Berry

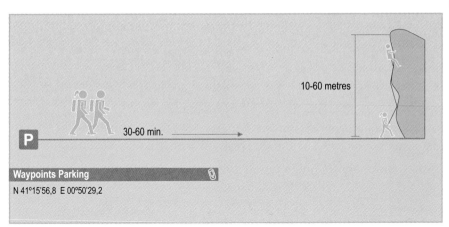

Waypoints Parking

N 41°15'56,8 E 00°50'29,2

Type of rock	Limestone coated conglomerate
Family friendly	No

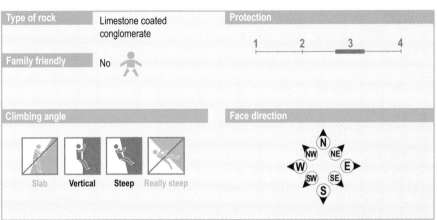

Protection

1 2 3 4

Climbing angle

Slab **Vertical** **Steep** Really steep

Face direction

Number of routes & Grade range

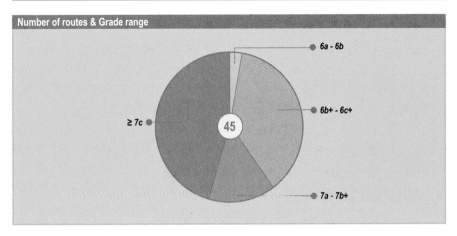

● 6a - 6b

● 6b+ - 6c+

≥ 7c ●

45

● 7a - 7b+

Climbing area Mallorca

Mallorca is one of those perfect sun drenched islands with an abundance of limestone that also serves as a major package holiday destination. Without doubt, it is one of the world's top venues for deep water soloing and a great destination for sport climbing in general. Also as it has a wealth of accommodation, cheap car hire, and plenty options for rest days. It is a place you'll definitely want to come back to.

The island, 96km in length and 78km in width, is surrounded by sea cliffs and in its heart lies the dramatic Serra de Tramuntana. These steep mountains drop off into lonely bays and it's there, where the grey limestone merges with the clear blue sea, that you'll find the best spots for deep water soling. DWS is becoming more and more popular in Mallorca and, especially in September, you'll not be alone in the water.

Spring   Summer   Autumn   Winter

The sport climbing venues on the island are quite evenly spread. There are a number of crags on the coast but the majority are inland. The climbing in the mountains has an amazing atmosphere and great views. There are a mixture of single and multi pitch routes, the walk-ins are generally short and flat, and you'll always be able to find the perfect crag for any weather. The variety among the crags is huge - unpolished slabs, steep overhangs, "juggy tufas", stalactites, roofs, and cracks all in beautiful surroundings.

The only disadvantage with Mallorca is that because both the climbers and the crags are so spread out, it doesn't have much of a "climbing scene". It is not a place to go on your own but it is a great place to go to with a group.

Cala Magraner, photo by Paul Lahaye

When to go

In summer Mallorca is home to hoards of holidaymakers from Germany and Britain, who mainly come to appreciate the beach and the nightlife. Despite the island's reputation as a tourist hot spot you can be there in high season without being bothered by the crowds. The island is of a reasonable size and the nightmare package holiday resorts are quite concentrated. The only thing is that it can be very warm in summer and you definitely have to stick to shady crags or get your swimming kit on and go soloing. If it really gets too warm you can always chill out on the beach.

In winter, the island is deserted and this is the perfect opportunity to get away from the cold weather at home - flights and accommodation are extremely cheap this time of year. Spring and autumn are the best seasons to visit Mallorca, but even winter is on the cards too.

Crag

Ⓐ Mallorca

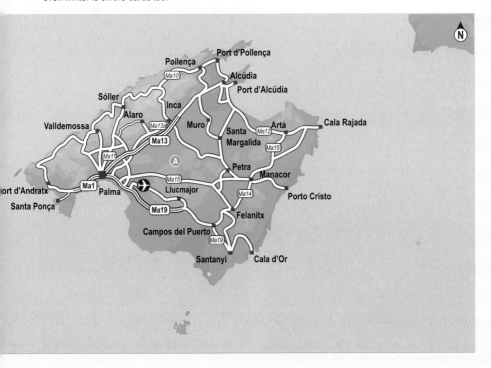

How to get to the area & how to move around

Renting a car is really the only way to move around the island and visit the various crags. Luckily car rental is quite cheap here. Bus and train services are poor and do not get you to the right places.

 By public transport

During the "normal" tourist season you can opt to book a package deal including both the flight and a hotel room. Otherwise book a flight ticket with one of many airlines that fly to Palma de Mallorca. EasyJet and Ryanair, amongst others, have year round flights from the UK and Germany.

 By car

With your rental car you can get to all the climbing spots on the island. Factor in a bit of extra time when estimating journey times. What may look like a straight road on the map will wind endlessly and small villages will continually slow you down.

Monastery of Lluc

Where to stay

You have a few options for your base, depending on which crags in particular you fancy. However, the island is not too big and it usually doesn't take more than 1½ hours to get to anywhere from anywhere. If you stay in Palma you'll also have access to decent nightlife. Another aspect that you might want to consider is closeness to the sea and beaches.

Camping is not a big thing in Mallorca and wild camping is illegal: you will have to choose between staying in a hotel, apartment, or villa. The best option if you are with a group is to rent a villa. These are very pleasant places and often come with a private swimming pool. Villas can generally accommodate 4 -12 people. There are lots to rent (more than apartments) and it can work out

Mallorcan coastline

Almost all villas for rent have a private swimming pool

very cheaply, especially if there are more of you. The price totally depends on the season and the villa size. Bargaining is often possible off season, due to low demand. Start your search with *www.mfh.co.uk* or with *www.fincaferien.de*. Apartment rentals are less common but do exist. Try *www.friendlyrentals.com*. Hotels are abundant and are best booked as part of a package deal. This might also be the cheapest option if there are just two of you. Hotel Sóller Garden in Sóller seems to offer the cheapest accommodation in bungalows. Then there is only one option for legal camping at the free campsite at the Lluc Monastery.

Campsite Lluc

 N 39°49'17,6 E 02°53'29,7

Open	Year round
Price	Free of charge

This is a free campsite near the Lluc Monastery with plenty of space under the trees. There are basic toilet facilities.

Directions
Directions: Drive towards the Lluc Monastery. The campsite is on the right, 300 metres before the big car park before the Monastery.

Campsite at the Monastery of Lluc

Julián Gonzalez dropping an Egyptian on La Noche me Confune (7b), Gorge Blau

Adam Tegg said seduced once again by the superb Es Pasto (6b+), El Calo de Betlem

The beach has plenty to do for kids

Hotel Sóller Garden

✉ Plaça Reis de Mallorca, 5
07108 Port de Sóller
☎ Tel +34 971 638046
🌐 www.sollergarden.com

Open   Year round

Price   €40 for a 2 person bungalow

A holiday style village of type wooden bungalows set amidst the gardens in the Port of Sóller. Basic but very clean accommodation, simply furnished. Ideal for those on a low budget.

Where to buy groceries

Near Palma there are many "centre commercial" areas with hypermarkets. Look out for signs on the motorway. Of course, every village has a supermarket too.

Where to find the local climbing guidebook

Rockfax has both a guidebook for sale and a mini DWS guide for Mallorca, which can be downloaded from *www.rockfax.com*. The guidebook is on sale at the climbing shops in Palma and Pollença or can be bought beforehand.

Bon Cami Outdoor
C/ Roger de flor, 36
Puerto Pollença

Foracorda
Carrer Miquel Marques 20
Palma de Mallorca

What else is there to see & do

Beaches
The whole coastline boasts incomparable scenery with many official beaches but there are more tiny, hidden, sheltered coves that make an excellent place to spend a rest day. The coves (calas in Spanish), in particular, have invitingly clear water and are ideal for snorkelling.

Palma
There are many important sights worth visiting if you feel like indulging in a bit of culture. La Seu is the imposing cathedral built over a period of 500 years and completed in 1601. Pueblo Español can be best described as an outdoor museum with scaled down replicas of Spain's most celebrated monuments. Around Plaza Mayor is the Ramblas where you'll find an extensive range of shops.

Villages to visit
There are many charming little villages that are worth a visit to truly get to know Mallorca. Fornalutx is a pretty village that enjoys a wonderfully idyllic setting surrounded by The Tramuntana Mountains.

Mallorca has mountains too

A typical Mallorcan landscape

Along the east coast Cala Figuera is a pretty fishing village where fishermen still sit around the old harbour mending their nets. The Monastery in Lluc is also worth a visit. It is beautifully situated 35kms to the east of Sóller. The view from the cross at the top of the hill is magnificent.

Hiking

Hiking in Mallorca is quite popular and is linked to the island's cultural heritage, as most of the land is still used for agriculture. The trails through the Tramuntana Mountains are very old and were used to connect the remote fincas to each other and with the bigger villages. As a result, there is a wide range of routes, from a half-day trip to an excursion of two or more days. Many popular trails are marked but it still is a good idea to get good maps of the area. They are for sale at the climbing shops in Palma

Adam Tegg enjoying a hot summer day at Puerto Christo, photo by Mia Linder

A superb dinner spot at Pollenca

Mallorca is also great for cyclists

Hikers have been visiting Mallorca for decades

and Pollença. Sóller and the Lluc Monastery are the most important - and most popular - starting points. There are something like a dozen peaks which have elevations higher than 1,000m and the highest is 1,443m.

Biking
No matter where you go in Mallorca, you'll see cyclists dressed in brightly coloured lycra whizzing by. It is a very popular place for both professionals and amateurs. You can enjoy flat rides as well as hills that challenge even the fittest cyclist. Bikes can be rented in the larger towns, such as Sóller or Pollença.

Canyoning and Caving
Mallorca is pretty well known among canyoning enthusiasts and canyoning and caving is possible between spring and autumn. The network of caves

is renowned for it's opportunities for quality trips. There are many outdoor agencies offering these activities with a guide. Check *www.mallorcadventurecenter.com* or *www.rocksportmallorca.com* for more information.

Sea Kayaking
Paddling from bay to bay under your own steam is a very good way to discover Mallorca's hidden coastal treasures. Sea kayaking is not so weather dependant: a flat calm sea allows you to make good time and explore the rocky inlets and coves; the bigger the waves the more exciting and challenging it can be! Check out www.kayakmallorca.com.

Boat cruises
There are several options for half day or full day boat cruises exploring the coves in a more comfortable way. Check *www.nofrills-excursions.com*.

Plenty of hard and steep routes at the Blue Grotto

There are many different crags on Mallorca and all together there is climbing to suit everyone's taste. What follows now is a description of the most interesting crags to help you to make your choice.

Cala Magraner

A perfect spot on winter days and this is one of the best areas for climbers with children. It's in a lovely position at an isolated sea inlet and it offers climbs of a wide range of difficulty with, compared to other crags on the island, a relatively high number of shorter lower grade routes. Although the beach is not the best on offer, it is perfect for a lazy day. There is also a mega steep cave with hard routes that face the sun. Altogether, this is a crag for the spring, autumn, and winter, and is best avoided in summer.

Tijuana

Another coastal location and sometimes referred to as Santanyi after the nearest town. It is a very good sun-trap in winter and a place to get completely sunburnt in summer as there is no shade at all. The routes, 50 in total, are largely vertical to mildly overhanging with technical climbing. The starts are often annoyingly tricky with wide roofs to span before you can go anywhere. Swimming after the sweat-fest is best done at the beach at Cala Santanyi, where you'll also find cafes and bars.

Carmen Elphick on Elvigilant de la Platja (4), photo by Pete Bradshaw, Cala Magraner

Fraguel, photo by Paul Lahaye

Alaro

One of the most impressive walls on Mallorca with phenomenal mega tufas. Only a very small part of this wall is developed (50 routes) due to its location on private property and the landowners forbidding climbing! Nevertheless, climbing here is a must if you love tufas. The sun shows up around noon.

Fraguel

A stunning crag has the best hard sport climbing on the island with an impressive series of perfect lines in the 8a and up. Almost all routes are steep tufa pumps with the exception of a few fingery routes on a vertical wall. Those routes are the only routes in the 6th grade; honestly the real fun here starts at 7a/7b! There are around 60 routes in total and

Nympha Stassen on one of the easier routes at Fraguel, photo by Paul Lahaye

you can find routes both in the shade and the sun. The access road is blocked in summer from June to September due to the risk of fires.

Port de Sóller
A small crag in a beautiful position above the sea and the port. It has 27 routes and most of them are between 6b and 7c. It has a mixture of steep hard routes, and slabbier, more moderate lines. It is a good crag for early birds in summer and, when it gets too hot, take some refreshment at the Nautilus bar at the car park.

Xon Xanquete
An extremely steep cave that faces northwest and is thus ideal on warm days. The routes are in the 7th grade and all require some strength and stamina. The location is beautiful but the approach is a bit awkward.

El Fumat
An imposing wall with about 25 routes. The routes range between 5c and 7c and, since it catches the sun late in the afternoon, it is a good place to visit on warm days or to get the evening sun on colder days.

Sa Gubia

The positive approach to improving your climbing

*Trad*CLIMBING+
The positive approach to improving your climbing

*Sport*CLIMBING+
The positive approach to improving your climbing

Starting Out
Gear
Placing Protection
Ropework
Technique
Tactics
The Mind
Multi-pitching
Training for Trad
Destinations

Adrian Berry
John Arran

ROCKFAX

Adrian Berry
Steve McClure

ROCKFAX

the **+Series** *from*

ROCKFAX
.com

La Creveta
A small crag and worth a visit if you love slabby routes on compact limestone, where good footwork is required. The 30 slab routes range between 5a and 6c. A new sector is currently being developed with harder overhanging routes. Around 15 routes are already in place.

Sa Gubia
The largest and most varied crag on offer with over 100 routes and one of the best options for groups of mixed abilities. It is situated in a beautiful gorge where climbing is possible on either side - climbing in the sun or shade is always possible. The variety of climbing is huge and it only lacks super steep routes. There is also a wealth of truly classic longer trad climbs.

El Calo de Betlem
A delightful little crag where it is possible to bring young children. One sector has powerful shorter routes and the other sector has some technical gems on a vertical wall. There are 28 routes in total and the grade range is fairly evenly spread. It gets the sun during the afternoon.

Paul Lahaye on Sostre den Burot (7a), Valldemosa, photo by Nympha Stassen

Gorge Blau

The gorge offers very nice climbing on both sides and is a great place to climb on warm days. The breeze through the gorge also helps to cool things down in summer but makes it uncomfortable in winter. The 50 routes vary between mildly overhanging middle grade routes and very overhanging difficult routes with a lot of 7th and 8th grade challenges. It is possible to bring young children here due to the very short approach and the abundance of flat ground underneath one of the walls.

Valldemosa

A very accessible crag, right next to the road, and therefore very popular. It totally lacks the great atmosphere of most other crags on the island but climbing here is very convenient. It has a large concentration of 6 graded routes with 50 routes in total. It is a good place to visit on the way to the airport. The sun gets in just after noon.

Gorge Blau

Mia Linder soaking up the tranquil atmosphere in El Calo de Betlem

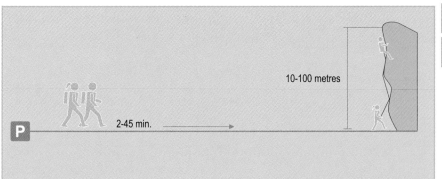

Type of rock
Limestone

Family friendly
Yes for Cala Magraner, Gorge Blau,
El Calo de Betlem

Protection

1   2   3   4

Climbing angle

Slab   Vertical   Steep   Really steep

Face direction

N, NE, E, SE, S, SW, W, NW

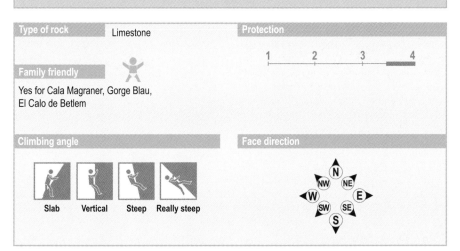

Number of routes & Grade range

850

- ≤ 4c+
- 5a - 5c+
- 6a - 6b
- 6b+ - 6c+
- 7a - 7b+
- ≥ 7c

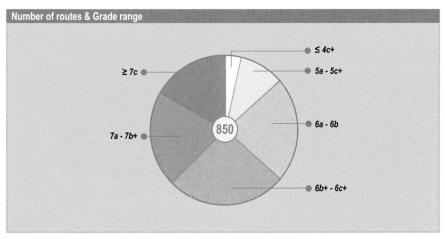

A fall is nothing to be worried about, photo by Mia Linder

First of all a special word of gratitude goes to Irene Pieper who is responsible for the graphical design and to Daniel Jaeggi who is our editor. We are again very pleased with their contribution to this Rock Climbing Atlas. Secondly, Paul Lahaye (*www.lahaye.ws*), Klemen Demsar, and Eoin Lawless deserve a special thanks for their generous contribution of photos.

In France we would like to thank Alan Carne for his friendly help while we were in the Gorges du Verdon. Furthermore we thank Adam van Eekeren, Fred van Nijnatten, Robert van den Broek and Thomas Rijniers for their help on the Calanques section. We thank Thierry Souchard and Bertrand Maurin for helping us out on Corsica.

For their help on the Italy chapter we would like to say thanks to Sjaak de Visser, Alberto De Giuli, Paolo Vitali and Harald Röker. On Sardinia we were fortunate to have met Peter Herold & Anne Mc Glone. A big thank you for showing us around and the enjoyable climbing! We wish that more people would just follow their heart and enjoy life as much as you do!

Andrew Warrington, Claudine Gatt, and Helga Cutajar helped us a lot while doing our research on Malta and we absolutely owe them a big thank you. On Gozo it were Xavier en Alexandra Hancock that made sure we had a great time there while discovering the beauties of the island. They made the right choice to follow their dream and move to this wonderful island. We also would like to acknowledge the help of the Malta Tourism Authority that provided us with all kind of information and photos.

Our trip to Morocco wouldn't have been the same without Theo van Bokhoven and Vincent Massuger. Thank you guys for the great time we spent in the Todra Gorge. Our stay in the Taghia Gorge was fantastic due to the friendly Youssef Rezki. We also received the help of some very nice French climbers, amongst them Mathieu Corpet, Xavier and Sylvie Legendre, Huug and Hellen.

In Portugal we would like to thank Marcos Delgado, Simon Day and Zé Maria for sharing their knowledge with us.

Gaby Kostermans and Kim van Leuken helped us on the research in the Costa Blanca and Malaga areas in Spain. Thank you girls for your contribution and great company! Fons Pijpers joined in Valencia and with him we spent a fantastic time in Albarracin and Montanejos. For their help in La Pedriza we would like to thank Juan Pablo Trigo, David Merchante and Isabel Morcillo. Then a very warm thank you to Christine & Jean-Bernard Hofer who shared their knowledge with us about El Chorro. Sam and Rich of The Orange House did the same on the crags in the Costa Blanca. We wish both couples all the luck in the world running their beautiful accommodation spots. In Siurana we thank Toni Arbonés for his help. Last but definitely not least we thank Adam Tegg and Mia Linder for showing us around on Mallorca and the great time we spent together.

Other people that one way or the other contributed to this edition of the Rock Climbing Atlas are:
Alan James, Cody Roth, Guy Maddox, Adrian Berry, David Pickford, Marcel Eijdems, Frank Koppens, Daniel Tulp, Elsje van Beek, Matthias Braun, Jorg Verhoeven, Stefan Glowacz, and of course our families.

Thank you all!

Wynand and Marloes

Climbing

UIAA	French (Sport Grade)	USA	British Tech	British Trad	Australia
1	1	5.1			9
2	2	5.2		M	10
3-					
3		5.3		D	
3+	3a/3c+				11
4-		5.4		VD	
4				HVD	
4+	4a/4c+	5.5			12
5-		5.6		S	13
5	5a/5b	5.7	4a	HS	14
5+			4b		15
		5.8			
6-	5b+/5c+		4c	VS	16
6		5.9		HVS	17
	6a				
6+		5.10a	5a		18
6+/7-	6a+	5.10b			19
7-		5.10c		E1	20
	6b				
7		5.10d	5b	E2	21
7+	6b+	5.11a			22
7+/8-	6c	5.11b	5c	E3	23
8-	6c+	5.11c			
8	7a	5.11d	6a	E4	24
8+	7a+	5.12a			25
8+/9-	7b	5.12b		E5	26
9-	7b+	5.12c	6b		
9	7c	5.12d			27
9+	7c+	5.13a	6c	E6	28
9+/10-	8a	5.13b			29
10-	8a+	5.13c		E7	30
10	8b	5.13d	7a		31
10+	8b+	5.14a		E8	32
11-	8c	5.14b			33
11-/11	8c+	5.14c	7b	E9	34
11	9a	5.14d			35
11+	9a+	5.15a			36
12-	9b	5.15b	7c	E10	37

Bouldering

V grade (Hueco)	B grade (Peak)	Fb (Fontainebleau)
		4-
V0	B0	4
V1	B1	4+
V1+		5-
V2	B2	5
V2+	B3	5+
V3	B3+	6A
V3+	B4	6A+
V4	B4+	6B
V4+	B5	6B+
V5	B5+	6C
V5+	B6-	6C+
V6	B6	7A
V7	B7	7A+
V8	B8	7B
V8+	B9	7B+
V9		7C
	B10	
V10		7C+
V11	B11	8A
V12	B12	8A+
V13	B13	8B
V14	B14	8B+
V15	B15	8C
V16	B16	8C+